MW00577968

FORBIDDEN GIFT

WILLOW BROOK—SECRETS OF THE PEN
BOOK ONE

Endorsements

Forbidden Gift is deep, rich, and captivating! Debra Torres brings a lovely new voice and unique twists to the Amish genre.
—**Cindy Woodsmall**, New York Times best-selling author

Author Debra Torres is a unique, new voice in Amish fiction. In her debut novel, *Forbidden Gift*, Torres explores the devastating consequences when a terrible secret kept for forty years is uncovered and lives unravel. Christian romantic suspense readers will enjoy this page-turner.
—**Kelly Irvin**, best-selling author of the Amish of Big Sky Country series

Enter Amish woman Johanna's world where the passion for writing stirs strong in her heart, while the Bishop of her district is determined to extinguish such things. Don't miss this story of unexpected endings.
—**Jerry Eicher**, author Amish fiction including *When Hearts Break*, the Adams County Trilogy, the Hannah's Heart books, and the Little Valley series.

Forbidden Gift, Debra Torres's debut in the Amish fiction genre, is an engaging, suspenseful story that addresses deep spiritual themes readers will relate to. Torres has a deft touch with suspense and characterization. The unexpected twists and turns of the story kept me turning pages to find out what would happen next up to the satisfying conclusion. I highly recommend *Forbidden Gift!*

—**J. M. Hochstetler**, coauthor with Bob Hostetler of the award-winning Northkill Amish series

Would you still pursue your dreams if it cost you everything you've been taught to hold dear? Torres explores this question and more in her well-researched debut novel, *Forbidden Gift*.

—**Jolina Petersheim**, best-selling author of *How the Light Gets In*

FORBIDDEN GIFT

WILLOW BROOK—SECRETS OF THE PEN
BOOK ONE

DEBRA TORRES

ELK LAKE PUBLISHING INC

PUBLISHING THE POSITIVE
Plymouth, Massachusetts

Copyright Notice
Forbidden Gift—Willow Brook—Secrets of the Pen: Book One
First edition. Copyright © 2021 by Debra Torres. The information contained in this book is the intellectual property of Debra Torres and is governed by United States and International copyright laws. All rights reserved. No part of this publication, either text or image, may be used for any purpose other than personal use. Therefore, reproduction, modification, storage in a retrieval system, or retransmission, in any form or by any means, electronic, mechanical, or otherwise, for reasons other than personal use, except for brief quotations for reviews or articles and promotions, is strictly prohibited without prior written permission by the publisher.

This is a work of fiction. Names, characters, businesses, places, events, locales, and incidents are either the products of the author's imagination or used in a fictitious manner. Any resemblance to actual persons, living or dead, or actual events is purely coincidental.

Scriptures taken from the Holy Bible, New International Version®, NIV®. Copyright © 1973, 1978, 1984, 2011 by Biblica, Inc.™ Used by permission of Zondervan. All rights reserved worldwide. www. zondervan.com The "NIV" and "New International Version" are trademarks registered in the United States Patent and Trademark Office by Biblica, Inc.™

Cover and Interior Design: Derinda Babcock
Editor(s): Sue Fairchild, Deb Haggerty
Author Represented By: Ambassador Literary Agency

PUBLISHED BY: Elk Lake Publishing, Inc., 35 Dogwood Drive, Plymouth, MA 02360, 2021

Library Cataloging Data
Names: Torres, Debra (Debra Torres)
Forbidden Gift—Willow Brook—Secrets of the Pen: Book One / Debra Torres
350 p. 23cm × 15cm (9in × 6 in.)
ISBN-13: 978-1-64949-267-8 (paperback) | 978-1-64949-242-5 (trade paperback) | 978164949-243-2 (e-book)
Key Words: Amish Books; Amish Romance Novels; Amish Fiction; Clean Romance Novels; Christian Fiction Family Healing; Inspirational Fiction about Women Writers; Bonnet Book
Library of Congress Control Number: 2021938969 Fiction

DEDICATION

To my brother John for showing our family how to face hard times with endurance, grace, and a little bit of laughter.

Acknowledgments

On this road to publishing my first novel, I didn't want to walk alone. God knew this, I could tell by all of the wonderful people he sent to journey along with me.

Thanks to my literary agent, Wes Yoder, who believed in this book and in me.

And a deep gratitude to all of my beta readers, editors, and encouragers: Diane Austin, Drew Menard, Michael Torres, Sue A. Fairchild, Jenny Leo, Heather Day Gilbert, Scott Lamb, Amanda Melton, Pam Miller, Jason Pope, Rena Rawlings, and Len Stevens.

Thanks also to Victoria Duerstock, Jim Fisher, Tyler McBee, John Scott Port, Debi Schull, Kevin Williams, and Tammy Karasek who graciously shared their talent, knowledge, and resources with me.

I also want to thank the amazing people who helped to make this book's beautiful cover possible: Katherine Shepler, Doug Miller, Stephan Schultze, Beth Passburg, Michael Torres, Audrey Torres, Annabelle Torres, and, of course, Derinda Babcock.

Thanks also to my Street Team made up of incredible people and devoted readers who helped tell the world about this book.

And heartfelt gratitude to Deb Haggerty at Elk Lake Publishing who has given me a chance.

Thank you to my husband, Michael, and our five wonderful children for your support, understanding, and patience. I love you dearly, and I could not be at this place without you.

And finally, to Jesus who always fulfills his promises.

Soli Deo Gloria

CHAPTER 1

JOHANNA

I couldn't stop my hands from trembling. I hadn't written a word in two weeks, and it was killing me. Now I understood what life was like for Mammi, whose heart had always yearned for the pen. May she rest in peace.

Trying to settle my hands and my mind with hard work, I quickly finished giving all the calves on our veal farm their noon bottles. I found my brother David working on the well pump in the back of our barn and told him I'd completed the task.

"Ahead of yourself today, ain't?" David got the pump started and went back to washing out the jugs we used to mix the calves' milk replacer. Water sloshed onto his heavy boots as he worked.

I put my trembling hands behind my back. *"Jah."* Normally chatty, it was all the conversation I could offer my brother today. I just wasn't myself.

Grabbing a basket, I headed out to the kitchen garden to pick the last of the season's tomatoes. I'd found that keeping my fingers busy was the important thing.

I saw that the deep, dark spots that covered most of the yellowed leaves on our tomato plants had spread. Only a few dozen of them had escaped the disease. Mamm called it the blight. But I called it ugly. The garden was one of my few joys now after I'd finally quit writing for *gut* in obedience to the *Ordnung* a few weeks ago. And this blight only added to my anxious mood.

Miracle, the long-haired gray cat I'd rescued from the barn rafters when she was just a kitten, rubbed against my black stockings. Stooping down, I gave her a *gut* scratch behind the ears. Miracle loved the garden almost as much as I did and did her best to keep it free of snakes.

I stood up and let out a sigh. Moving deeper into the garden, I passed by the withered plants and found those that had been spared. I took a few minutes to let my mind wander and enjoy how the morning sun brought out the red in each tomato hidden in the green leaves.

Finding them and dropping them into my basket for the last canning of the season felt like a treasure hunt. My mind went to the jewelry *Englischer* women wore while shopping at our summer vegetable stand. Glinting in the sunlight, ruby reds or emerald greens wrapped their fingers and dangled from their ears.

Before I could stop it, the beginnings of a new story formed in my head. I frantically searched the oversized pockets of my apron for my journal and pen. I knew I had to capture the words when they first started flowing.

A smile swept my face as I thought about how many columns I'd secretly written for our local newspaper this way. No matter what I was doing, when the words came, I would disappear to our barn or just into the woods to climb our large outcropping of rocks for a minute or two.

Now where was my journal?

Ach! I remembered. My journal, along with my writing pen, were hidden under a large haybale in our barn, just where I had put them. I wanted to run there and fetch them now, but couldn't, even though my black sneakers started to point in that direction as if they had a mind of their own.

The journal called to me, just like it had the dozens of other times I'd vowed to stop writing. For Mamm, for the bishop, for the whole Willow Brook community, I'd tried to quit.

Really, I did.

I picked a few other tomatoes and brought one to my cheek. Its tight skin felt so warm and smooth against mine. There were the jewels again. I looked around the garden, once lush, but now fairly bleak with the end of the season. Suddenly, I had the setting for my story. I raised my eyes to our barn, its brick red a beacon of what lay under its hay.

"Johanna, *Kumme!*"

The sharpness in Mamm's tone shocked me and the story fled. Heat prickled the top of my head, and I pushed at the confines of my prayer *Kapp* to let the air in.

"I'm coming!" I rushed out of the garden's fence to find my mother.

The kitchen door swung open, and Mamm now stood out in the yard calling louder.

"Johanna!" She said my name with more anger this time even though I was only a few steps away. "The bishop is here. He wants to see you."

Her tone made my palms grow clammy. She took my basket, only half full, while I hurried toward the house.

"Fix your *Kapp*," she hissed as I passed.

Smoothing my head covering and taking a deep breath to steady myself, I walked into the living room where the bishop waited, my mother following close on my heels.

"*Guder Daag*, Bishop," I said, trying to sound cheerful.

He did not return the greeting, but stood unsmiling, his sour expression sending a chill down my spine. Something was coming. I could feel it.

He reached inside his black coat and pulled out a copy of the *Mountain Laurel Star*.

I sucked in my breath. How in the world had he—

"You need to stop writing, Johanna," he thundered.

Visions of being shunned flashed across my mind as my mother wrung her apron, her confused glance darting from me to the bishop and back again.

"What does he mean, Johanna?"

Fear. I heard it clearly in my mother's voice—as familiar to me as her sharp tongue. In most of my twenty-five years, it was always one or the other with my mother.

The bishop held up the *Star*, but since I hadn't written for a few weeks, my writing shouldn't have been in there. Maybe he was just trying to get me to talk.

I steadied myself and met the bishop's heated glare. "What do you mean, Bishop?"

He unfolded the newspaper then and went right to page three where my column had appeared for two straight years. Instead of replacing me with someone else, I saw that the editor was running a "Best of Ima" series. It felt *gut* to not be forgotten. Even with the bishop's glare, I couldn't help but look at the story installment fondly. This story included one of my favorite scenes on how I had "rescued" Miracle, just a new kitten then, from the rafters of our barn. I couldn't help but smile.

"Johanna!"

I winced at my mother's snap. Mamm was horrified, I knew. But she shouldn't have been too surprised. Her own mother's blood ran through my veins, after all.

The bishop folded the paper back up and then rolled it. "This is not the first time you've been caught with this sort of deviance. It could lead to the *Bann* for you."

The bishop went on to explain how he knew the writing must be mine, even though the story's byline read "Ima Righter." I tried to focus, but the gray hairs in the bishop's thick, scraggly brows made me think of the wizards in the books my brother Mose and I, hidden behind stacks of hay, took turns reading when we were young.

That feeling washed over me again. My hand itched for my pen. Studying the bishop's quivering brows, I wanted to take notes. A new character was emerging in my mind, and I had to fold my hands to keep them still.

There would be no writing anything with the bishop watching.

Why was there such a deep sternness from the bishop on this? And threatening me with the *Bann* was a bit strong for my type of sin. What about Aaron and Emily? My *Bruder* and his new bride had gotten off mighty easy when their first baby was born large and healthy two months before their due date.

No, something deeper bothered the bishop about my writing. Something that maybe had little to do with me. This rule against writing was one I could never understand. My love for the pen was as much a part of me as my Amish roots. And I was being forced to choose between the two.

"What do you have to say, Johanna?" Mamm's voice was cold, her lips thin.

Dat should have been the one dealing with this, not Mamm. But his stroke had taken away his speech. Suddenly, my heart hurt all over again for what we'd lost in my father. A wave of guilt washed over me, and I felt badly for the trouble I was causing Mamm and our family. We both knew problems with the bishop could negatively affect our entire family, and here I was pushing him.

I bowed my head and let my words fall to the floor as I spoke. "I'm finished writing. I've stopped submitting columns to the newspaper."

I couldn't look at either of them after that—wouldn't. The pain felt too great. Hearing the bishop's dismissive grunt, I turned and walked slowly to the barn to get my journal and pen.

My passion to write would have to die. And it was up to me to kill it.

Heading to the river just past the road, I threw off my *Kapp* and let the chill September wind have its way with my hair. Large, unruly curls with a mind of their own escaped the prison of my bun. Mamm would frown if she saw me now, her brow furrowing under her own collection of trapped, snowy locks. But after what just happened, I was having a hard time caring about what Mamm would think.

I felt a familiar twinge of guilt but pushed it back, deep down inside, where it had plenty of company. Hopping on our river swing, I swung out over the rushing water below, letting my thoughts go.

Curls, lots of them, relished their moment of freedom right along with me. They swayed in rhythm with the old wooden swing.

I must have looked rather comical out here, pumping like mad over the rushing Shenango River. An old Amish *Maedel* like myself. Being unmarried at the age of twenty-five wasn't a common thing among the Amish, and I tried to not think about what giving up writing would do to me. Writing filled a lot of empty spots in my life. What would be my purpose now?

If I tried, I could fly out to where my black sneakers touched the sky. The rush of the old swing over the flowing water made me dizzy, but I didn't care. I didn't care about anything at all. I just needed to escape the conversation that had just taken place.

The wooden swing, worn smooth by all eight of Mamm's brood, had its share of wear from my own legs. Short and stubby at first, they had grown sleek and toned with a bit of muscle that came with hard work. I was a bit too skinny for Mamm's taste, and she wasn't afraid to say so. Stoutness and sturdiness was all she'd wanted from her only daughter. And I wasn't either.

My hands hurt from the constant scratch of the weathered rope, but I didn't care about that either. With each pump, warm memories of growing up with seven brothers came flooding back, and I swung more fiercely to catch them.

Dat had picked this spot because it pulled away a *gut* bit from the rush of the river and offered just the kind of swimming hole his hot and sticky brood needed. One by one each *Bruder* would swing out as far as he could over the water and let go. A whooping and hollering mess of legs and arms, he'd crash down into the river just seconds later.

Every last one knew how to work the swing so he could get to the blackest part of the hole where the river was deep and the current mild.

The dark spots in the green water used to make me queasy until Mose taught me how to swim one day. Poor, softhearted Mose had nearly drowned trying.

But he did what he'd set out to do. After that day, no one loved the swing as much as I did. Content to let me swing over them, my *Bruders* would laugh and carry on in the river below. All seven were grown and out of the house now—fine-looking Amish men living in the way of Willow Brook's *Ordnung*. Not one chose the "sinfulness of the world," as Dat had called it back when he was able to speak his mind.

Since I was the only one left living with Dat and Mamm, the full force of their worry had been unleashed on me. What once had been fairly divided among the eight of us was now all mine.

Their worry seemed plain in every look, sigh, and extra line on Dat's face and in Mamm's extra sharp tongue.

Soon they would have even more time on their hands when they moved to the *Dawdi Haus*. The small addition had been vacant for a few years now. My heart squeezed at the empty space Mammi Miriam used to fill there. Fresh grief took me by surprise. Nobody understood me like she had.

Soon as my youngest brother, David, along with his pinch-faced wife Mary, moved their family into our home, there were bound to be some big changes. David would be filling Dat's shoes as head of the main house, and Mary would take over the kitchen and Mamm's garden.

The garden. How I would manage with Mary lording over me there, I couldn't say.

My hands stung as I clung tighter to the scratchy twine. The pain helped to push back thoughts that threatened my peace.

Life would be different then. And as for me, well, I wasn't sure yet where I was going to end up. David said I could stay in the house, but the look in Mary's eyes said different.

A soft creak came from somewhere deep inside the old oak's branch and brought me back to the present, reminding me of the bishop.

And my trouble.

I had a choice to make, and I knew it. I'd already told the bishop and Mamm I was giving up writing for *gut*. The problem was, I didn't know how to do that. Writing made up such a huge part of who I was. My thoughts, my feelings, my ideas—even my memories—all came through my pen. Writing made life real to me.

I pumped the swing harder, letting out the tension of my choice as I swung back and forth.

The problem was, being Amish made life real to me too. These were my people. This way of life helped to define me just like my writing did.

If I kept writing, I would be put under the *Bann* and would be unable to eat with or maybe even speak with my family and friends. At least not until I publicly confessed and repented of my sin to the People. The harshness of the *Bann* varied from community to community, and Bishop

Amos was not a soft man. I'd seen the *Bann* separate families—for *gut*.

Funny, I'd lived in fear of the *Bann* my whole life, and now with it looming over my head, I still wasn't sure what to do.

I had to think of my family.

I had to think of my writing.

Ach. This was all Lizzie's fault.

I smiled, though, when I thought of my friend. She'd come up with the idea to write for the newspaper, tossing the plan out to me at a desperate time in my life.

Mammi Miriam had just died.

Lizzie had a Mennonite friend, Morris, who was doing deliveries for the paper. When Morris told her the *Star* was looking for a columnist, it was all she needed to put her plan into action.

We'd met in our usual place—the outcropping of rocks in our woods. I had thought she'd come to console me about Mammi's death, but I was in for the biggest surprise of my life.

"Guess what?" Lizzie tossed me an impish grin.

"What?"

She reached into her basket and pulled out a copy of the *Mountain Laurel Star*.

I flinched as if she'd pulled out a snake. "Where'd you get that?" She knew as well as I did that the *Englischer* newspaper was *verboten* for Amish like us to read.

She'd giggled and opened the paper. "Here, on page three." She pointed.

I started reading. All at once, my heart sank in my chest.

"Why, this is mine." I felt confused. "This is my story."

She'd grinned. "I know."

"But it's mine. How did they get a hold of it?" Indignation had risen in my chest and threatened to boil over. I glanced at the byline. "Who's this Ima Righter person?"

"It's you!" Lizzie looked very pleased with herself.

A headache formed at my temples. "Me? What are you talking about?"

"It's your story. I sent it in to the editor."

"You what?" I screeched. "Are ya crazy? I could get in deep trouble for this."

"That's why I didn't put your name on it, silly," she said calmly. "Ima Righter is your pen name."

"My what?"

She rolled her eyes. "Your fake name. Think about it. 'Ima Righter.' Get it?"

It was my turn to roll my eyes. "But why would you do such a thing?" I snatched the paper from her. Seeing my story in print gave me a feeling I'd never felt before. I really couldn't stop staring.

She reached out and touched my hand. "I did it because you're a wonderful writer and you're *schmaert*, Johanna. No matter what the bishop says about it, your stories deserve to be shared with someone other than you, me, and Miracle. To me, even if it's just this one time, it was the worth the risk."

I had blinked back tears then. Besides Mammi Miriam, no one had ever called me a writer.

That's when Lizzie told me about the columnist position that Morris shared with her. And I couldn't move fast enough to apply. After seeing that first story in the newspaper, a hunger consumed me to have all my writing in print. Writing for myself was one thing, but sharing my gift with others was an entirely different feeling. And I wanted more of it. Morris, sworn into secrecy, became my own personal delivery man.

The editor of the paper, Hilton Hughes, allowed me the freedom to write what I wanted for the column, as long as it was in his hands by Monday at noon. That gave me till Friday at noon to have it to Morris when he delivered the paper to our *Englischer* neighbors. Sometimes, I wrote poetry for that week's submission. Other times a story, separated into segments, came to me. I would write about our calves, the farm, the garden, and especially the river. The Shenango often filled me with creative thoughts.

I'd done my best to keep my Amish identity out of the paper. And tucked away as we were in a small Amish district, separate from the larger New Wilmington Amish communities, it wasn't hard to keep my identity hidden from my readers. But the bishop was forever suspicious.

Only two months later, Lizzie met me out at the outcropping to share the sad news that she'd been put under the *Bann* by the bishop.

Her words had made my skin crawl. My best friend under the *Bann*? Since I was a baptized member of the Willow Brook community, our relationship would drastically change.

"What? Why?" I asked it even though I knew the reason. Morris had become more than just a "friend" to Elizabeth.

Baptized Amish could only marry baptized Amish. That was that. And Lizzie was baptized Amish. So Morris was off-limits.

I had been afraid for her, but she didn't seem afraid herself. A little sad, maybe. But not afraid.

"Where will you go, Lizzie? What will you do?"

Lizzie had taken both of my hands in hers. "*Gott* knows where and what, Johanna." Her warm eyes looked deeply into mine, making me squirm just a bit. I was, after all, disobeying the *Ordnung* myself with my writing.

That was the last time I saw her. Sometimes I wondered about her life beyond the community, and daily I felt grateful for what she had done for me.

A hawk swooped past, bringing my mind back to the river. I had stopped pumping, and the swing was nearly still. Maybe it would make things less painful if I got around to doing what I came here for. I patted the pocket of my heavy cape where I'd safely stashed my journal and pen.

Thick with acorns, the oak's largest branch hung lower than ever. I pumped my legs again, and my swinging shook some acorns loose. I watched them disappear into the blackness of the water below. I shivered, thinking about how cold the water was this time of year, but I didn't want to stop.

If I was going to do this, I was going to do it right. Slowly, I pulled out the journal my grandmother had given me when I was ten and prepared to drop it, tattered and worn into the river. It wasn't my only journal, but, because it had been a gift from Mammi, it was more special to me than any of the others I now had tucked under my mattress. My eyes stung at the thought of parting with any of them. But this one was going to be the most difficult. It was where I had some of my most heartfelt writing.

I held my journal tight along with my pen, whispering a prayer that *Gott* would help me do the deed. It certainly wasn't something I could do on my own. My resolve wavered, I could feel it.

The journal held all of my best poetry and short stories that I had written since that day Mammi Miriam had discovered my love for writing. The pen with its delicate engraving had been a secret gift from Lizzie before she fell under the *Bann*. In order to keep my promise to stop writing, I knew I had to give up both treasures, and the rushing waters of the Shenango seemed like the perfect place to let them go.

Wouldn't Lizzie be proud to know that I had been writing for the newspaper now for over two years?

Ach, it didn't matter what Lizzie thought though, did it? The bishop had made his point clear.

Enough already.

I had to choose.

A crack shot through the air like lightning, and the jolt of it seared through my body. The journal and pen flung from my fingers, and time seemed to stop as the thick branch split right up the middle before my eyes. Wood that had withstood the worst storms that Northwestern Pennsylvania dished out for the last hundred years turned to powder in less than a second. The moment happened so fast and yet I saw it all so slowly as the gnarled old branch crashed into the swollen river taking me right along with it.

Fear and black water enveloped me as I desperately clawed my way to the surface. My cape dress caught tight on the sharp edge of the broken branch, and I couldn't be free of it.

CHAPTER 2

JUDAH

The reporter in the cubical next to me thumped hard at his keyboard again. I got that he was under deadline, but he was the loudest one in the office and hard to block out. To distract myself, I opened today's newspaper. The "Best of Ima" section took me a little by surprise. Never had I seen my editor, Hilton Hughes, reprint anything in the *Mountain Laurel Star*. To him, "old news" was not worth the ink.

But things seemed way different where Ima was concerned. Since her first unsolicited submission had been dropped in his mailbox a few years ago, she'd become the bread and butter of the *Star*. Now that she'd missed her deadlines for two straight weeks, Hilton's hot little head didn't know what to do with itself.

I'm not sure I believed the buzz she'd disappeared. She probably just wanted to stop writing. I didn't see what the big deal was.

I ducked behind my cube wall when I caught a glimpse of Hilton walking out of his office. You never knew what was going to come out of his mouth these days, and I had an important story to write. The county bank had just been robbed, and I was about ready to slip out the door to start asking some questions. The story would be big for me, and I didn't want to blow it.

"You've got to find her," Hilton hurled in my general direction.

Hoping he wasn't talking to me, I kept my head down and grabbed my coat to leave for the bank. I nearly ran into him just outside my cube wall.

"Oh hi, Hilton. I was just—"

"The few times she'd mailed her columns, it always came with the county postmark. That should narrow things down a bit."

"Hilton, I'm headed to the bank for the—"

"Bertram's got it."

Bertram. The new hire. The guy was still a rookie, for Pete's sake. Bertram Hochstetler had a hard enough time looking you in the eye, let alone covering a bank robbery. What was Hilton thinking?

This job had been tough enough for me to land, and the last thing I wanted to do was lose it over a case like Bertram.

And what if somehow the guy knocked the story out of the park and ended up on Hilton's "nice list"?

That would be just my luck.

Bertram emerged from around a corner. A real heartthrob, he had begun to bald at the ripe old age of twenty-three. His thick-framed glasses slipped down his greasy nose. Hilton must have liked something about him, or he wouldn't have even given him a chance with the *Star*.

Hilton told him to wait a minute and focused again on me.

"Listen, we have a delivery guy who picks up her pay and sometimes delivers her columns to me. Says he's sworn to secrecy about her true identity. I'd threaten to fire him, but he's our only link to Ima. He's leaving for the day, and I need you to tail him. Maybe he lives near Ima. If not, she's got to be somewhere in the area."

Had Hilton lost it? There are over one hundred thousand people in Mercer County not to mention wherever the delivery guy lives. Thanks a lot, Hilton.

But I really couldn't blame him. Ima Righter's column had been a bit of a phenom the minute it was in print. People were drawn to her for some reason. During the time she'd been a columnist for the *Star*, she'd done quite a few stories, submitted in installments. And our audience ate every word up. Advertising and subscriptions had blown up after Hilton had accepted the woman's request to work for the paper.

The pieces I'd read made me feel uncomfortable, though. Maybe it was because, if I was honest with myself, I knew I couldn't write that well.

Although he hadn't been so kind when he'd first received her unsolicited submission. "What does she think—she's somehow different than all the other writers trying to get their teeth into this paper?" Always the hothead, Hilton had taken her story into his office at the far end of the newsroom.

I'd waited for the mocking session that was sure to follow. Hilton had a way of tearing apart someone's work.

And I had the scars to prove it.

But then things grew quiet over on Hilton's end of the newsroom. A little too quiet. I'd gotten up, craned my neck around the edge of my cubicle, and peered through the glass of his office at the rare sight of Hilton digesting a story.

No red pen in sight.

Why doesn't he just toss it down and say he hates it, like he hates everything else?

Hilton hadn't hated Righter's story, and neither did our readers. Our publisher later said it was one of the best decisions Hilton had ever made to add Ms. Righter, or whatever her name was, on the editorial page.

FORBIDDEN GIFT

Her current silence didn't matter to me. As far as I was concerned, the fewer writers to compete with around here, the better.

Hilton was talking to Bertram now about the bank story. My story. I went back to my cube to find my keys.

The Swagon was a '97 Buick Roadmaster station wagon with real faux-wood paneling on its doors. The car's third backseat faced backward, and it had no AC, but I loved it. Other guys my age were giving in to the lure of trucks, SUVs, or sports cars, but those came with monthly payments I wasn't interested in. The Swagon not only didn't break my budget—when it wasn't in for a repair—but also had sentimental value to me because it had been Dad's.

Driving it, I felt close to him somehow.

I did my best to follow the delivery guy in the pickup, but I forgot to mention to Hilton that the Swagon only went so fast before she started to shake. I lightened up on the gas pedal to calm things down and watched the pickup slowly edge out of my sight. It wasn't long before the truck was completely gone. Backtracking, I tried to follow one of the lonely country roads the guy might have turned down, but after a while, the fields of drying corn all started to look the same, and I got a little turned around.

Trying to turn on my GPS, I remembered the charge on my phone had been low when I left the office, and it was now dead.

The Swagon uttered its signature groan as I hugged a curve too tightly. I felt like joining in. Being employed by a newspaper had been harder than I'd thought it would be.

And now with my editor on a rampage, I was getting fed up with it all. Sure, I loved being a reporter, but dealing with people like Hilton Hughes hadn't been taught in any journalism class I'd taken.

Trying to move up at the paper hadn't been easy either, not with people like Bertram taking my big stories and Ima's writing always catching Hilton's eye. A few weeks ago, I had been excited to find out that Roger, the senior writer, forgot to fact check something in a front page story. His subsequent exit was my big chance.

But here I was, stuck out in the country, looking for a writer I didn't want to find.

As far as I was concerned, Ms. Righter could fall off the map.

What if she came into the office one day looking for a full-time position? Hilton liked her so much, he'd hire her on the spot. Even if there were no open jobs available, he'd find a place for her, all right.

I just had to make sure that place wasn't my cubicle. Then again, if she was never found, where did that put me? Forever on assignment, scanning the countryside for someone I didn't care to find?

No, until all this died down, this looked to be my life, and after seeing the determination on Hilton's face earlier, the end was nowhere in sight. Somehow I needed to locate her, but make sure she never wrote for the *Star* again.

I wanted to move up so badly at the *Star*, I could taste it.

Sure, there were bigger papers and bigger opportunities out there, but this paper meant something to me. It was the one Dad and I had talked about whenever I told him I wanted to be a reporter. Even though I was just a kid then, Dad told me working at the *Star* was possible if I set my mind to it. And here I was proving him right. Although I wanted to advance in my career, I wanted to do it at the *Star*. Not for some other paper I didn't care about.

My parents had run a newspaper before moving to Riverview, and they loved the *Star*. Now that I had lost both of them—my dad to death, and my mom to what was going on between us—in a weird way, the newspaper felt like home to me.

The Swagon rattled along, and as I continued to search for the delivery guy, I thought of my mother. The last time I saw her had been rough. I had just graduated from college and, in celebration, she had pulled Dad's grill out of the garage and made burgers on it for the first time ever.

She never grilled. Not even when Dad was alive. Why did she need to start then?

Our little "party" had consisted of just her and me, and I couldn't shake the thought that Dad had been the grill master of the family. Grilling without him made me feel weird inside. Weirder than I had felt in a long time. At least since he died.

"Since when did you learn how to grill, Mom?" I'd asked her.

She smiled. "It's really not as hard as it's made up to be. I just read the instructions on the back of the lighter fluid bottle. I could teach you."

I took another bite out of my burger. It was good, but I couldn't shake the feeling Dad should have been here today watching me graduate and making the burgers. Mom shouldn't be living out this stage of her life without a husband. The whole thing made me angry at myself all over again. I had never told Mom how my own stupidity had led to Dad's death. I'd let her believe what I wanted her to believe.

Maybe, though, I should have told her. Some days the guilt was too much. It made me irritable, almost like I wanted to hit something. And now, I could feel it building up again.

Why did Mom have to go and learn how to grill?

"I'm thinking of trying chicken wings on the grill next. Your dad made some good wings that way. And after that, I could try his barbecue—"

"Yeah, you know, I really don't want to talk about Dad right now." I'd set my half-eaten burger on my plate.

Mom seemed a little upset at that. She was always talking about wanting to "keep his memory alive" so we could heal. And here I was shutting her down again.

"Why can't we just talk about him sometimes, Judah?"

I rolled my eyes. "Do we have to go there ... right now?"

"I would think that now would be the perfect time to talk about your dad. He would have been so proud to see you today."

I got up abruptly then from the deck chair, making the pitcher of lemonade slosh. Mom didn't seem to care. She just stared into her lap.

I don't know why I wanted to add to her pain, but I just didn't care. I had been living with Mom all through college to save money, but when I started interviewing for jobs, I felt like it was a good time to think about getting my own place. I had to look out for myself. I was done feeling like I had to talk about Dad all the time.

"Now's probably the best time to bring this up, Mom." She kept her eyes on the uneaten burger on her plate. I just wanted to get this over with. "As soon as I land a job, I'm going to be getting my own place."

"Nice time to tell me this, Judah." Mom raised her eyes to meet mine. She was angry, but I didn't care. I had to look out for myself. "You can't keep running from what happened."

"Maybe, but I don't have to keep reliving it either." Going into the house, I gathered my things and headed for the front door. I didn't know where I would spend the night, or how long I would be gone, but I knew I needed to get out of there.

I slung my backpack over my shoulder and stepped out the door. Mom had followed me into the house and now faced me in the doorway.

"This isn't who your father and I raised you to be."

Why did her words always have to sting?

"Well, last time I checked, my father was dead."

I hadn't meant to say that, but there it was, lingering between us like some bad smell and hurting her more than if I had struck her.

"Your father died saving you."

"Yeah, well, sometimes I wish he hadn't bothered."

Mom turned away from me then and slammed the door in my face. I heard the lock click.

That had been two years ago, and other than grabbing my things and my dog when I knew she wouldn't be home, I hadn't been back since. I couldn't face the guilt anymore.

A fraying sound coming from the Swagon's engine brought me back to my mission to find Ima. The noise was followed by an acrid, burning smell, and I slowed down. This was just what I needed. And no working cell phone.

Seeing the buggies on the road signs and wide shoulder, it looked like I had broken down right in the middle of Amish country.

Rolling down my window, I made my way to the curb, careful to stay out of the buggy path. No need to make the Amish folk angry, after all. If I couldn't figure out what was going on under my hood, I'd have to trek it for some help, and there was a good chance there would be a buggy involved in my rescue.

Rolling hills, a picture-perfect autumn countryside, and the sound of the rushing Shenango river greeted me. It was enough to make anyone stuck at a desk all day swoon.

But not me.

I grabbed my water bottle, glad I had filled it up before leaving the office, and took a look at my engine. Car repair wasn't one of my strengths, but I had learned a thing or two in keeping the Swagon running. I lifted the hood with my fingertips, careful not to get burned by the hot steam. After the smoke cleared, I noticed my fan belt had decided today was a good day to shred to pieces. And I didn't have a replacement. Running my fingers through my hair, I leaned against the Swagon and planned what to do next. For starters, I made myself forget about Hilton, Ima, and the *Star* for just a few minutes.

A turkey buzzard found its perch high in the hickory tree across the road. I watched the bird for a bit while it preened its feathers without a care in the world. And then an odd sound traveled with the breeze.

At first, I thought the bird had made the noise, but the more I listened, the more I had trouble placing what I heard. The sound wasn't the typical type of noise you'd hear on an empty road. Maybe the game commission had brought in another wild animal to help kill off the last overpopulating animal it had introduced.

The hairs on the back of my neck stood up when I heard the noise again. The sound seemed almost human.

Eerie, how it would stop and start again. Almost as if ...

I squinted out toward the river.

CHAPTER 3

JUDAH

Water, anything but water.

My heart beat like crazy as I made my way through the knee-high weeds to the river.

The racing Shenango had been swollen for weeks after the crazy fall rains we'd had. The fear of water I'd successfully hidden for over a decade began to surface and race along with it.

Coming closer in, I heard the sound again—definitely human.

"Where ... where are you?" A voice I barely recognized came from my lips.

Scanning the bank and the fast-moving water beyond, I could see a thick branch floating about twenty feet away. I reached out to an old oak, steadying myself.

Who had cried out? Had I imagined it?

The water looked black out where the branch floated. A sure sign of a drop-off. I knew about those all too well.

A soft ripple came from somewhere near the branch. A prickle ran up my spine as a woman's hand reached out in a desperate attempt to grab hold of the branch. The wood rolled at the grab, and the pale hand slipped slowly back under.

I threw off my jacket and, when I did, half my belongings flew into the weeds behind me. I let out a word that shocked even me and waded out. I tried to call out to the woman, but my voice caught somewhere deep in my throat. I slipped on the algae-covered river rocks and fell. The water was cold, too cold.

Why was I here? Of all people to help a drowning person, I was the worst pick.

I could leave her. No one would know. She'd probably be dead by now, anyway. What would be the point in saving someone who's already dead? But the image of her reaching hand made my legs move. Somehow, I just couldn't live with that.

A chill ran through me, heightening my sense of urgency. I had to move fast. I searched the sky for help for the first time since my dad died.

Wading waist-deep out to the drop-off, I took big sweeps with my arms under the water, hoping I'd find her here where I could still touch bottom.

My breathing grew heavier as the water deepened. I explored the river bottom with my feet, feeling out where the drop off began. Finding it, I stood at the edge and noticed that the flow of the river had cocked one end of the thick branch toward me.

A surge of adrenaline exploded into reckless valor, and I made the jump out into the deep, black water.

My landing took my breath away, and the branch tried to turn under me, but I shifted my weight and steadied myself on a leafy part of the wood laden with acorns. The branch couldn't have been long in the water if fresh leaves and even acorns still clung to it. Looking up, I saw the fresh gash in the oak above.

Why didn't the log move with the current? Was it stuck on something or maybe someone?

Then I noticed the two thick ropes wrapped around the limb.

My mind started to make connections, and desperately I made heavy sweeps with my free arm and legs in the water below the branch. My fingers felt so cold now, I could barely move them.

"God!"

I begged someone I didn't believe in anymore. What was wrong with me?

Wet fabric, lots of it, brushed my cold, stiff, searching hand. I made a grab and missed, my slowed reaction losing the cloth to the current.

I had one chance and, not thinking, plunged after what I figured was her dress. A stupid choice, I knew. I could write the headline myself, "Non-swimmer Dies in Futile Rescue Attempt."

Flailing to get to the surface, I ended up with another fistful of fabric and, clutching it this time, pulled the woman up with me. But together we sunk back under. Cold and painful memories of that day I nearly drowned as a boy washed through me.

And here I was drowning all over again. Only this time Dad wasn't around to die trying to save me. I was glad for that at least.

I must have been losing it, though, because there he was, under the surface with me, holding something out. Reaching for it with my free hand, I felt the scratch of a swing rope.

I pulled the rope with all I had and, keeping the unconscious woman's head up, hooked one arm over the log. Kicking like mad, I was able to bring one side of the stuck log to where my feet could almost touch.

Stretching for a foothold, I finally found one and, after pulling her dress free from the log, I thrust myself and the woman forward up the bank. Clutching to her desperately—her layers of fabric made it difficult—I made my way up the bank and laid her where the ground was finally flat. Grateful for the CPR training Mom made me take after Dad died, I clawed at the front of her garment, straight pins pricking my thawing hands.

Didn't these people believe in buttons?

My hands tingled as I started compressions and opened her airway.

CHAPTER 4

JOHANNA

I laughed as I made my way through the field of wheat stalks. Golden brown bristles ready for harvest tickled at my palms.

It was a beautiful autumn day. Perfect on all accounts, and I was headed to meet my beau. Our courtship had been kept secret for all this time.

Wouldn't Mamm and Dat be pleased with my surprise?

They still saw me as a Maedel, but I knew different. And the secret was so much fun to keep—at least for now.

When me and my beau were published, then all of Willow Brook would know. And the wedding plans would begin.

We'll plant a hundred stalks of celery, just to make sure we'll have enough to decorate each table. Taking in a long breath, I felt as if I could even smell the roasht chicken casserole with its buttery stuffing.

It would be quite the celebration.

The sun shone bright and seemed to be growing brighter by the minute. I had to admit, the sun's glow seemed a bit strange for autumn in Willow Brook. The days were normally cool and cloudy this late in September.

We did have our occasional "blue sky" day, though, and this was a beautiful one.

It matched my mood, and I was glad for it.

Now that I was to be wed, my parents' minds would finally be set to rest. No more worrying about my future. No more long talks at the kitchen table with Mamm about what was to become of me.

Being single and Amish had been an uncommon mix. And it put too much pressure on Mamm and Dat—way too much.

And it had stung to be "passed over."

But now that I had my beau, all that had changed. Odd that I couldn't place his name. Probably just all the excitement.

The sun shone even brighter now, and its warmth drew me in.

Just past the wheat field, the sun looked to almost touch the horizon in the distance. I changed my direction then and began to walk toward the glow.

My beau had passed this way—I just knew it. I could feel his presence still in the air … but where was he?

It was as if I could reach out my hand and grab hold of him.

I let my eyes roam the field as I walked. My man was nowhere in sight. Odd that I could feel him at all. The closer I walked toward the bright sun, the more I felt I could touch him.

Just a few more yards now and I would reach the light. Never before had I seen a sunset in this way—it beckoned me.

Reaching out now, I could feel its warmth on my fingertips.

JUDAH

I was losing her, I could tell.

She had been under too long. If I'd only hurried a little more or decided to help a little sooner. I seemed to only be looking out for number one these days. If I was honest with myself, it was a crappy way to live.

Opposite, actually, of the way Mom raised me.

Between compressions and breaths, I berated myself for who I had become.

Would I really have just walked away, leaving her to die? The truth slapped me hard in the face. She couldn't die. What I wouldn't give to have Mom here about now. She and I could tag-team. We'd trained enough for a moment like this. I'd even settle for Bertram's help—I was that desperate.

The woman's lips had started out cold when I pulled her out of the water but were beginning to warm up. Was it my warmth or hers? I couldn't tell. Exhaustion, that's all I felt.

I held my ear just above her mouth, listening carefully for breathing, just like I had been taught. Nothing yet. Mouth-to-mouth resuscitation was totally different on a real person. I had been great on the dummy. Maybe I was losing my touch. Or maybe I was losing her. She wasn't breathing on her own yet.

Five more breaths in, and I could see her chest rise and fall with them—a good sign that there was no obstruction. And her heart seemed to be beating, although slow.

Pushing up the long sleeves of her dark blue dress, I felt her wrist again to confirm her life, but this time I could barely find a pulse.

She was letting go.

A thick swell of grief welled up in my chest and caught me off guard.

"No!"

A pair of mourning doves fluttered in alarm from their perch in the old oak.

What was I doing? I didn't even know her.

Unfamiliar feelings sprang up. She couldn't die.

Bertram had hung a sign on his cube wall just a few days after he'd been hired. We all have a story to tell.

I had been annoyed at the time and thought the guy was trying to tell me how to live my life, but oddly, I thought of that sign now. He could be right about that one thing: *we all have a story to tell.* And I could tell this Amish lady had more to say.

Maybe it was because I had risked my life for her. Maybe that's why I couldn't let her go.

Pump, pump, pump, pump ... breath, breath.

Again, I wished I had someone to help me. I totally understood why my CPR instructors always pushed the "tag-team" approach. I felt tired and cold from the river. Looking around for a car or a buggy, I found nothing.

I couldn't do this anymore. My hands had grown numb, and the air was only getting colder as the sun started its slow descent in the sky. I felt the beginnings of hypothermia setting in as another round of shivers ran up and down my spine.

I had nothing left to give and wanted nothing more than to lie down, to take a break. And then I could work on her some more.

My knees started to give out when a song popped into my head, and I remembered the "Stayin' Alive" CPR technique we were taught. The tempo of the song almost perfectly matched the number of compressions per minute needed in hands-only CPR.

Ha!

A surge of energy coursed through me, and Travolta, the Bee Gees, and I worked CPR on the Amish woman tirelessly after that. I even belted the song out loud at some point. I didn't know where the strength came from, but I definitely didn't have any more to give on my own. I wasn't asking any questions, and I wasn't going to give up on her now. I knew I would die trying to save her if I had to.

Another grueling fifteen minutes went by, and suddenly a flash of pink came into the young woman's cheek.

Had I imagined it? No, there it was on her other side. A small cough followed and then a larger one with half the river along with it.

JOHANNA

Just seconds ago, I basked in the warmth of a glowing light, and now I hurt all over. A shiver shot through me from head to toe.

My mouth tingled as if I'd been kissed, but I was afraid to open my eyes. I had a sneaking suspicion I had been caught in some sort of dream.

Disappointment cut like a knife, but I couldn't open my eyes—wouldn't.

Someone turned me over, and I was sick. So much stink. I thought I would die. Whoever was helping me probably wished they were dead about now too.

"Are you … are you all right?" A strange voice—not from the People.

I opened my eyes and sat up.

The sunlight glistened off the crown of his head just so. Hair the color of harvest wheat dried in what was left of the sunny afternoon.

I scooted back across the weeds, putting some distance between us. He looked at my chest and then turned bright red. I noticed my cape was missing and my bodice torn. I covered myself with my arms. What exactly had gone on here?

He shook his hands in front of him as if to say I had the wrong idea.

"You fell in the river." He nodded his head in the direction of the water as if that explained it all.

The river.

Shivering some more, I looked in the direction where he had nodded at the rushing green of the Shenango. He stood then, walked away, and came back with a checked fleece blanket. I saw a car parked on the side of the road, where a buggy had just pulled up. Someone else was coming to help.

Whoever this man was, he seemed genuinely concerned for me. How had he gotten me out?

Before I could ask, he told me what had happened and warned me recovering from CPR could be tough, saying even broken ribs could result. I could see now his clothes were as wet as mine. I checked my sides for pain, and the fleece slipped. He reached out to recover my shoulder. I opened my mouth to thank him when the bishop startled the both of us by roughly pushing his hand between us.

"Let her go!"

My lips pursed as I saw our scene through the bishop's eyes. I did my best to silence a groan. As if I wasn't in enough trouble with the bishop.

Quickly, I tried to put more distance between us, but the world started to spin. The man reached to steady me, and at his touch, I felt his warmth.

"None of that now, Johanna." The bishop pushed the man's hand away and roughly pulled me up.

"Now, hold on there." The man came to my defense. "She fell in the river. My car broke down over there, and I heard a noise, and ..."

My foot caught on the fleece and it dropped to the ground, exposing the sad state of my cape dress. I fumbled with the material, trying to right the wet fabric and clutching it to myself.

The bishop's look betrayed his thoughts.

"I don't know who you are or what you're doing here." He flung his words over his shoulder toward the man as he pulled me forward. "But you need to go back to where you belong."

He shot a shameful look at me and roughly led me to his buggy. He slapped the driving lines to the horse's sides, looking forward to sharing my latest sin with Mamm and Dat, no doubt. I wished with all my heart I didn't feel so weak. There was so much wrong in the way the bishop had treated us.

Feeling the man's eyes on me, I stole one last look from the side of the buggy. He raised his hand ever so slightly.

Ach! I hadn't even asked his name.

JUDAH

The old man had caught me completely off guard, and I'd been too stunned to speak. The elation I'd felt when the young woman had finally breathed on her own still coursed through my veins.

She was alive.

But just as quickly, she'd been taken. What had the man called her?

Johanna.

I hadn't heard the name before, but I liked it.

When the buggy was just a black dot on the wooded road, I took a walk back to the river and eased myself onto its bank.

Filling my lungs with the late afternoon air, I sat taking in slow breaths and willed myself to calm down. With the way things looked now, I could easily let myself believe nothing had just happened—that I'd just imagined the whole thing. But I was wet and cold. And I couldn't stop shaking.

I knew I'd better get myself dry and warm soon, or I might regret it later. The sun would soon set. I couldn't make myself get up though—not yet. Wrapping myself in the warm fleece Johanna had dropped, I gazed out across the river and was surprised to see the log still bobbing in the distance.

The current had succeeded in moving the wood further out, but it seemed to still be caught on something underneath. Whatever held up the branch, I was glad for it. Without that old log, I would have drowned right along with Johanna.

My fingers grew numb again, and I stretched them out behind me, trying to get feeling back. As I did, they rolled over something smooth and hard.

Fumbling to grip the object, I brought up a pen covered in mud. No ordinary pen, though, judging from its shape and weight. This one felt like a Parker. I'd always had a thing for pens. A box under my bed held all the dropped and forgotten ones I had ever found.

Finding a pen always made me feel like I should keep writing. I couldn't even begin to count the number of times I had been ready to throw in the towel on the whole thing, and then I'd find a pen lying in a parking lot somewhere.

I swiped the mud from the pen, but the engraved letters on its barrel were still hard to see. I rose and sloshed the pen in the river to clean it. Squinting in the waning sun, I saw that my hunch was right on it being a Parker, but that's not what caught my eye.

"Johanna" was engraved in beautiful curling letters across the barrel of the pen.

Why would an Amish woman bring an expensive pen—a writer's pen like this—down to the river? From what I knew of the Amish, they weren't writers. They were land workers, garden tillers, and pie bakers mostly.

Taking time out to sit by the river and write just wasn't their thing, as far as I knew. And what was she writing? I scanned the bank, hoping to find something to fill in the blanks for me.

CHAPTER 5

Kelly's head hurt.

She'd been working hard on an article for the *Pittsburgh Post-Gazette* and had just hit "send" on her email to her client.

"Glad that one's done." Her words echoed a bit off the walls in her study. She sighed.

Finishing a story had always been a big deal when her family was there to celebrate her accomplishment. These days, it felt a bit anticlimactic.

Life as a freelance writer was still rewarding to her, however—if not a little hectic. The fast pace wasn't as bad as being publisher of a mid-sized paper, though. Kelly shook her head at the memory and smiled nonetheless. The ten years she and Jack ran *The Messenger* paper in Upstate New York were some pretty special years of her life.

Kelly organized her writing space and decided it was time to head to her garden. She needed to clear her mind, and a little prayer wouldn't hurt either. Sitting on the bench in her mudroom, Kelly pulled on her boots. As she stood to head outside, a gardening glove fell from her hand.

Bending down to retrieve it, she got full view of all that had collected under her bench.

"Ugh!" The dust bunnies had multiplied, and it looked like the spider webs were planning a takeover. Grabbing her broom and dustpan, she swept up what she could, reaching the broom into the far corners while hoping she wouldn't send a big spider crawling out.

Her sweeping set a red ball into motion that rolled across the vinyl flooring and bounced off the baseboard. The ball came to a stop just a few inches from Kelly's boots. She stopped sweeping and stared.

The ball had belonged to Liza Lou, the Catahoula leopard dog that had filled their home with energy and love for ten years. If she were here right now, Liza would be pushing Kelly with her snout, wanting her to get moving so they could head outside. The ball would be in her mouth, with her tongue probably hanging out the side.

Kelly shook her head and braced herself emotionally for what was coming next. Thoughts of Liza Lou were always followed by memories of her son.

Judah.

Kelly hated what her relationship with her son had become after he'd left that day she'd grilled their dinner. Judah had come back to get his things a few times, but always when she was at church.

She cried on the Sunday she came home to find he had taken Liza Lou along with her toys and food bowls. She was his dog, after all, and the two of them had always been close. Liza belonged to Judah, there was no doubting that, but Kelly felt heartbroken even still.

It seemed like God was taking all she loved the most away from her.

She'd tried every way she knew to apologize to Judah for slamming the door on him. There was plenty he needed to apologize for as well, but she'd decided to overlook all that. Their relationship had a rift that needed to be fixed. If it had to start with her, then so be it. She wasn't beyond admitting she'd made a mistake.

But apparently Judah was, because he'd chosen to ignore every one of her efforts to mend what was broken between them.

Eventually, she'd decided God would have to fix their relationship. And with that decision came the peace she had been looking for.

Still in the mudroom, Kelly opened the door a few inches and breathed in deeply. The air seemed cooler than usual and felt good in her lungs.

She had grown tired of living in an empty house. As she stood there in the doorway, thinking and praying, a crazy thought popped into her head. Kelly smiled. She grabbed her keys and headed over to the Riverview Humane Society.

There was a time when she was a girl that her family had more barn cats than she could count. Jack had never liked cats, and after they got Liza Lou, there was no chance of bringing one into the house, especially not with a breed of dog known for its unique ability to climb trees.

But today was a new day.

Kelly entered the cat section and picked out a long-haired orange-and-white cat that had been named "Peaches" by her previous owner. A sign on the cat's cage said she was great with people and that she'd been given up for adoption due to the previous owner's lack of space.

Well, space was something Kelly had plenty of. After sitting for a while with Peaches nestled up against her in the Humane Society's cat room, she decided it was time her small family of one become two.

CHAPTER 6

JOHANNA

Mamm, Dat, and the bishop had been in the kitchen a long time. Too long for it to be *gut* news I'd be hearing when they were done.

Sitting inside the bishop's buggy, I banged my head several times against the side. How did I get into this mess? The bishop hadn't even let me go into my own house when we pulled up. He just handed me a lap robe from the back of his buggy and roughly told me to stay put.

The truth was, I hadn't felt well since the incident at the river and breathing had become difficult. What had the man said about CPR and broken ribs?

The accident still seemed a little fuzzy for me, but I knew I had to get my story straight before Mamm started her questions. I remembered the sound the branch made when it broke and the feel of the cold river swirling above my head.

I knew I was going to die in the river.

Why doesn't the bishop hurry up and get on with it? If I'm the one on trial here, I ought to be in there.

Now here was a story, wasn't it? My brain started outlining it, and I wished for my journal and pen. A sick feeling rose in my stomach.

That's why I had been at the river in the first place—trying to put a part of me to death so I wouldn't be put under the *Bann*. At least that's what I was supposed to be doing. I never could quite come to do that deed though. Part of me was glad for it. The other part … *Ach*!

Shivering overtook me despite the lap robe and wouldn't stop no matter how many times I rubbed at my arms.

I needed to do something. The sun would soon set, and sitting here wasn't helping me at all. I stepped down from the buggy. They could find me in the barn where it was warmer.

Inside, I discovered my younger cousin Benjamin finishing up some chores. Since Dat's stroke, my *Bruder* David had already taken over a *gut* deal of work on the farm. He paid some of my cousins to help, and they often spent more time over here than they did at their own homes.

My heart yearned for what once had been—Dat young, spry, and able to talk with me like he used to. And the *Bruders* all here with us.

Ach. What *gut* did it do trying to dream up something different? David would be calling this his place soon enough. Just as soon as Dat decided to move into the empty *Dawdi Haus*, taking Mamm with him. And I would probably be stuck living with David and Mary.

This old barn would then officially belong to David's family. I shut my eyes and deeply breathed in the sweetness of the meadow hay David and our cousins had hauled in to winter the horses.

This had always been my barn.

Benjamin was hitching up his buggy—getting ready to head home. I shivered again and grabbed Mamm's barn shawl off the peg. Hadn't the man by the river said something about having car trouble?

"Ben, I need ya to do a favor for me."

"What do ya need?"

It was *gut* I'd run into shy Benjamin in the barn. My other cousins would have been too nosy.

After giving Ben my instructions, I asked him to move quickly so that the bishop wouldn't stop him on his way out.

The barn wasn't as warm as I thought it would be, so I made my way quietly into the house where I softly sat down on Mamm's hickory rocker, waiting to be let in on the conversation going on in the kitchen.

From the sound of things, the bishop still seemed pretty angry and Mamm, I was sure of it, was wondering at the rebellion of her only daughter. She'd raised seven sons with very little trouble. But I was a different story. I knew that. She'd always said I had a talent for bringing trouble right to their doorstep. I was too much like her mother, my grandmother, Mammi Miriam. And that was the problem right there, she'd often say.

My grandmother and I shared a love for writing that put a dagger of fear into my mother's heart. More than once she'd told me about the time when she was a little girl, and the bishop found out her mother had been secretively writing.

She'd been playing in her living room and hid under a quilted table runner when the bishop angrily entered the room with her Dat. He had warned him to take control of his wife and her writing or else he and his family would need to find another place to live. He'd threatened the *Bann* on Mammi and a private shun on their entire family.

Dawdi made Mammi Miriam give up her writing after that, and it nearly killed her. Mamm said she suffered so from the depression that resulted.

Without writing, Mamm said her mother had seemed lost. She didn't write for others like I was doing, she just wrote for herself and maybe for *Gott*.

Mamm said she could always tell whenever her mother set the bishop's ruling aside and wrote on the sly because the depression lifted and a sense of joy returned to their home.

But that's when fear would set in. My mother didn't understand how writing could ever be worth risking their family's security among the People.

Mamm thought the fear would go away when her mother died, but she had been mistaken. Somehow the burden had passed to her own daughter, right under her nose.

I swallowed hard at the memories and had some compassion for what Mamm would be feeling now in the kitchen.

The bishop had the power to make things go wrong for our family. Very wrong. And with Dat's health the way it was, where would we turn if we didn't have the People? Willow Brook took care of its own when it had the bishop's blessing. But the way his voice raised in the kitchen right now, I knew we were at risk of losing that and a whole lot more.

I heard the bishop ask twice for some more coffee and shook my head. Mamm must be pretty upset to have not heard him the first time. Finally, I heard the chair slide over the hardwood followed by the clink of ceramic.

I hoped she didn't believe all that the bishop was telling her about me and the *Englischer*. The thought crossed my mind to enter the kitchen and defend myself. But physically, I didn't think I was up for it. I tried to remember the last time I'd eaten.

From the bishop's tone, I could tell he was building up to something big. If only Dat could help in some way. I wished again that his stroke had been more merciful. I knew he understood what was being said against me, but there was very little he could do about it.

It was up to Mamm to handle the bishop now. And I wasn't sure she was up for the task, given her fear of him. Over the past six months, Mamm had taken on more and more of Dat's responsibilities than she'd probably realized. I knew that took a toll on her as well.

I started to drift a bit, thinking about Mamm, Dat, and the fate of our family, when the bishop's loud voice carried into the living room.

"And that's why I've decided to discipline your daughter with the *Bann* until she gives a public confession for her sin."

Just like that, the bishop's words dropped like lead onto my shoulders. I sucked in my breath.

CHAPTER 7

After settling Peaches in her new home with a bowl of food and some toys, Kelly sat down at her computer to see what her son was up to these days. She was grateful Judah hadn't thought to block her from his social media channels.

After checking out Judah's latest posts, she moved to the sofa and picked up the newspaper. A family in town had experienced a fire and lost their home. She took a minute to pray for them and to jot down their names and address. Mentally, she figured out what she could do to help. The *Mountain Laurel Star* had always held a special place in her heart and now even more so since her son had landed his dream job there two years ago. Reading his articles made her feel connected to him even though they weren't speaking.

When he'd first started at the paper, an article would appear now and then, but now, after being there for nearly two years, he had one every day. She could tell that the editor, Hilton Hughes, trusted him with some of the more significant stories now. His byline showed up on the front page a few times each week.

Following her son on social media and reading his articles in the paper was a one-way connection with her son, she knew that, but she would take what she could get for now. Kelly spent a lot of time on her knees praying for a soft heart for her son, one that listened to the voice of the Holy Spirit. She couldn't understand why Judah would shut her out this long and was sure it probably had something to do with his dad's death. He'd never really dealt with it. She'd asked God more times than she could count for the healing she knew he needed.

She'd even found herself praying for the other writers on the paper's news team and particularly grew in fondness for the writings of a Miss Ima Righter. When Kelly first read that pseudonym, she had just taken a sip of Earl Grey and almost lost it.

Ima Righter? She'd shook her head and smiled, holding her mug of tea in midair. But she found herself intrigued by Ima's raw writing style. She held nothing back, and her words pulled on Kelly's heart more than anything she had read in a long, long time.

Kelly felt sad to see that, lately, the paper had been running a "Best of Ima" series, and wondered what was going on with the writer. She hoped this was just a short leave for her and wished she could ask Judah about it.

Heading to her computer, Kelly checked to see if the *Star* had set up a website yet and was disappointed to find they hadn't. Her freelance writing skills included web writing, and if Judah weren't connected with the newspaper, she would have called them by now. But the way things stood between them, she felt awkward about approaching her son's employer for work.

Kelly's concern for the *Star* had been growing over the past few years. Having some experience in newspaper publishing herself, she knew it took advertisers, lots of them, to keep a newspaper running. And having a digital edition was key in today's day and age.

Kelly picked up her latest copy. The newspaper seemed thinner than she remembered. Skimming through again, she noticed fewer advertisers and names on the masthead. Most articles now, other than Ima's column, were written by Judah, a Bertram Hochstetler, and just a few other people. It wasn't that long ago the paper had a large staff and was thick and filled with ads.

The paper meant a lot to her and to this community. She hoped for her son's sake and for Riverview it wasn't in trouble.

JUDAH

I'd found my phone and wallet where I'd frantically dropped them on the riverbank, but couldn't locate my reporter's notebook, and it was nearly dusk. I needed that notebook to get all my facts straight for a story I'd been working on.

At least I had on some dry clothes. The old coat and snow pants I'd found in Mom's "in case of an emergency" box she'd tucked in the trunk when I first started college were pretty tight but warm.

Clutching Johanna's pen tightly in my hand, I searched the grass with the old flashlight I kept in the Swagon's glove compartment. I spun my head at the sharp, hollow sound of horse hooves on the pavement and nearly slipped on something slick wedged in the mud of the riverbank. The item made a sucking sound as the mud gave it up—not my notebook, but some kind of journal.

I looked at Johanna's pen and wondered if the journal also belonged to her.

I shoved the items under my coat and turned toward the approaching buggy. I held out my thumb, hoping for a new ticket to town.

The young man in the buggy couldn't have been more than seventeen.

"Hullo." He scanned my clothes that were two sizes too small and looked away, I guessed to hide a grin. "Heard ya might need a ride into town." He cleared his throat and then nodded over in the direction of the Swagon.

"Sure could," I rubbed my muddy hands on my tight snow pants. "Thanks."

I stepped up into the waiting buggy and tried to keep conversation going as we traveled back to town. Through a series of questions, I found out my driver was Johanna's cousin Ben, and she lived at the veal farm down the road in Willow Brook.

JOHANNA

At last, they called me into the kitchen. I braced myself against the smooth edge of our family table and considered the odd look Dat gave me.

The bishop's eyes seemed cold as he explained the extent of the *Bann*. Because each Amish community had variations of it based on its *Ordnung*, he wanted to make sure we got it right. I couldn't help but wonder how much of an influence he'd had on the Willow Brook *Bann*.

Oddly, he addressed my parents instead of me.

"Dorcas and Jakob, because of Johanna's continual disobedience, including what I saw by the river today, you're not to eat with her or receive any kind of help from her until she kneels before the congregation in public confession."

I thought he was done but there was more.

"And in order for Johanna to understand the seriousness of this matter, your communication with her should be limited."

The bishop left quickly, not even bothering to say goodbye.

The resentment bubbling up in me concerning that man was difficult to squash. I had nearly drowned, but he had added what happened this afternoon to my list of wrongdoings.

The thoughts seemed rebellious, and if I didn't put them in their place, I'd be in worse trouble. The bishop was *Gott's* chosen man, and it was his responsibility to look out for us. After all, what had happened in the last few hours must have made me look fairly tainted in his eyes.

I slumped back into the ladderback chair that had been my place at the table since I'd been weaned. My stomach growled and something didn't feel right in my head. I took a nervous glance at my mother and wished I hadn't.

Dat shuffled past me without saying a word, his shoulders stooped. I watched as he stopped at the door that connected the kitchen to the *Dawdi Haus*. He opened it for me and then left to go upstairs.

CHAPTER 8

JUDAH

As the buggy jostled along down the country road, a strange feeling came over me about the journal. I knew I should give it to Johanna's cousin—it was most likely hers. But I wanted to read it. I mean, what does an Amish woman write about? And maybe this could somehow be a lead in finding Ima. I hadn't thought about that until now, but if the *Star's* delivery guy lived out here somewhere, maybe Hilton was right and Ima did too.

Reading someone's journal felt wrong though. It had been a long time since I had felt guilty about anything, so the feeling was a tough one to place at first. When I was a young boy, I aimed for a clean conscience, and I'd let guilt get the best of me. Multiple confessions a day to Mom or Dad became the norm.

But as I neared my teenage years, I got pretty good at ignoring my sensitive conscience. And after Dad died, I found I couldn't handle any type of guilt at all.

The pressure was way too much. But I couldn't tell Mom the part I'd played in Dad's death. Not ever. So, I guess I just pushed the truth back. If I stayed on top of my thoughts I rarely felt guilt about Dad or anything anymore. And if I did, I hoped it was when I was home alone, and I could drown my sorrows in whatever I chose to medicate them with that night.

Why was this bothering me then? What was the big deal?

I guess it was because the journal was hers, after all, and she would probably be wondering what happened to it. What right did I have in keeping it?

But no matter the guilt, I couldn't make myself bring up what I'd found stuck in the riverbank back there.

I needed to look through the journal first, to see what kinds of things an Amish girl writes about before she nearly drowns.

The cousin dropped me off at Hal's Rivermart, a small grocery chain that served the rural areas. A cold, hard rain began to fall, and people covered their heads and quickly rushed in to get a jug of milk, or whatever. Most ignored us, although we must have been an odd-looking pair.

I thanked Ben and hopped out of the buggy. As I did so, the journal slid out from under my too-short coat and made a loud slap on the wet pavement.

Quickly, I reached to snatch it up, but my frozen fingers fumbled with the spine. Grasping it finally, I made a quick decision and quietly slipped it onto the worn buggy seat.

Whatever. Let her have her journal.

With what I hoped was a look of composure, I said goodbye to Ben.

But I couldn't help but wonder at the glint of curiosity in the young man's eyes as he nodded and took one last look at me before urging the horse onward.

JOHANNA

Mamm stood to clear the table. I started to help her, but she gestured for me to stop. So I told her what had happened instead—the swing, the river, the *Englischer*, all of it. I even told her what happened to my treasured journal and pen. Not that she would have felt badly for their fate, but I wanted her to know just the same.

And then I waited.

After all that, surely she would have something to say in my favor, now that the bishop had left and Dat had gone upstairs to bed. Mamm and I had our share of troubles, but she was my mother after all. Surely she didn't believe all that the bishop had said. She *knew* me. Especially now she had heard the truth about what happened at the river.

While I waited, my stomach pains increased.

After she dried and put away the last mug, Mamm kept her back to me. With both hands on the edge of the butcher block counter top, she hung her head.

I wondered if I should leave, but before I could, she spoke.

"Do you realize what you have done?" Mamm's tone was low and stern. "What your selfish writing, and now what the bishop thinks he saw at the river, has cost our family?"

They were questions I didn't want to answer. Because deep inside I knew.

"Mamm, it's *my* sin to bear alone. Why does the bishop need to bring the family into it?"

Mamm sat down and laid her head in her hands.

"Because, Johanna, what *you* do impacts others around you. And for some reason, out of all the rules in the *Ordnung*, writing upsets our bishop the most. Because of what you have done, he will make it harder on us all. He'll get the People to agree and eventually find a way to drive us out."

I grew tired of hearing this. Mamm had been warning me about staying out of the bishop's wrath since I was a little girl and had discovered my love for the pen. Our family had tiptoed around him all our lives. Now that the

Bann had come, strangely, I only felt courage rising up in me. Why couldn't Mamm feel it too?

I spat the words. "I almost drowned today. Do ya even care?"

Mamm gave me a long, hard look. "You're under the *Bann*, Johanna. I need to stop talking to you now. You'll be spending most of your time and taking your meals in the *Dawdi Haus* until the bishop is satisfied with your kneeling confession before the People."

I got up then and made my way through the open door to the *Dawdi Haus*. After quietly shutting the door, I sat down hard at the small table.

You're under the Bann, Johanna. I need to stop talking to you now.

The words chilled me. Mamm was just doing what the bishop said, but her words stung just the same. We were pretty bad off, she and me. And if I was honest with myself, we'd been that way for quite some time now. Our relationship hadn't always been this strained. We'd had some bumps along the way, but my trouble with the bishop seemed to set it off downhill quickly.

And now the *Bann*.

She and the bishop hadn't even tried to find out my side of the story about what happened at the river.

Anger flushed my cheeks, and I stood on wobbly legs. Slowly, the chair fell to the ground behind me. Everything felt fuzzy.

I walked further into the *Dawdi Haus*, breathing deeply, and I could nearly catch the scent of my grandmother. My greeting was already out of my throat, and I had to cover my mouth to stop it.

Mammi Miriam.

I knelt at her rocker and let myself remember a time when I was thirteen and had followed my well-worn path into the *Dawdi Haus*. My face was tear-stained, and my heart in need of comfort—nothing new to my grandmother. She received me with open arms like she'd always done.

"I hate her," I'd said. Most of the People would have been shocked, but Mammi Miriam just smoothed my hair and rocked away the hurt.

"*Gott* knows."

She'd waited patiently for whatever would come next out of my mouth.

"I don't even know where to start."

"Begin at the beginning."

She always told me to do this and those words often helped me calm down and organize my thoughts. Quietly, she listened to my most recent problem with my mother. It had been wash day, and I had been helping to hang the clothes. The sky was blue, the rose of Sharon were in bloom, and I could see the Clydesdales in the neighbor's fields. The day was so beautiful, I couldn't help but sing—it just came out. I'd belted a few lines before Mamm seemed to notice, and I thought it would be okay.

But fear of the bishop and all his rules had a solid grip on my mother's heart.

"Where did ya hear that song?" Mamm stood in front of me.

I'd jumped a little and clammed up, remembering the bishop's rule in the *Ordnung* and what it said about writing anything.

Mamm angrily pointed her finger at me. "Your grandmother wrote that song."

Why did everything I did make her so angry?

I'd left my mother and her finger then and ran all the way to the *Dawdi Haus*—to the waiting arms of Mammi Miriam.

Resting my head on my grandmother's soft arm, I'd let the story spill out. I didn't care if I ever saw my mother again.

And then Mammi Miriam said something that had struck a chord deep inside me. I sought to remember it now because the words had given me strength to not give up on my mother.

"Everybody deserves another chance."

After Mammi had spoken those words, she'd looked quickly around the room and then slowly pulled out her thick journal from the folds of her cape dress.

"You know I don't write anymore, Johanna." She winced then. "Well, at least I try not to, at the order of the bishop."

I couldn't keep my eyes off the book in her hand. I knew it existed, but had rarely seen her forbidden journal since it represented a deviance from the *Ordnung*.

"But I do read what's in here from time to time. It ... it comforts me. It lets me know where I've been and reminds me of where I'm going. Your own journal ..." Mammi Miriam stopped then to wipe moisture from her eyes. "I'm not sure I did right in giving you that."

I squeezed her hand. I had already filled many pages. My journal was my deepest treasure.

"You have a gift, Johanna. One that not many people have. Use it as comfort in situations like this. There will come a time when I won't be here to comfort ya. But *Gott* will. And your writing will."

Mammi Miriam had pressed her journal to her heart then and hugged me close with the book snugged in tight between us.

A mouse skittered across the cold hardwood, bringing me back to reality.

I shook my head and eased myself into a standing position.

What I wouldn't give to have my grandmother here. And for what seemed like the hundredth time since she'd passed, I thought about Mammi Miriam's journal. Where it had ended up after she died had always been a mystery to me. The day after her funeral, I had secretly searched the *Dawdi Haus* up and down looking for it. I knew I couldn't ever ask Mamm, and Dat probably wouldn't have remembered even if he had known where it was. *Dawdi* had gone on before Mammi Miriam, so he hadn't been around to ask either. Not that he would have told me. He'd watched her like a hawk when it came to writing and that journal.

My grandfather was one of the reasons why she'd hid her words so well, I figured. That journal had to be in the *Dawdi Haus* somewhere, but I had no idea where.

Sighing, I looked from the worn rocker over to the cookstove, where my memories brought back the times we mixed the pumpkin we had canned with sweet cream from the few dairy cows we kept on our veal farm. Mammi had agreed to bake fourteen pies for David's wedding—I'll never know why. But we worked hard, the two of us, with our hands deep in pat-a-pan crusts.

Why had it taken me so long to return to the comfort and solace of this place? These comforting memories lay just beyond the door to my own home, yet it took the *Bann* to get me in here.

Mammi had understood me like no one else. Sometimes even better than I did.

Blowing wispy curls out of my eyes, I crossed over to the bedroom, wondering for the first time in my life if it would be better not to be Amish after all.

I fell onto the bed, cold and damp from the river, my stomach still growling.

CHAPTER 9

JUDAH

Bertram picked up the phone on the first ring, and I felt glad the guy had no social life. He lived and breathed the newspaper and probably wished he could work the night shift too. But I needed his help and had decided that being nice was probably my best approach.

Bertram arrived at Hal's Rivermart in a little over an hour.

He eyed my muddy snow-pants get up. "Wow, you look horrible. What happened?"

Suddenly I felt cautious. Bertram was new, but he still had what it took to sniff out a story.

"I fell into the river."

Lying to him came harder to me than it had earlier today and that irritated me. Besides, Bertram didn't buy it, I could tell. But he did a surprising thing and clammed up.

I looked pitiful, and I knew it. I felt grateful for his silence.

By the time Bertram finally dropped me off at my apartment, the sun had long since set, and I'd started coughing. Before getting out of his pickup, I thanked Bertram for coming to get me and even patted him on the arm to show my appreciation. I resisted the urge to give him a hug.

Liza Lou met me at the door of my apartment, jumping up and smacking one paw on each of my shoulders so we could see eye-to-eye. I needed a long, hot shower, but my Catahoula Leopard dog wouldn't rest until I'd paid her some attention first.

"Hello, girl." I scratched under her arms while trying to kick dog toys and dirty laundry out of our way.

Although I couldn't feel my soggy toes anymore, I still lingered petting her. There was just something about the way Liza Lou filled my empty apartment that helped make it feel more like home.

I'd met Liza Lou for the first time at the Riverview Humane Society when she'd weighed only a few pounds. I was a lot younger then too—just eleven—and naive enough to believe that my beautiful puppy was all that the rescue shelter said she was.

They'd mistaken her spots and shaggy coat for the telltale signs of a mutt, but the "mixed" sign written in black dry-erase marker on her shelter cage couldn't have been farther from the truth.

In her first year, it seemed as if Liza Lou would never stop getting bigger and soon grew to her full size of the Catahoula Leopard breed that she turned out to be. She stood just a few inches shorter than the Great Dane that lived down the street in our small neighborhood, and I had to pick up a job after school to help my parents handle the cost of her food.

Getting a rescue dog at the humane society was something I had been proud of and maybe I'd bragged a bit too much about my "heroic deed" in selecting Liza Lou and saving her from potentially being put down.

But that was before Liza had saved my life.

Water had never been my thing, but my friends kept inviting me to go swimming with them. I felt pretty embarrassed that I couldn't swim and kept making excuses not to go. One summer, Mom had had enough and signed me up for lessons at our town's outdoor pool.

Even though I was a teen, I would share the class with a bunch of three-year-olds and told my mother I would only do it if she wouldn't watch.

She agreed and dropped me off every weekday that June.

It was the perfect set-up. Mom would drop me off and even give me a little cash for the pool's snack bar after the lesson. I would walk in and pretend I had to go to the bathroom. When I was sure Mom had left, I would walk back out.

My friend Gabe had a single mom who worked three jobs, so he always had extra time on his hands. For that whole month, I would load up at the pool's snack bar and then walk to Gabe's for an hour's worth of video games before running back to the pool. Then I'd go into the pool's bathroom and hit the showers.

By the time Mom got there, I'd be waiting on the bench outside with my beach towel flung over my shoulder—wet and still out of breath.

Mom had been so proud, and I had been pretty happy about my perfect plan. I talked up my lessons and answered all of her questions with the limited knowledge I had of swimming strokes that I'd read from a book I'd checked out of the library.

Who needed to swim anyway? I figured I could stay away from water for the rest of my life.

That was until Mom and Dad threw a surprise party for me out on the lake the day I turned thirteen. A birthday party at the lake was just the place where I could show off my new swimming skills, they said. They'd paid for the lessons, after all. Why shouldn't I feel comfortable swimming with all my friends now?

Mom kept bragging to the boys about all the things I had told her I could do in the water. I had to be sure no one found out my secret so I took a blow-up raft and floated out to where my friends were playing in the lake. That had to be enough for my parents. I was "in" the water after all.

But this act wasn't enough for my friends. They flipped the raft, and I began struggling for my life.

I learned that day that Catahoula Leopard dogs are great swimmers. While some dogs have some webbing between their toes to help them swim, Liza Lou's breed has more. In fact, their webbing extends out almost to the end of their toes. When Liza Lou heard my cry for help, she plunged right in. Dad had been grilling some burgers when he heard Liza bark. Without even taking off his shoes, he dove in as well.

The swimming spot had been a new pick for my parents, and they were unaware of the dangerous undertow that could creep up in that area until it was too late. After Dad swam to me and shoved me toward Liza, he was caught up in the undertow.

Clutching Liza's harness, I let her pull me to shore, the whole time thinking of the excuse I would use with my friends. Massive stomach cramps seemed the best way to go. I'd gone in too soon after eating. That had to work. And it would have if my friends had been focused on me when I got out of the water.

But they weren't.

They had formed quiet huddles on the small beach, pointing back out to the water from time to time. I couldn't figure out what was happening until someone told me a few minutes later that Dad never made it out.

Clearing my mind from the memory, I took Liza out for a short walk so she could do her business. When we returned, I filled her dog bowl and flicked off the light. The shower would have to wait.

JOHANNA

Sunshine crept in through cracks in the green shade, and I awoke with the slap of the *Bann* still stinging my face. Thinking about my chores, I tried to get up and help Mamm, but for the first time in my life I didn't get up, couldn't get up.

And then I remembered the bishop saying no one could receive help from me anyway. Rolling back over, I let sleep take the pain away.

A few hours later, sharp stomach pains and nausea pulled me awake. Along with them came an irritating guilt.

How was this my fault? Falling into the river hadn't been my plan.

I needed peppermint tea to help my stomach, but knew my presence in the kitchen would only make Mamm uncomfortable today, so I settled for what I could find in my grandmother's small kitchen. She'd died just about two years ago, but maybe there were still some tea leaves she'd dried before her death.

If only this awful fog in my head would lift.

I let out a small cough as I reached for the knob on one of Mammi Miriam's cupboards. Mamm, in her concern for Dat's health, could have overlooked the chore of completely cleaning these out, and I had been too absorbed with my own grief to care.

Opening the cupboard, I caught Mammi's scent again. A homey mixture of pine and dried goods. I sighed.

Mammi, I need you.

What would she think of me, under the *Bann* and hiding out in her home? *Ach*, it would have been more than Mammi Miriam could bear. She'd always had such high hopes for

Mamm's only daughter. And she had been the only one besides Lizzie who had encouraged me to write. Now, look at where that had gotten me.

I shook my head, needing to think about something else.

A hot steaming cup of mint tea and maybe some light biscuits. That's what Mammi would have made me on a day like today.

After she had given me an earful.

I fumbled in the cupboard looking for the tea, feeling lightheaded.

It was *gut* my journal sank into the river. Gut that my favorite pen stayed buried deep in the mud.

My head knew this, but the truth of it still hadn't reached my heart. Writing had always helped me reorder my jumbled thoughts and now that it wasn't an option, things were even more of a struggle. Although Mamm may never understand it, my writing had become my way of drawing closer to *Gott*. Using my gift had become a form of worship.

Sometimes my words seemed like a song or a prayer. And other times, they came out more like a poem. Lately, for the newspaper, I had written longer pieces and sent a series of installments to them as they came out from me. Sharing my writing for others to enjoy was a thrill larger than life.

Once, when I'd had another argument with Mamm, I'd grabbed my journal and left the house through the back door. Sitting quietly on our outcropping of rocks, I prayed for the first time the way Mammi Miriam did. I'd experienced *Gott's* love in a fresh way that day, and the poetry I'd written in my journal couldn't come fast enough.

Thinking of that poem's watery grave in the river now made me sad.

Writing was my outlet, and it never felt wrong—despite what the bishop said. Even now, something big festered in me, and I needed to write it down.

But I had no paper.

How people got along in life with no way to describe it on paper, I had no idea. Without the pen, I felt voiceless.

Letting out a sigh, I reached into the cupboard as I continued my search for tea.

CHAPTER 10

JOHANNA

I could hear my parents "talking" on the other side of the door. Mamm would talk, and Dat, who still had mobility in his right hand, would scratch his response on a small slate board. I had been dragging myself past the door in dire need of the toilet when a tone of desperation in Mamm's voice made me stop.

Eavesdropping had always been strictly forbidden by my parents, but I couldn't get myself to move on. My ear just sort of glued itself to the knot in the pine door.

"I've wanted to open that door all morning, Jakob. There can't be much food in there. And I ... I was pretty upset about the mess she's gotten us into with her writing and now that *Englischer*. But ... maybe I said too much."

I heard some scratching of the chalk.

"I know we can't speak to her. But we can offer aid in time of need. There may be a need. How do we know there is a need if we don't ask?"

More scratching.

"Give her time? Jakob, I don't know how much time we have. You know what this could do for us and for the rest of our children. Things never go well for families who get on the bishop's bad side. Not in Willow Brook, anyway. And we've worked so hard to keep the peace."

Judging from the way her voice rose at the end, I figured Dat had walked away. I heard some shuffling and then the front door open and close.

He was gone to do what he did every day to help lighten David's load. I knew my father's schedule fairly well. I also knew his lack of patience when it came to Mamm's "worry talk" as he used to call it.

"I've come up with a plan, Jakob ..." Mamm's words sounded weak and measured now. Why she said that after the door shut, I don't know.

From what I could gather, they both weren't sure what to believe about me and the *Englischer*. A strange feeling rushed through me. Didn't they know me better? My face grew hot, and before I could stop myself, I quietly turned the knob.

I thought I was ready to defend myself, but when I saw Mamm staring out the window looking older than her years, I grew weak. A sick feeling suddenly rose up in my stomach. Trying to fight whatever was going on inside me, I held my head high and even began to raise a finger in debate, but it felt useless.

Nausea rushed in with a vengeance, and I retreated into the *Dawdi Haus*, making a mad rush for the small bathroom.

Mamm, I noticed, did not come to my aid. That hurt more than the heaves that took over my body.

As I labored over the toilet, it struck me odd that the bishop would be lenient about such a convenience, allowing indoor toilets just in my lifetime, and yet ban writing.

How I struggled to respect Bishop Amos. I knew I sinned with my angry thoughts, but now that I was sick, it felt harder not to give in to them.

Oh, help my wicked soul.

Sitting in her study with Peaches on her lap, Kelly worked on a large website for a local university where Judah had taken a few advanced classes when he was a senior in high school. The school's marketing department had hired her to write articles for high school seniors like Judah had been. She stopped a few times to rest her thoughts and run her fingers though Peaches' thick orange fur, feeling a little sentimental.

The university had asked if she was familiar with the age group of their audience. She'd smiled at that, remembering the day her son left with his brand-new college backpack to take his first class.

The memory also brought a heart full of pain. Judah had been so lost after his dad died, to the point where she'd become concerned for his mental health.

And she had some suspicions that he was smoking pot then too.

Judah had such a need for healing and forgiveness but had shut her out even then. As a new widow, she had spent a good part of those first years praying for understanding and also banging her head against the wall waiting for it to come. There were still so many things that just didn't make sense.

Peaches jumped down to check out her food bowl, and Kelly decided it was a good time to take a break. She needed some fresh air, and her garden beckoned.

Kelly returned a wave to her neighbor, Sam, as she walked out her back door. Also widowed, Sam was quite a bit older than Kelly, but he tended to forget that and would often sit and chat for hours. Although a fun guy for his age, she didn't feel up to talking to him right now.

Kelly quickened her pace and glanced back to Sam's house, breathing a sigh of relief as she saw him reenter his back door.

The day was cool, and she had just pulled on the extra hoodie she'd brought out with her to the garden when Gabe's shock of red hair caught her eye. She called for him to come out to where she had been pulling stink bugs off the last of her zucchini plants. There were still a few plants producing despite it being late in the season, but the leaves had been wilting and turning brown. The change had been a mystery to her until she began to notice the brown bugs with the shield-like back roaming around her plants like they owned the place. One by one, she had been slipping them off the leaves and into her mason jar to avoid the stink they gave off when they were upset.

"Uh, hello, Mrs. Barton."

Gabe had been one of the kids Kelly and Jack had wished Judah would have left out of his friend circle. She smiled anyway and motioned for him to come inside the deer fence her husband had built for her years ago.

While he wound his way through the various black plastic paths she had constructed to separate her plants, she grabbed a plastic grocery bag and started picking zucchini and the tomatoes she had left for Gabe's family.

"Judah's, um, not here, Gabe. But I've picked some things for you to take home." As Gabe stepped over a few stray pumpkins, Kelly noticed how tall he had gotten. She'd heard he was training to be a mechanic.

"Actually, I came to talk to you, Mrs. Barton. You see, Judah and me, we aren't friends anymore."

Wiping the blank look off her face, Kelly invited him to sit on her garden bench. Any other day she would have been happy to hear that Judah wasn't spending time with

Gabe. But not today. The news felt like a sign that her son had just pushed one more person out of his life.

"What happened?"

"I'm not sure." He looked down at his hands. "I really don't want to talk about that."

"Okay." Kelly took off her garden gloves and sat on the wood beams that divided her blueberry bushes from her strawberry patch and waited.

"I actually came to get something off my chest."

"I'm listening." Kelly's face flushed. She tried to keep her mind from racing to all of the horrible things Gabe could say.

"First of all, I never really got to tell you how sorry I am about Mr. Barton's passing."

Kelly hung her head for a moment as she tried to hold her emotions in check. When she raised her head back up, she was surprised to see that Gabe's eyes were filled with tears. She felt the sting of tears in her own eyes and a few minutes passed before either spoke again.

Gabe cleared his throat and said, "What I came to say was that I feel partly responsible for your husband's death."

"What?" Kelly hadn't expected that.

He held up his hand. "Not in any way that's illegal. It's just that I was there with Judah each time he skipped out on his swimming lessons when we were kids. We actually came up with the idea together."

She swatted a bug flying around her head a little harder than she needed to. "Skipped out?"

"I thought Judah might have told you, but I'm guessing he hasn't. And since we aren't friends anymore, I'm going to because ... because I need to."

Gabe told the whole story to Kelly then, and bit by bit, the puzzle pieces fell into place. She finally understood why her son had withdrawn from her and God.

What an awful thing to bear all by yourself.

Gabe was on his feet and almost out of the garden before she was able to speak.

"Wait, Gabe!"

He stopped and turned around. Kelly grabbed a few more tomatoes as she made her way to him. She pressed the bag into his hands and looked him straight in the eye.

"I forgive you, Gabe. Thank you for telling me."

Gabe had to wipe his eyes on the front of his shirt this time. Then, he nodded and was gone.

JUDAH

I woke with a start. Sunlight filled my room. *What time is it?* The clock indicated midmorning and I rubbed my eyes to rid them of the last bit of sleep. I felt as awful as I smelled. I shuffled out to the living room and fed Liza Lou, then let the steam of the shower take away the memories that needed to go if I was going to keep it together today.

Despite the drum of the water, I heard again the loud clap the journal had made when it fell out of my hands and slapped onto the pavement.

The memory made me cringe.

If the Amish guy hadn't been such an introvert, I'm sure he would have at least said something about the journal.

I'd surprised myself by giving the journal back and laying it on the seat. Why couldn't I have just tucked it back up in my coat? Or smiled and given him some lame excuse?

But the memories of what happened yesterday seemed still clear in my mind. Although the water was warm in the shower, I shivered at the thought of the near drowning.

A memory flash of that chestnut hair caught me off guard. Curls drying in the September breeze. Big green eyes made sadder by something far greater than what had happened in the river.

It became clear why I hadn't taken the journal now.

Giving the journal back had been a rare moment for me. But it was most likely her book after all, and I didn't want to contribute any more to her pain.

CHAPTER 11

Kelly sat down on her garden bench and wept—a hard cry, harder than any she'd had in a long time. But as the tears flowed, she realized God had answered her prayer.

Finding out after all these years that Judah had deceived her into thinking he was taking swimming lessons made her angry, but when she worked through the anger, she started to see the bigger picture.

She finally understood. Her son's behavior made sense now, and she was almost knocked off her feet with a fresh wave of pain when she understood the fullness of what Judah must be feeling.

He had skipped out on the lessons.

He never learned to swim.

He had been forced to participate in a swimming party.

He nearly drowned.

And the last one was the hardest to swallow.

Because of his foolishness, his dad died saving him.

Kelly shook her head. How one seemingly little sin could escalate into something so big, so heart-wrenching seemed too amazing to bear. She guessed that was why God hated all sin.

Searching her heart, she realized she had forgiven her son the moment Gabe told her what he had done. That felt good to discover. She didn't want to be caught up in a trap of unforgiveness.

Judah had enough of that for the both of them.

A small breeze caused the big yellow blooms on her sunflower house to nod in her direction. Packing up her bug jar and gloves, she decided it was time to get back to her freelance work. Before leaving the garden, she stopped at the entrance to her sunflower house and, peeking in, found a small blanket she had left there the last time she'd needed a break from life.

Kelly had planted the sunflower seeds in a good-sized square this year. The variety she'd chosen promised to be one of the tallest in the world and with the biggest flower. The claim seemed a pretty steep one, but she was satisfied with the way this one had turned out.

When Judah was a boy, they had checked out a book from the library that showed them how to make a sunflower house. And each spring after that, they'd experimented with different varieties of sunflowers from the seed catalogs that came like clockwork in the dead of winter.

She laughed, remembering the year they'd tried a new variety but the sunflowers hadn't grown taller than her waist. And their blooms hadn't been any larger than Judah's hand. They felt disappointed at first until they saw that the blooms came in different colors.

Judah used to love to come out to the garden and hide among the sunflowers when he knew she was headed out to weed or pick vegetables. Just as she got busy, he'd start howling like a wolf or hooting like an owl. She'd play along, standing up to scan the horizon and placing her hand over her eyes to shield the sun.

Kelly smiled at the memory. That had been before Jack died. Before she'd lost the two men in her life who mattered most.

She stooped to enter the sunflower house now and enjoyed the shade that the giant leaves provided. This year, she had tied string across the tops of the towering flowers and the last of the morning glories now wound their way around each string, creating a sort of roof.

Judah would have loved to see this addition.

She put the blanket over the black plastic and lay face down on top of it.

Quietly, she poured her heart out to the only One who knew her completely, and who would carry her through to her next step.

Whatever that was supposed to be.

CHAPTER 12

JOHANNA

First hot and then cold. Couldn't my body make up its mind? What was the matter with me anyway?

Giving up my second search for peppermint tea, I sank deep into Mammi's chair and rested my head on the kitchen table.

The idea of not being Amish consumed my thoughts. How would I? What would I? Where would I?

My head hurt with the thought of it.

My body ached.

Now, what was Mammi doing waiting on me? She set a cup of steaming tea at my side and went to slide the biscuits into the cookstove.

"Mammi? Is it really you?"

The old woman shuffled about the kitchen without speaking, but serving me while not really seeing me. Gray, frizzled strands of hair poked out from under her prayer *Kapp*.

"Miriam!" The voice boomed from the bedroom.

Dawdi?

"Where did ya hide it this time?"

Mammi's hands pressed into her pockets, searching. She reached up to smooth her frizzled hair and then looked about the room.

I knew that look.

Mammi was trying to remember.

Footsteps hit the hardwood in the next room of the *Dawdi Haus*, and I watched as Mammi's eyes darted in a panic about the room. The lines on her face smoothed when her gaze rested on the utensil drawer. She took a deep breath then, and her eyes rose to meet her husband's, but not before they caught mine. Wrinkles curved as the edge of her lips formed a small smile.

Things became fuzzy then, and the small table where I sat rattled as something hard hit the floor.

JUDAH

I'd been in bed most of the day, still struggling with exhaustion. Good thing my editor had given me a few days to search for Ima. I needed some rest before heading out again.

I should research the after effects of saving someone from drowning. The adrenaline rush that the human body goes through in life and death situations had to be off the charts, so I expected physical fatigue, but hadn't anticipated emotional exhaustion.

It was times like these I wished I still talked to Mom. Somehow, I knew she would understand how I felt. And I knew she would be proud too. Imagine, me, the world's worst swimmer, saving someone using the CPR training she'd initiated. She'd be glad to know I finally put it to some use.

I reached for my phone and then remembered Dad. What a hypocrite I was, touting my lifesaving skills when I was practically responsible for my own father's drowning. There had been no one to save *him* that day.

And why was that?

The current had taken him farther under than anyone would have known to look. When they dredged the lake and finally found his body, he had been gone for two days.

I slammed the phone down on the nightstand. Nope. And probably for the hundredth time since I'd left that day, I promised myself I would never contact Mom.

Talking to her brought way too much pain.

Shoving all those thoughts and memories back where they belonged, I found I still couldn't stand not knowing how Johanna was doing. If she felt anything like I did, she had to be having a rough time. Recovering from receiving CPR was difficult too, if I remembered what the books said correctly. Most times, people were hospitalized afterward—if they even lived, not dragged off soaking wet in a buggy.

A wrestling match went on in my head. One minute I truly didn't care—she had her own life, after all. Then, however, I kept asking myself questions I couldn't answer.

I needed to take another nap so I could forget everything for a while.

The angry *pound, pound, pound* of my downstairs neighbor's broomstick handle woke me.

Pound, pound, pound.

I slapped my head. What was it this time?

My neighbor had trouble understanding that a big dog like Liza Lou made noise when she walked—and sometimes ran—across the floor. And too bad for her that Liza, despite her age, had made a game of playing fetch with herself and a tennis ball in my hallway.

Over the pounding, I heard my cell phone ring. I grabbed it, making a mental note to jog around the apartment later with extra loud steps.

Neighbors.

"Have you found her yet?" Hilton's voice barked through the phone.

"Well ... no, sir."

"Well, get on it. The publisher is upset that advertising is down without Ima. And Harper Inc. is threatening to pull all their ads if she doesn't start writing again. We're getting threats of a shutdown. I may need to start cutting some staff."

A wave of fear ran through me. This thing just kept getting bigger.

Hilton kept going. "I know what we need to do to get things moving here." The volume of his voice crept up with each word. "We need to blow the lid off this thing. Find her, and you can do a cover story on her life. What she likes for breakfast, where she gets her nails done ... I don't care."

"But what if she doesn't want to be found?" Why would a successful writer up and leave unless she had a good reason?

"What do you know, Barton?" The sneer coming through the phone was palatable.

I wished I'd shut my mouth before saying anything.

I decided to roll with it—make him think there was a story here. At least it might buy me some more time to look. Could the paper really be shut down over this? I ran my fingers through my overgrown hair. When was the last time I'd gotten a haircut?

"Not ... not much really." I tried to sound casual, making him believe I had more than I did.

"You've got something, Barton. What did you uncover yesterday?"

"Not a whole lot." Which was the truth.

When I didn't elaborate, Hilton's anger only grew. "You have one week, Barton. If you don't bring me the writer, I'll fire you, I swear!"

"I'm on it, boss." I opened my mouth to say more when Hilton hung up the phone.

I ran both hands through my hair, making it stand on end. I didn't care though. It matched how I felt inside.

Bertram was working late on a story when he overheard Hilton's call to Judah. His boss had been in his office with the door closed, but his voice carried through the air conditioning vent even clearer than if the door had been opened. He'd meant to tell Hilton about this at some point, but Judah had told him not to.

"If you do that, we'll never know the truth about what's going on around here," he'd said.

Still, Bertram didn't like listening in on people's private conversations.

"Hey." Whoever this new caller was, Hilton seemed pretty comfortable with them. "It was a lot to put on Barton. I know that. Sending an investigative reporter out without any leads was just plain stupid."

Funny. Bertram had thought the same thing.

"I had no choice, you know that. My back was up against the wall. If I'd been completely honest with Barton about the state of the paper by telling him the whole truth about where we were at, it would have stopped him in his tracks and sent him packing."

Bertram slunk in his chair. This was way too much for him to hear.

"I can't afford to have my reporters quit—not yet. We still have another issue to get out, anyway. I'm about to write a front-page story that no editor-in-chief should ever have to write."

Just one more issue? What was his boss saying? Bertram froze when he heard Hilton's door open.

As Hilton passed, the scent of whisky stung his nose.

CHAPTER 13

JOHANNA

I was in and out of consciousness for the next few days, but that didn't stop Mamm from speaking her mind.

She'd said she heard the thump of my fall and come running into the *Dawdi Haus*. She'd picked me off the floor and brought me, with the help of two of my nephews, to my grandmother's bed, where she'd changed me out of my still-damp clothes.

After getting Dat's permission to speak to me, considering the circumstances, Mamm chided me for wearing damp clothes, for not keeping a fire in the hearth, for not eating anything, and for losing my *Kapp*.

I tried to put a pillow over my head to drown out the sound of her voice.

The fever gave me a break, though, and I slept through a *gut* part of what she had to say. Sometimes I would wake to find her still talking to me and wondered what I'd missed.

"It was a miracle of *Gott*, you know, that the branch broke when it did. He, in his sovereignty, knew you would have had trouble throwing your writing things in the river."

Oh, how I still longed for my journal though.

"It was the push you needed, if you ask me."

Although no one had asked her.

Now, after I'd had a few days to recuperate, she'd propped my head on the pillow and was spooning nourishing broth down my sore throat as her non-stop chatter continued. She'd even shared stories of her girlhood and every last fear she'd suffered because of her mother's writing.

Mamm probably felt relieved that my throat was too sore for me to speak, and I was too weak to run. She knew she had a captive audience until I regained my strength.

After a while though, an odd thing started to happen. I started to understand my mother a little better.

Mammi Miriam's determination to write, even though writing was banned in our community, ruined my mother's childhood. Well, Mammi's writing didn't exactly do that. The bishop and his way of scaring Mamm out of her wits did it. And having her own Dat fail to take a stand for his wife and family over a rule that made no sense had contributed to my mother's fear all this time.

Maybe that's why I always had a hard time relating to her. My bond with Mammi Miriam came so easily. But for Mamm and me, that fear always stood between us.

And now, since I had no choice but to listen to her stories, I began to understand my mother's need to protect her family. And I guess she saw my writing and the writing of my grandmother as kind of a threat—the one thing standing between her family and peace with the bishop.

And peace with the bishop translated to peace in Willow Brook.

I also discovered it wasn't me she'd been mad at all these years, but what was inside me.

Mamm already hated writing because of what she'd experienced with her mother. Finding out I'd taken up the pen, too, must have been a shock and a burden.

JUDAH

As I scrambled my eggs the next morning, a knock at the door made me jump. If it was the lady downstairs, I didn't know what I'd say, but I'm sure it wouldn't be pretty.

Liza Lou barked like crazy, and I considered letting her plant a wet one on the lady.

I grabbed Liza Lou's collar to hold her back and opened the door. I felt almost disappointed when the grumpy neighbor lady wasn't the one leaning on my doorframe. Bertram grinned sheepishly down at me and gave a little wave. When did he get so tall?

"I thought you could use some help."

Just what I needed from the one who most likely would have my job by the end of the week.

"Help with what?" I didn't mean to snap, but there it was.

Bertram straightened and coughed a little. "Well, unless you've already had your car fixed?"

My car. I palmed my forehead. I needed to figure out how I was going to get it back. I'd been holed up here in my apartment and hadn't wanted to deal with ... well, anything.

Bertram turned to leave when an idea came to me.

"Uh, hold on a minute, Bert. I think I *could* use a hand getting my car back."

Bertram perked back up. He was like a puppy, really, this guy. I had a hard time trying to figure him out. If he was after my job, he had a funny way of showing it.

I let him in and pointed in the direction of my couch. "Wait here for a minute."

He and Liza Lou got acquainted while I headed back into my small kitchen. I forked my eggs straight from the pan into my mouth and washed them down with orange juice from the carton.

Then, I grabbed my keys, gave Liza Lou a quick pat, and we were out the door.

"Hey, Bert, why do you help me out so much?"

I figured we might as well get things out in the open so there'd be no surprises getting in the way.

"I mean, what's it to you if I get the Swagon—I mean, my car back?"

We were on our way now, so at least I'd get a ride out of him before this awkward friendship ended. Bertram didn't strike me as the lying type, so I braced myself for whatever he might say.

"Oh, nothing, really." Bertram took a big breath.

Here it comes. This had Hilton's stink all over it.

"It's just something my pastor said last Sunday."

"Your *what*?"

"Yeah, well. Forget it."

And just like that Bertram's face flushed red, and he turned a stony eye to the road.

Now what was that all about? I hadn't pegged Bertram as a Jesus freak. But now that I thought about it, he could fit the mold.

I knew exactly what Bertram was trying to do. Growing up in a Christian home, we'd talked to countless people about the love of God and the free gift of salvation. It felt odd to be on the receiving end of evangelism now. Poor Bertram, he had his work cut out for him trying to talk to me about Jesus.

Because whatever faith I thought I had as a kid died the day God took my dad.

JOHANNA

I woke to the sound of Mamm and Dat having a "conversation" in the kitchen of the *Dawdi Haus*. The sun's morning rays shone through the bedroom.

"I know that the bishop is angry with us. But we can't let this to get out of hand, Jakob. This goes beyond whatever happened to Johanna down at the river. You know that."

Beyond what happened at the river? Whatever Mamm was talking about, she sounded weary. She'd been waiting on me for days, plus taking care of Dat's needs. All this after the visit from the bishop and his announcement of the *Bann*.

I imagined Dat writing on his small slate.

"Yes, Jakob. I do think this is about my mother. When ya come right down to it, it's always been about my mother and whatever happened between her and the bishop forty years ago."

What was Mamm talking about?

"I have a plan, Jakob. One that will help mend what's been broken between the Yoders and the Zooks for decades. One that will get our daughter off the *Bann* and give her purpose among the People. And it will give ya the rest your body needs."

I heard the door to the *Dawdi Haus* quietly shut.

I thought about Dat then and was surprised to realize I hadn't really considered his needs in all of this. I'd been thinking about what I wanted, but poor Dat, his body still suffered from the effects of the stroke. He and Mamm had planned to move soon into the *Dawdi Haus*, only now his wayward daughter occupied the space. I wondered how he was taking all of this on the inside. We had always been so close.

In that moment, something inside me broke.

What was I doing, allowing my selfish plans to threaten my family and its place in our community? With Dat still ill from his stroke, I saw now how exercising my gift could harm the people I love the most.

Mamm was right. It was *gut* the branch broke when it did. There was no way I could have thrown my pen and journal into the river myself. It had been the hand of *Gott* that allowed it to happen.

And to that, I needed to submit.

The morning paper hit the door hard. Kelly's delivery boy was getting better with his aim. Most mornings, she fished the paper out of her nasturtium bed.

Kelly's tea kettle whistled, and she figured it was time to give the computer a break and see what her boy had written for the day.

In mid-pour, she saw the news and almost burned herself.

The paper could shut down?

Kelly took the paper over to her computer to read Judah's editor's explanation. His news was point blank. Ads and subscriptions were down and the publisher, Walker Press, a New York City company, had deemed the paper a failed investment and would only consider continuing if Ima Righter could be found.

"Found? I didn't even know she was missing." Kelly petted Peaches' long fur as the cat raised her head from her favorite spot in the curve of the counter-height kitchen chair.

Not satisfied with the story, Kelly opened her laptop and did her own search. On some of the larger news sites, she found the *Mountain Laurel Star* wasn't the only "failed investment" Walker Press was dealing with. The whole publishing company seemed to be in trouble. Print was a difficult business for anyone these days, and without a strong online presence, a newspaper could pretty much set itself up for failure.

Kelly rechecked her computer, hoping she may have missed something the last time she'd checked, but the *Star* still didn't have a website. Kelly wondered if their demographic dictated the lack of online presence. Riverview was a large town, but most people were older and probably wouldn't read the paper online. Maybe the town just wasn't big enough to sustain a newspaper anymore. Even without the impact its closing would have on her son's life, Kelly felt sad.

The *Star* had been a big part of their lives. Getting a subscription had been at the top of their list when she and Jack had moved to Riverview a few years before Judah was born.

"You've got to know where the hurting people are if you're going to minister to them," Jack had said when they talked about subscribing.

Kelly had never thought of that as a reason for getting a newspaper, but it made sense to her. Countless times they would look up addresses after reading a story about someone's tragedy or job loss. Praying for those people and cheering them with a visit and something she'd baked soon became a family ministry that even Judah had enjoyed as a boy.

This news just didn't make sense to Kelly now. If the publisher wanted to get out of the business, why had they waited this long when someone else could have stepped in long ago to make positive changes? And why did so much depend on Ima Righter?

None of it made sense.

The water for Kelly's tea grew cold as she did her own investigating into Walker Press. The whole company seemed to be going belly up, from what she could see. Her anger flared as she read about how the *Star* and other small-sized newspapers were being blamed for the shutdown. Just because the publisher had failed didn't seem to be enough reason why the *Star* couldn't still run with a new owner.

Maybe Walker Press was deflecting the responsibility of its shut-down on its clients instead of publicizing an underlying issue. Kelly understood things were much tougher on newspapers now than when she and Jack were publishers in Upstate New York before Judah was born. But it still seemed that something could be done for the *Star* before they called it quits.

Searching more online, she saw that *The Call*, a small weekly newspaper in New Jersey, was also being shut down this month and also had the Walker Press publishing logo on their outdated website. She looked for their number on their contact page and dialed its editor-in-chief before she really thought through what she would say. Her efforts would probably come to nothing, but something inside her just had to know more. Having her newspaper shut down was one more loss in her life she wasn't prepared to handle quite yet.

"Hello?" Kelly put her kettle back on to boil. Someone had picked up the phone, but she only heard a lot of background noise and no answer.

She heard more shuffling before a man said, "Roland Scott, editor. What can I do for you?"

"Um, I'm not really sure. This is Kelly Barton. Our local paper is shutting down, and I see that yours is being affected as well. My husband and I were former publishers of *The Messenger* in Upstate New York quite a few years ago. I guess I'm just looking for answers."

There was a bit of a pause and then the sound of a door being shut.

"Have you called your paper's editor?"

"No ... for personal reasons, I can't. That's why I called you. What's going on with Walker Press?"

Kelly knew her question dove into the personal very quickly, so she dropped a few names of people in the business she still connected with on her freelance writing gigs. Her tactic seemed to work as Roland Scott started to talk. He seemed angry and shared with Kelly all he knew, delving straight into what had happened and how Walker Press had made risky investments that tanked, causing a lot of small-town newspapers to shut down over the past few years.

"But that's not right. What if the paper itself was doing well in its town?"

"Without the investment of a good publisher, a town newspaper can't keep its head above water these days, Ms. Barton. We're searching for another publisher now, but very few companies want to take the risk on a newspaper that may or may not have had a hand in helping to cause a large publishing house to go belly-up."

"I see."

"If you know of anyone looking to invest in a New Jersey newspaper that had no fault in its shutdown, please send them my way."

"I sure will." Kelly said her thanks and then set down her cell phone. She really didn't know how well or how poorly the *Star* was doing. And she didn't know how to find out without revealing who she was to Judah's editor. If the *Star* was spiraling in the same path that *The Call* was, however, she could only see things ending in disaster.

CHAPTER 14

JUDAH

I studied Bertram out of the corner of my eye as we drove down the road. Besides the thinning hair, he was also a bit pear-shaped.

I tightened my toned abs and ran a few fingers through my thick bangs.

But there was something about the guy that made you feel like he wasn't caught up in his looks. Like he was okay with his own nerd self or something.

Weird.

The truck came up on the Swagon faster than Bertram must have expected. It shimmied to a stop, making deep ruts in the soft gravel as he moved off the road.

Bertram had jumped out of the truck and fished through some kind of toolbox in the back before I opened my door.

"It's the fan belt, Bert. Sorry ... I should have mentioned that."

Bertram waved me off like he had everything under control.

Looking out into the river, I swallowed hard. Strange feelings came out of nowhere and caught me off guard. I had to look away but then decided to cut myself some slack. It's not every day you save an Amish woman from drowning or have to face your deepest fears by digging around for a body in the dark water of the Shenango.

Had that happened only a few days ago?

I began to think about Johanna. Really think about her. And all that thinking made me really want to find out if she was okay.

It surprised me how much I cared.

Slowly, I got out of the cab of the pickup while Bertram tinkered over to my right with the Swagon's engine. He looked like he knew way more about cars than I did so I let him do his thing.

And besides, I wanted to see the spot.

I walked through the weeds and found the old oak. I even thought I could see the log with the ropes wrapped around it caught just a bit downriver.

A strange rush of concern for Johanna made me almost buckle. I shook my head. What was wrong with me? Johanna was probably fine—surrounded by burly Amish men who would like nothing better than to make a pie out of me.

If Amish men even made pies.

I didn't know a ton about the Amish. Although the community in nearby New Wilmington was one of the largest in the state, the church districts near Riverview were pretty small in comparison. And up until a few days ago, I'd never even spoken to an Amish person.

The clip of hoofs on pavement broke into my thoughts, and I squinted across the bank of weeds to see who might be coming.

Something fluttered in my stomach.

The tan buggy slowed, and I saw an Amish man get out and speak with Bertram.

After a quick exchange, the man got back in his buggy and was gone. By the time I made my way back to the Swagon, Bertram had stuck his head back under the hood and gone back to work.

"Hey, Bert, what was that all about?"

"Mmmph?"

I went around front and asked again. "The Amish guy. What did he want?"

Hands busy and mouth full of car parts, Bertram gestured with his whole head toward the front seat. His gaze headed back to the engine.

I sucked in a deep breath at the sight of Johanna's journal sitting shotgun.

"Ah, Bert?"

"Mmmph?"

"Why did the buggy guy drop this off?"

"Hersrsd—"

I put my hands on my hips and raised my eyebrows. Sensing my frustration, Bertram freed his mouth to speak.

"He said it was yours. You left it in his buggy the other night."

I could feel my jaw drop but sensed Bertram's eyes on me. I had to think fast.

"Oh, great. Yeah, glad to get it back."

Bertram looked at me for another moment before disappearing back under the hood.

Later that evening, as I sat on the couch in my living room, the stories in Johanna's journal trapped me. My stomach growled and I really needed to use the bathroom, but I just couldn't stop reading. I checked the time on my phone. Fixing the Swagon had taken most of the afternoon, but I'd gotten home nearly three hours ago. Yet I couldn't seem to tear myself from her writing.

My abs were sore from laughing, and I was pretty sure I would never tell anyone about the pile of wet tissue on the floor next to me. When Johanna wrote about her grandmother slowly slipping away in their little *Dawdi Haus*, her hand becoming still in Johanna's grip, I'd lost it.

Johanna hadn't wanted to say goodbye—ever.

I understood.

Johanna wrote about her Amish life in a way that felt surprisingly honest. With my own writing, it seemed like I always tried to be someone I wasn't. Letting the world know the real me was something I hadn't even considered and, frankly, it scared me to death.

Her writing also gave me an insider's view of a culture I knew very little about, even though I'd lived near Amish all my life.

Growing up, I had gawked with the rest of my friends as their horses trotted in their "buggy lanes." Amish kids dressed as miniature versions of their parents stared right back at us.

We'd snickered and pointed at the neat piles of manure left in the "Amish Only" parking spots in the far corner of the grocery store lot. And we'd held our noses in the store when a farmer who probably didn't even own a stick of deodorant passed by.

If I was honest with myself, that kind of distance from those people had been just fine with me.

But these people in her journal felt so real. I could almost touch them.

How could someone who never went to college and who didn't even have access to the internet write like this? I felt relieved I didn't have to compete with someone of this caliber at the newspaper. Johanna had the skills of every one of our staff in the tip of her little finger.

She wrote about anger, pain, regret, and deep resolve so vividly, I felt it too. Reading such emotion was hard to take.

But the writing was so vibrant, I lived what she felt right along with her.

The shadows in my apartment grew long as I started to read Johanna's last entry. She seemed to be writing a goodbye of sorts. The emotion in her words felt almost palatable. *Goodbye, my heart,* she wrote. My chest tightened. Whatever she was being forced to leave behind, she loved it more than life itself.

JOHANNA

Mordecai Zook.

My mother had literally just dropped his name right into my lap while I sat propped up after eating corn soup with rivels in Mammi's poster bed.

I stared at the slate for a long time while the name stared back at me. Mamm must have left the slate for effect, maybe to let me warm up to the "plan" she'd been talking about. One that, in her mind, would forever mend the breach between our family and the bishop. I read the name on the slate again.

Mamm had to be kidding.

I had decided to give my writing up for *gut*. To confess to the bishop and to the People about my sin—to do whatever it took to get off the *Bann* and ensure my family had the ongoing support of the community.

But I would not—could not—marry Mordecai.

"I'm sure he's changed," Mamm said, coming back into the room with a piece of apple tart on pat-a-pan crust. My favorite.

I'd seen her look like this before. Her face like flint.

She'd be ready to take whatever I would dish out concerning the bishop's grandson. But when I dug down deep for my argument, I saw my father's face, and, just like that, I had no more fight.

After agreeing to give up my writing for the sake of my family, marrying Mordecai would just be a final way to seal my fate.

My mother knew that, I was sure of it. But what she'd missed in all her calculations was the abuse I was in for if I chose to marry Mordecai.

I never told Mamm about my experience with Mordecai at one of the few Singings I had attended. Why should I tell when it would only dig a deeper rift between our families? But there were things about Mordy that would make Mamm cringe if she knew.

Mordecai had worn out his first wife, Rebekah. There was no other way to say it. He'd kept her pregnant and quiet about what went on behind closed doors at their house. She'd died during childbirth just this past spring.

Mordecai's time of mourning would be about over, and Mamm knew, just as I did, that he would be looking for someone to take Rebekah's place quickly. He needed someone to make his meals, do his laundry, tend to his brood of six, and fill his bed.

Rebekah had been shy and never spoke much at our canning frolics or quilting bees. She didn't have to explain to me the bruises I'd spotted that day when her toddler pushed up her sleeve.

Because I already knew the reason.

As the bishop's grandson, Mordy kept things clean and friendly on the outside, but he was a different man when he had you alone.

When I was sixteen, I was old enough to attend a Singing and even to accept a ride home in a boy's courting buggy. Although Mamm had well prepared me for the Singing experience, I felt shy and new to the Amish courtship scene.

Not to mention awkward.

Mose brought me to the Singing but had his eyes set on his sweet Linda, whose cheeks glowed a pretty shade of pink the whole time we all sang together in the Kings' barn. I know because I sat next to her and couldn't help but notice. Mose kept quiet about his intentions, but I knew he wanted more than anything to be able to take Linda home alone in our buggy.

Halfway through the event, I'd decided to walk home after it was done. The Singing made me nervous anyway, and I needed time to clear my head after all the googly eyes that were going on from where the boys sat on one side of the barn to where the girls sat. So, after the Singing was over and the couples started pairing up, I told Mose he could have the buggy all to himself.

"What do you mean, Johanna? Dat said I'm supposed to take you home."

Thinking quickly, I tried to look coy and told what I hoped wasn't a lie. "Not if I've found another way home."

"Ah."

Mose looked around, thinking he would spot the boy who supposedly asked to take me home. Not seeing anyone waiting for me, he seemed unconvinced. I could see him waver in his decision, but then his eyes caught Linda's, and he nodded.

Phew.

I'd started down the dark road lost in thought as I fleshed out the characters in a story I had been working on. It was then that Mordecai, then seventeen, caught up to me.

"Hey, Johanna, ride with me."

It was more of a command than a request, but I was too young to tell the difference.

If I got a ride home from a boy on my first Singing, maybe Mamm would let up on me about going to another one for a while.

I didn't know him very well. Mordecai was only a year older than me, but for some reason, my brothers had always kept their distance from him. But I figured as long as I didn't have to talk too much with him I would be okay.

But I soon found out Mordecai seemed interested in more than talking. After passing the courting buggies parked on the sides of the main road, Mordy took a side road that led away from our farm.

A small chill made its way through my body when he stopped his buggy.

Mordy reached for me, rough and large for his age and not gentle by any means. I tried to push him away and caught a slap from him across my face.

Fear coursed through my veins. I was too shy then to cry out, but not too shy to run. I could still hear the ripping sound my best cape dress made as I tore away from his grasp and on into the wood. Mordecai's angry shouts thankfully faded behind me.

Branches whipped my face, and wild blackberries scratched zigzagged lines in my skin, but I didn't stop running until I arrived safely in our barn, bleeding and bruised from the wood.

My emotions were all over the place, and I was glad I had some time to steady myself before Mose returned with his courting buggy from the Singing.

When he saw me, he let out a small groan.

"Johanna."

"I'm okay, Mose. I just need you to go to my room and get me my other dress."

"I shouldn't have left ya."

Tears threatened, but I kept them at bay. "Just the dress, Mose."

"I saw who picked you up on the road."

I waved his words away. "He's the bishop's grandson, Mose. He does what he wants."

"Not to my sister." Mose grew red in the face. "Did he?"

"*Nee*, Mose. But I've learned my lesson. I'll stay away from him." And from any more Singings, for that matter.

It took some convincing to keep Mose from heading over to the bishop's house right then. For just a few seconds, he seemed to forget we were Yoders and Mordecai was a Zook. But eventually, he trudged into the house and brought me out my other dress, along with a cloth and some water to wash my wounds.

With a fresh dress on and most of my scratches covered, I figured I could pass for normal as I entered the house.

On the inside though, I knew I would never be the same.

I stared back down at the slate now. Marry Mordy? Mamm had no idea what she was asking.

JUDAH

The coffee I'd made earlier had grown cold, but I drank the last sip anyway. As I turned the final pages of the journal, Johanna's words grew more intense. Her heart was breaking, almost torn in half. And I felt it.

Images of Dad played on in my head—so real I could have reached out and touched him.

Dad. I really miss you. Why didn't you let me die? Mom would much rather have you alive than me. Plus, she doesn't know that I was responsible for your death. And I've been pretty horrible to her.

Why was all this surfacing again?

I wanted to get up from the couch. Move away from my pain. But the journal held me fast. Johanna spoke of a man then, someone who was making her give up her dream.

Someone with a heavy hand. Someone who, I felt, was trying to play God.

This man, "Bishop," she called him, pulled her away from the thing she loved, warning her there would be consequences if she kept it up.

I didn't get that part. Mom's pastor had been more than encouraging in everything I tried, especially my writing. In fact, he had written the recommendation letter I needed to get into my college's journalism program. And he'd handed me a graduation card with a sizable check.

"I know you'll put it to good use." He had looked me in the eye and placed a hand on each of my shoulders. "I'm proud of you, Judah. And I'm excited to see how God will use your writing gift."

I hadn't appreciated the encouragement then, being so wrapped up in what I didn't have that I'd let it consume me. And change me.

I remembered what I had done with the pastor's money too. He wouldn't have been so proud of me if he knew.

There was just one more page in the journal. I decided to make a fresh cup of coffee—decaf this time—so I could savor the writing. But as I got up, the ceiling fan caught the page and it turned. I went to flip it back and had to sit down again when I caught a glimpse of the final line.

Goodbye, Ima Righter.

CHAPTER 15

JUDAH

It took me a few minutes to understand what I was seeing. Then, without really thinking, I picked up the phone, ready to expose her to Hilton.

I could almost smell the promotion I'd been longing for. Hilton, the hothead, had threatened to fire me just days ago if I didn't find her. My head spun at the new possibilities. I couldn't believe I'd actually done what he'd asked me to do. As the phone rang, I ran through what I would say, but when Hilton picked up, something inside me did a backpedal.

There was more to this story. This could also be big news, really big news, for the *Star*. Something that would put us back in the running with the advertisers who loved Ima.

Furthermore, if I broke the bigger story, it would mean even more leverage for me. I could see myself sitting in the now-vacant senior writer office.

But I had to play it smart. Obviously, Johanna didn't want the world to know about her writing gifts. She probably hadn't let many people in on her writing secrets. Especially not that geezer who accused me of molesting her after I had just saved her life. And what about this bishop guy? What power did he have over Johanna?

There was a secret somewhere in all of this. And if I exposed her now, something big would be lost, I could feel it.

"Barton ... Barton, is that you?"

How was I going to explain this call?

Hilton had been a journalist for too many years. He'd pull my story right through the phone if he could.

"Yeah." I tried to sound defeated. "I can't find her, boss."

"Don't quit." I couldn't believe he was falling for this act. "I talked with Walker Press earlier today."

Was he letting me in on publisher business? I stood up a little straighter, sure now, by the significant slur to his words, that he had stopped at the bar on the way back to the paper.

"Yeah?" Man, could I sound any dumber?

"They're shutting us down ... with ... without Ima on staff."

"What?" I snapped Johanna's journal shut. He couldn't see it. I knew he couldn't. But just to be sure.

"Have you seen today's paper?"

I slapped my forehead. I hadn't. A good journalist always sees his own paper. *Excuse, c'mon, come up with an excuse.*

"I've been out looking for Ima."

"That's good. You keep looking. The advertisers like her. Our audience likes her. She's what we need to keep running."

"I'll find her."

"Ah, Barton. You and I both know it's a needle in a haystack."

Was Hilton throwing in the towel here? If he did, forget the promotion. I would be out of a job.

"I'll find her."

Hilton didn't know what I knew. He had to keep the paper from dying until I could submit the story of my life and somehow get Ima back on staff.

"We've got one less day now. I've let our readers know we're shutting down unless we find her. Our key advertisers made it clear they won't be placing their ads in our p-paper."

There was a long pause, and I could hear the tinkle of ice in his glass. I was about to hang up when he started talking again.

"If you find her and bring her to work here ..."

My ears perked up.

"You've got the senior writer slot."

He hung up then, probably heading home to sleep off his buzz.

I stood there for a while, just holding the phone as a war raged in my brain.

Of all the people to find in Mercer County, I take the Swagon out and am led right to the one I'm looking for. No wild goose chase. No needle in a haystack. Just a drowning woman and a guy who can't swim. I realized I did need to give the delivery guy some credit, however. He probably did live near Johanna. So even though he lost me, he led me to the right location.

I needed time to think. I couldn't tell Hilton I'd found her. Not yet. Johanna was too good. She'd have my job, or a level up, in a heartbeat if she decided to work for the *Star*. And judging from how much she loved to write, an offer like that would be pretty tempting. Even if she was Amish.

I had to figure out a way to bring this whole thing to my advantage. I'd found her, after all. That had to count for something.

No, I wasn't going anywhere if I could help it. The paper had to be saved and, somehow, I needed to come out on top as the hero in all of this.

The problem was, I had no idea how to make that happen.

JOHANNA

Someone knocked on my door. Or was I dreaming? I opened one eye at a time. I checked Mammi's wind-up clock and saw that I had only been asleep for an hour and the night was as dark as ever. Who would come to see me at this time of night?

Someone who was about to forsake the *Bann*, that's who.

I cracked the door and spoke out into the blackness of the night.

"Hello?"

"Johanna?"

The voice sounded excited and maybe a little desperate. Something in it I recognized.

"*Jah*?"

The person pushed into the door and gave me a big hug.

Touch. Just a few days on the *Bann*, and I was starved for it. Caring little about the source of the hug, I hugged back.

Lizzie pulled away then so I could see her, and she could see me. Tears flowed, and neither of us could say anything for a few minutes. I tried to swallow the lump in my throat, but it wouldn't go down, so I just stood there looking at her. She was a sight for sore eyes.

"*Ach*, Johanna. Look at ya! I came as soon as I heard."

I nodded and tried to smile. Heard? She'd heard about the *Bann* and still she came? It was more than I had done for her.

I shook my head. "Lizzie, you shouldn't have come. You know what can happen."

She put her hand on my arm. "Nothing more can happen to me. At least not from Bishop Zook."

I gave her a questioning look, still wiping my eyes and trying hard to speak without blubbering.

"I'm not Amish anymore, Johanna." Lizzie smiled. Her face filled with light as she explained how she had grown closer to Jesus at a Mennonite Bible study.

Lizzie looked the same as always—still dressed plain. Then, she surprised me by holding up her left hand to show me some twine she had wrapped around her ring finger. And then she stood sideways to show me her swollen middle.

My jaw hung, and Lizzie laughed.

"Morris and I wed four months ago." She sighed and looked out the window into the night. "Mamm and Dat, you know, they do whatever the bishop says. I couldn't live like that anymore." Her eyes grew misty. "I do miss them, though."

I still couldn't speak, but Lizzie giggled and grabbed my hand.

"After my *Bann*, there wasn't anything else for me to do, Johanna. I tried other Amish communities where I have friends and relatives, but somehow, news of the *Bann* always arrived ahead of me, and after living there for a short time, I was always asked to leave and go repent to my bishop."

I couldn't imagine going out on my own like she had— searching for help and friendship. Neither of which I had offered to her. I admired her strength and bravery.

"Lizzie, I'm so sorry ..."

She gave me another hug. "Now don't ya worry about any of that. That's not why I'm here."

I shuffled over to put the tea kettle on and took out some friendship bread Mamm had left when she was in the *Dawdi Haus* earlier. My friend must be hungry, eating for two now.

Lizzie held up her hand. "I'm not here to stay long. At least not for now." She took a bite of friendship bread even as she spoke. "Morris is outside waiting for me in the car."

I handed her a cup of milk to wash it down.

"I have to tell you what I learned living in other Amish communities—brief as that time was."

I sat down and just watched her. I hadn't realized how much I missed my friend until now. Lizzie had been one of the few who believed in me and my gift to write. I had forgotten how *gut* that felt.

"Pay attention, Johanna! This is important."

I smiled. Feisty as always. "I'm looking straight at ya!"

"*Ach!* But you're not listening. Focus on what I'm saying. I don't have much time. If Morris starts beeping out there, we'll both be in a heap of trouble."

I sat up straighter and leaned in.

"The People in Smokey Hollow and the People in Piney Gap are permitted to write creatively."

"What?"

"They write. Well, not many of them do, but those that want to can. There's no rule against it."

I stared. "Why, then, can't we?"

Lizzie shrugged her shoulders. "That's a *gut* question. Our bishop must have created that rule, got the People to agree, and added it to Willow Brook's *Ordnung*."

"Well, maybe it's been in our *Ordnung* longer than our bishop."

Lizzie shook her head. "*Nee,* I checked that too. A great aunt in Piney Gap let me stay with her for a few days after I left Willow Brook. I asked her about Bishop Zook and his ban on creative writing, and she said she had never heard anything like that from the bishop who led before him. In fact, she said Zook stopped allowing creative writing just a few years after he became bishop. That it was uncommon for a bishop to put a rule of that sort on his People. And my great aunt"—Lizzie reached for another slice of the sweet bread—"writes poetry."

As I let that sink in, anger rose in my chest.

"Lizzie, all my life I've been told that writing is a vain pursuit that leads to prideful living. It's something I've always felt guilty about because I thought *Gott* was against it. But what you're saying ... you're saying it's the bishop's rule he wanted added to our *Ordnung* and it's not necessarily *Gott's* rule?"

Lizzie beamed. *"Jah*, that's what I'm saying."

A short beep sounded outside.

"Ach! Morris! He should know better." My friend gave me a quick hug, pressed a small book into my hand, and was out the door before my head had a chance to clear.

"But how will I—" I looked out into the night as the door shut and the car pulled away.

I started to worry that Mamm would have heard the beep or the car, but caught myself. How much worse could things get? I was already under the heaviest discipline the bishop could give me.

I began to think about the *Bann* and how Lizzie had said the bishop had banned writing just a few years after being ordained. Mammi Miriam would have been most impacted by this. She must have been writing freely up to that point.

I couldn't imagine having my greatest passion taken from me, just like that. The pain would be too great to bear.

And yet Mammi had endured it.

I had so many questions. Why did the bishop target writing when it hadn't been in the *Ordnung* before he came to Willow Brook? If I found the answer to that, maybe I could bring about some change that didn't involve marrying Mordecai. My thoughts went to Mammi's journal.

There had to be answers in there. Knowing Mammi, she would have written down her deepest thoughts on the subject before giving up her pen for *gut*.

I wished Lizzie had more time to talk. It would help to have a friend at a time like this.

But she was gone, and I had no way to contact her. The teapot whistled and I rose, setting the small book my friend had given me on the table.

The book! I turned back and looked at the cover—a book of poems published by her great aunt. On the inside cover, in Lizzie's best penmanship, were these words:

Write your story.

And under them she'd written her new last name and address. Smiling, I pressed the book to my chest and went to pour my tea.

JUDAH

Sleep would not come. I stared at the ceiling, my brain working hard to try and figure out this story.

If I couldn't write it all, at least I would be the one who broke the story. It wasn't much, but if I nailed this, maybe I could ride on the wave of Johanna's success.

I'd keep everything I knew quiet until I was ready to drop the story. But until then, I needed more.

I had to talk to her. Why had she stopped writing when she was doing so well? Why had she kept everything so secret?

Man, what a great cover this writer had. I pulled off my blanket. I'd start my research tomorrow, but, for now, I had to write down what I knew.

Sometimes writing seemed labor intensive. Stories on city council meetings and ribbon-cutting ceremonies were boring but had to be done. Churning them out gave me the satisfaction of completing the assignment, but I'd never felt anything like this. Writing this story took me to a place I had never been with my craft. Tonight, I became a composer and my computer keyboard a baby grand. The article came together quickly and felt like a work of art.

When I finished typing what I knew, I read over the words and decided this first part was good stuff. Maybe even award-worthy. And I knew Hilton would agree if he could bring himself to admit it.

My best story yet. This article was the first installment of a series of investigative stories that would uncover the whereabouts of Ms. Ima Righter. And hopefully bring her back to the *Star*, ensuring the paper's success instead of its shut down.

A negative thought about Johanna and her bishop came to me then, but I tried to push it out. The more I looked over the story, the more it tried to grow roots and spoil my moment.

What bothered me was that part in Johanna's journal where she wrote about giving up writing. Her bishop had found out her secret, and it looked like she had to decide whether to keep writing or leave her Amish community.

I mean, I'd never heard of an Amish newspaper writer. That's probably why she'd chosen an alias.

What would happen to her when news like this got out?

Bad news always traveled faster than good news. And the fact that Johanna changed her identity to write for the *Star* and may have violated some kind of Amish rule in the process seemed definitely bad for her.

Our readers would love it, though, and the story would spread like wildfire. People would probably be showing up on her front doorstep.

I had to turn it in to Hilton. The paper would die without this. He was hounding me for something anyway. And I had an obligation to the *Star* too. This story alone could whet Hilton's appetite and maybe even stave off the publisher from shutting us down until I could uncover more.

The sick feeling in my stomach grew stronger, but I pushed it down with a swig of water. I had every reason to turn this piece in. It was my story. My career. I had done what my editor had asked me to do—no, had pushed me out the door to do. Why shouldn't I benefit from it a little?

Especially since Johanna, or Ima, was likely to have one of our jobs before the week was out.

This would help her too, right?

And Hilton would be indebted to me. He would think twice before replacing me with Ima. I would be the one who broke the story, after all.

It felt like a win-win for both Johanna and me. I would keep my job and she'd get a new one. Hopefully, Hilton would keep his promise about the senior writer position being mine.

I attached the story to my email and hit Send.

JOHANNA

I sat at the small table in the *Dawdi Haus*, reading poems by the light of the rolling mobile propane lamp. The writing was beautiful. Captivating.

An ache developed in my heart for my own pen. I had to find Mammi Miriam's journal.

Energy sprang from nowhere as I hid the poetry book in a drawer and moved thoughtfully through the small home. I'd already looked for the journal right after Mammi died, but maybe it was hidden somewhere no one would ever think of looking. Knowing Mammi, that sounded about right.

Rolling the lamp around with me, I targeted the kitchen first. I looked behind a lone, outdated calendar, feeling the wall behind it. From there, I made my way through every cabinet and drawer. I even knocked on the floorboards, wondering if a loose one might hold the treasure I sought.

Then, I moved to the house's one bedroom, doing more of the same. The mattress seemed a great hiding place, but I resisted the urge to start cutting it open.

I pulled out the dresser drawers one by one and again knocked on every floorboard before tumbling into a heap on the bed.

Energy gone and heart aching, I slept without dreaming.

Kelly couldn't sleep. She hated it when this happened.

When Jack was alive, he would pray for her and hold her when sleep failed to come. Now she lie alone, unsleeping and staring at the ceiling fan.

Missing her husband took up a good part of her thoughts, but something else bothered her tonight. She just couldn't quite put her finger on it.

She rose, made herself a cup of chamomile, and began to look through the box in her study where she stored old copies of the *Star*.

Jack wouldn't have liked her saving them—the clutter would have driven him crazy—but she allowed herself this pleasure now. Sometimes when her heart hurt for her son, she would take out old issues and reread Judah's stories. It made her feel close to him in some weird way.

This time she wanted to look closely through the papers to see if she could pinpoint any areas where the *Star* had been failing. Maybe her own experience as a publisher would help her to see something, anything, that would warrant a shut down.

By four in the morning, she had read through all the issues she had—two years' worth. From what she could see, there had been plenty of advertisers to support this size of newspaper if they had been managed correctly. Only in the last month or two had the paper thinned and ads dropped off. Until then, the paper had been doing well.

Her research confirmed her suspicion the shutdown might be more an issue with the publisher than anything else.

And then there was the Ima connection.

After rereading all of her columns, Kelly decided she loved Ima's writing even more and wondered why they'd stopped so abruptly.

She reread the issue that had come yesterday, and the line about finding Ima Righter popped out at her again.

She couldn't wrap her head around that one. Where had she gone? Why had she quit? And why was the newspaper's existence hinging on her return?

God help Ima wherever she is. And show me how I can help the Star.

CHAPTER 16

JUDAH

What had I done?

Even though I had just hit Send, I was already regretting my decision to email my story to Hilton in the middle of the night. I covered my face with my hands. Why hadn't I waited until the morning after I'd thought it through more? Dad always said that nothing good ever happened after midnight. That expression had always rubbed me the wrong way even as a preteen, but, deep down, I knew he was right.

I should have remembered his warning before I hit Send. I didn't even want to check my email to get Hilton's reaction. He'd love it, no doubt. The newspaper would be saved. I'd be the hero. The end.

He'd probably want me to sit back down tomorrow afternoon and write the story's second installment.

Before he could do any of those things, I needed to get off the grid to think. He could try to call me later, but I'd already turned off my phone. I left my phone by my computer and went to bed. Vivid dreams sprang to life as soon as my head hit the pillow.

The bearded Amish guy with no mustache—a younger version of the man who had pulled Johanna into his buggy after her drowning—seemed angry. And there was something about his eyes that creeped me out. Maybe it was because they didn't move in sync with each other.

Because of his lazy eye, it took me a while to figure out I wasn't the object of his rage.

I looked behind me and saw her.

Her eyes were downcast and focused on her bare feet.

The man raised his voice. I should have been ready for what came next.

Johanna's head ricocheted off the barn wall with the slap of his hand on her cheek, but still she stood.

Anger surged through me, and I lunged at the man, only to find myself flat on my bedroom's laminate floor.

Gasping, I turned on all the lights and then rubbed my hands to stop the shaking. Liza Lou woke and started pacing the floor.

"No, girl, it's not time." But I knew I had blown it. She wouldn't stop whining and running from me to the door until I took her out.

And then there was the lady downstairs. She probably slept with her broom by her bed.

Grabbing my hoodie and Liza's leash, I hoped to make it quick. Liza lunged out the open door before I was quite ready. Hanging on tightly to her leash, I ran headlong into someone who was just getting ready to knock.

Flailing, I hit the crumbling concrete hard. And there went Liza, barreling at top speed down the road, her leash trailing behind her.

I'm sure I said something unsavory.

A figure hovered over me saying something, but his words seemed garbled. Why had he tripped me?

I hoped I was still dreaming.

Something felt cold on my head, so cold it hurt. Whoever tended to my wounds wasn't doing a very good job. A light went on, and I could see Bertram's face now. He looked pretty upset. A pile of bloody paper towels lay on my end table.

"Bert, what's going on?"

Relief spread over his face, and he mopped his balding head with a crumpled paper towel. "Judah!"

Remembering Liza Lou's exit, I scanned the room for her and then tried to sit up.

Bertram gently pushed me back down.

"Consuelo's looking for her."

"Liza Lou can't run the road alone. She'll get hit, Bert. Despite her age, she still races cars like they're ... Con ... who?"

"She's your neighbor, Judah, the lady downstairs. You don't know the name of your own neighbor?"

I let out some more words that made Bertram wince, and he got out some more paper towels, pressing them hard against my head.

"Ow!"

"Well, whatever you think of her, she was pretty quick to help after you ran into me."

"What were you doing on my steps at 4:00 a.m.?"

"Your email. Your phone was off, but you'd just sent it, so I thought maybe I'd catch you awake. I saw your light on, so I was getting ready to knock."

The email. Something deep inside me hurt. Why had I sent it? I hadn't even thought it through. Boy, had I messed up.

I remembered the dream and the man with the lazy eye. Sitting up too quickly, the room tilted, and I lay back down.

"I had to come. After you said you found Ima."

Hilton was fast.

"Who told you about her?"

"You did."

"Me?" My head hurt. "Don't lie for Hilton, Bert."

"Hilton's the one you need to look out for. If this gets out, it could really hurt Ima."

He wasn't making sense. I slid up on my elbows now. I was making progress, at least I could get this far up without feeling dizzy.

"I'm serious. That's what made me come over here in the middle of the night. That Amish community is rough on its members, especially the ones who go against Bishop Zook."

"How do you know this?"

"I have family who are Amish. If a story like this gets out, who knows how people are going to react." Bertram began to pace the room.

I touched the sore spot on my head and winced. "I know, I've probably ruined her life with that one stupid email." I squeezed back tears.

I felt embarrassed for Bertram to see me so upset. I lay my head back down on the couch and hid under the icepack.

It was the lowest I had felt in a long, long time.

JOHANNA

"You know, at the age of twenty-five, you aren't getting any younger." From Mammi Miriam's bed, I heard Mamm talking to me all the way from her own kitchen. She must have left the *Dawdi Haus* door open so I could hear her.

I let out a sigh.

The door to the cast iron cookstove creaked, and the sweet molasses scent of shoofly pie made it all the way to where I lay.

The bishop's favorite.

"It's perfectly honorable to marry a widower. A special thing, considering the children."

Children. I hadn't thought about Mordecai's six children.

"As new mother, you'll take on many responsibilities that will keep your hands and mind busy. After some time in this role, I'm sure you'll forget all of this writing foolishness."

I slid under the covers but could still hear her.

"You'll be the right fit for the grandson of the bishop. It's a plan so perfect, it must have come from the almighty hand of *Gott* himself."

I plugged one ear.

"Now I've made a bit of an offering here with these pies. I hope it's enough."

I sat up. Offering? What was Mamm talking about?

"The trick is to try to get the bishop to think he's come up with the idea all by himself, Johanna. That way, he's sure to stand behind the plan. He's the one who has to get Mordecai to propose, after all."

Propose? I knew I'd agreed to this, but my resolve wavered. She was going to talk to the bishop about it *now*? I stood quickly and the room spun.

"Mamm?" My panicked voice echoed off Mammi Miriam's bare walls.

The front door slammed shut and I was left alone with the smells of Mamm's pies.

The earthy scent of blackstrap molasses blended in the air with nutmeg, cinnamon, and clove, wrapping around me like a blanket and bringing me back to my childhood. When I was younger, I had been Mamm's constant companion. Even before I could reach the counter, I stood on a stool to help her. Back then we were two peas in a pod—baking, cleaning, and gardening together. Having a girl with all those boys must have been a treat for Mamm. Someone to keep her company.

The closeness changed the day Mamm discovered I had been writing. Mammi Miriam had given me a journal to write my thoughts, and Mamm about blew her lid.

I'd kept it hidden after that, but that didn't really matter to Mamm. She'd grown up with her mother. She knew the draw that came with the gift. Slowly, she withdrew from me, and I spent more and more time with Mammi Miriam who understood me.

I shook my head. Things were so different now. Mamm was on her way to the bishop's to seal my fate and my life was about to change drastically. And without Mammi Miriam's own journal, there was very little I could do about it.

The walls in the small *Dawdi Haus* started to close in on me, and suddenly, I wanted to be outside—anywhere but here.

I needed air.

Pulling myself up from the bed, I held on to the bedpost and steadied myself. Colors swirled in my vision and threatened to turn black. I took in slow, deep breaths of air and shapes reemerged from the shadows.

I can do this.

I pulled myself up, willed my jelly legs to be steady, and slowly made my way out the back door.

JUDAH

"One email?"

Bertram had been snoring on my recliner, but was now awake. I'd stayed on the couch, not trusting my balance.

The sun shone through the curtains now and Bert had refocused on the email.

"You only sent one email?" Bertram went from a reclining position to sitting straight up in less than a second.

"Yeah, you want to keep rubbing it in?" My face hurt from where I fell, and I didn't need him cramming what I'd done down my throat. Hilton was probably running the story right now.

"It's just that there was no one copied on my email. I remember checking because, well, I couldn't believe you would send something so, well, sensitive, to me." Bertram was on his phone now, rechecking the email. He smiled. "So, you had to have sent two, if Hilton got one too."

I got up a little too fast and came close to blacking out. "Get my computer, Bert. Um … please." Wow, I was being polite. But maybe, just maybe, I had made the best mistake of my life.

Bert dashed to my laptop and brought up my emails for me. Good thing, too, since my vision was a bit blurred and the words on my computer jiggled.

I tried to read, but a headache had started behind one of my eyes.

Bertram got me more ice and read the whole email to me, start to finish, including his name in the address line.

"No one is copied?"

He shook his head.

JOHANNA

The air felt crisp and a little on the cool side for September. I was glad I had brought Mammi's heavy shawl and pulled it close around my throat. The road that wound away from our house was filled with color. Orange sugar maples, yellow hickories, and red oaks made my eyes almost hurt with their brightness. Rolled bales of hay, harvested by my brothers and cousins, filled my father's fields. Mamm's kitchen garden looked like she'd already picked it clean of the last remaining tomatoes. Fat pumpkins sat in the straw where they'd basked in the sunshine all summer long—their shriveled vines a sure sign they were ready to pick. I longed to touch their smooth orange skin and knock on one to hear its hollow sound.

But Mamm might spot me, and she wouldn't approve of me being out so soon after being sick. I muffled a short cough into the cape and continued on. I moved toward the road so I could see the Clydesdales one of our *Englischer* neighbors raised for equine plasma and other animal blood products. The horses they used, my neighbor told me once, had saved the lives of countless animals across the country. But I just enjoyed them for their beauty and the calm they brought me.

The herd often grazed in one massive group by the fence that bordered our fields. I hadn't seen them in days due to my illness and wondered if the foals born last spring had gotten any bigger. I started along the road at a slow pace but spotted a tan buggy up ahead and ducked into a trail still shielded by thick stalks of drying dent corn. Picking my way through the corn, I took a path that led to the wood instead.

No need for anyone to feel uncomfortable seeing me on the road because of the *Bann*. The less of that, the better.

The crunch of autumn leaves underfoot made my walk sound somewhat like a melody as gusts caught trees and more leaves swirled to the ground.

I tired quickly and my steps slowed. Needing a place to sit, I strayed off the path a bit to our outcropping of rocks.

Scratching at the moss for a foothold, I finally found some leverage and pulled myself up to the flat surface of the largest rock. I found a sunny spot and curled into a ball for warmth—a silent spectator of all the fall colors around me.

After a time, I heard a light patter in the leaves below and was greeted with a bound by my cat Miracle. Her thick coat told me she was prepared for a long, hard winter. I snuggled into her and let the tears roll.

CHAPTER 17

JUDAH

I must have passed out at Bertram's news about the email because, the next thing I knew, Liza Lou was licking my whole face, and my apartment smelled like bacon.

"I think you'll be all right, really. Just a good knock on the head when you fell. You'll want to see a doctor if your headaches persist, though. Could be a concussion."

The woman's back was to me while she talked, giving me a full view of her house dress that ended where an impressive set of cankles began. As she cooked, she broke into a little salsa with the Latin music coming from her phone.

Bertram seemed to have vanished.

"Um ... hello?" Liza Lou sat panting beside me now. I couldn't tell if she was glad I was okay or happy about the lady and her bacon.

The woman turned and stuck her hand out. "I'm your downstairs neighbor, Consuelo." She laughed when she noticed my hesitancy. "You say it like this: 'con-sway-lo.' My friends call me Sway."

She handed me a plate of something that smelled delicious.

"*Huevos*—the way my *abuela* used to make them with olives, onions, and tomatoes—the works!"

I thanked her, and, as I tucked into the eggs, I felt a little bad about hating her and her broom.

"That dog of yours sure gave me a run for my money this morning."

"Thank you for that," I said, although I couldn't imagine Consuelo running for any amount of money.

"Oh, that's okay, *mijo*. I'm just sorry we hadn't met before. I thought you had a grizzly bear up here or something."

While I ate, Consuelo told me about her Cuban heritage and explained she was a nurse over at Shady Hill Hospital. She said she'd "checked me over and fixed my face" after Bert had left for work.

Raising my hand to my head, I felt the butterfly bandages, and an odd feeling ran through me. Mom had always been the one to tape me up after a fall ... or a fight.

I was about to thank her and probably say something sappy when the doorbell rang.

"Judah? Are you feeling better?"

Bertram sure was starting to be a regular around here.

"Yeah, man, I'm good."

Although I really wasn't good, and I had a feeling that both Bertram and Consuelo could see right through my act. I lay my head back down on the couch.

Consuelo left then, saying something about her shift and that she'd be back to check on me later.

After she'd left, a cloud seemed to fall over Bertram's face. I tried to shut my eyes, but I could feel him staring at me. Holding my hand to my temple, I fluffed the pillow under my head so I could see him better.

"What's the matter?" It came out more like a growl.

"Oh, um, well, Judah, I was thinking."

Bertram took off his glasses and started cleaning them with his polo. He put them back on, blinked a few times, and stared right at me. I looked away. Whatever it was, let him spill it on his own. My head hurt.

He cleared his throat and began. "I know that Hilton sent you to find Ima, and you did. You had every right to send that email. It was your assignment, after all."

I knew there was a "but" coming.

"But after meeting Johanna and maybe having an idea of what a story like this could do to her, were you really going to send that email to Hilton?"

I could hear it in the tone of his voice: disappointment. The feeling was familiar. I'd seen disappointment in my mother's eyes every day I lived with her after my father's death.

I put on my "I don't care what you think about me" front and turned to Bertram. "I was. What's it to you, Bert? What do you know about her community?"

"My grandfather was Amish before he left the church. But I still have some relatives over in the Willow Brook district. Do you understand what your piece could have done to Ima ... er, Johanna? Even if the bishop already knows and that's why she's stopped writing, it could still have done more damage to her and her family than this is all worth."

"Whatever, Bert. I had to think about myself here." I let him in on all that Hilton had told me the night before. He had to understand my desperation then. Maybe even think about how my idea could save his job too.

But I was wrong. When I'd finished, Bert was still on Ima's side.

"Think about it, Judah. If Zook finds out she's been writing for a local paper for two years, she'll be *bann*ed, or excommunicated, if she isn't already. What if she has a family or even kids?"

"She's pretty young, Bert. And she wasn't wearing a ring."

"The Amish marry young. Their culture is very different than ours. And they don't wear wedding rings. Personal jewelry is not allowed. They feel it draws prideful attention to their bodies."

The more Bertram spoke, the more I couldn't get my dream of the bearded man out of my head. I saw the man slapping Johanna over and over again. I squeezed my eyes shut to make it stop.

A small tingle crawled up my spine as I thought about the guy, and suddenly, I knew Johanna was in trouble. She might not know it yet, but she was.

And I did care, probably a little too much, and that scared me too.

That's when an idea started to form in my cloudy head.

I clawed my fingers through my shaggy bangs, and my mind made a jump to the last time I saw Mom a few years ago. She'd practically begged me to stop and get a haircut on my way back from work. Waving a coupon and a ten-dollar bill in my face, she'd given me the look that I did my best to avoid when I was living with her.

The look that asked—What are you doing with your hair? What are you doing with your life?

Whatever.

But as the plan took shape, I began to agree with my mom about one thing. I really did need a haircut.

It all came at me in a rush then, and somehow, I needed to slow it down. I needed to bounce my ideas off Bert.

"Who did you say still lived in Willow Brook that you know?"

The question came out without a lot of thought, and I wondered if Bertram would be quick to clam up after he figured out my plan.

"A great uncle. My grandfather's brother. I still visit him every now and then."

I grabbed some scissors and placed a large bowl on my head.

"I want to get into her community. I need to find out more about Ima Righter. And I ... I've got a funny feeling about that bishop."

Bertram shook his head. "I'm not so sure that busting into that Amish community is the right thing to do, Judah. The part of my family that used to be Amish there ... you should hear some of their stories."

"Well, that's just it. I'm not going to 'bust in.' I'm going to ease in. Sort of go undercover. What's it take, anyway?" I brandished the scissors. "A bad haircut and an Old MacDonald hat, right? What did you say your uncle's name was?"

"My great uncle. I didn't."

A knock came to the door. Forgetting I had put the bowl on my head, I let Consuelo in.

She gave me an odd look and then waved a container of something in my face. As she headed for the kitchen, she said something about a shift change and called for Liza Lou to follow.

My phone and Bert's rang then and, looking at each other, we picked up, hearing ourselves in stereo on a conference call from Hilton.

"Boys, I've got Walker Press here, and they say they're willing to give us a little time in our search for Ima Righter."

Hilton had his professional voice on, and I wondered how many people were in the room with him.

"That's great, sir," Bert said. "We're moving forward with your directive and are confident things will improve."

While I'd fumbled for a response, Bert had knocked out just the answer they all wanted to hear. He could blow the whistle on me right now, something I probably would do to him if I were in his shoes. Instead, Bert kept firing off comments to Hilton that were spot on. I managed a short "thanks" to the group before Hilton hung up. Bertram mopped his bald spot with a paper towel and plopped down on the couch.

I used the opportunity to push my idea.

"You heard Hilton, Bert. We have a little more time to save the paper. He says to find her or we're done. We're both done. I've already found her, and I know where she lives. The least I could do is pay her a little visit—find out if she's decided to stop writing for good. Or maybe she's got some more stories left in her."

"I don't suppose this little Amish lady is … I don't know … maybe *bonita* by any chance?"

How long had Consuelo been standing there? Long enough to get the gist of what was going on, that's for sure. She'd given Liza Lou the leftovers she brought for her and now stood at my island giving me a motherly wink.

"Well, I don't know if her looks are really—"

"She's beautiful." I cut Bert off before he could say more. What was wrong with me? I had a feeling I would be using the word "concussion" as an excuse for many days to come.

"Well, I'm pretty sure she won't be interested in a man with a bowl on his head." Consuelo smiled. I reached up, and my hand bumped into the plastic.

"Is that what this is about, Judah?" Bert's face grew from pink to red. "You want to invade an Amish community over a pretty girl?"

I had to be honest with Bertram and, oddly enough, with myself as well.

"She *was* pretty, Bert. But that's not it. I had a dream she was getting slapped around by someone who looked like a younger version of her—what did she call him—bishop?"

"Zook?"

"If that's who her bishop is, then yeah. He was the man who took her away in his buggy after she finally started breathing again."

"Breathing?"

We both looked at Consuelo. Bertram had gotten a bit of the drowning story in my article, but now I had to fill her in as well.

When I was done, Consuelo gave me an odd smile, like she was proud of me or something. I hadn't seen a look like that in a long, long time.

"Are we still talking about the bishop of Johanna's community, Judah?" Bertram paced again. What was with this guy?

"Yeah, Bert. The bearded guy with no mustache."

Bertram sat back down on my recliner and leaned back for a few minutes with his eyes shut. Together, Consuelo and I waited for him to let us in on what was going through his mind.

Finally, he slid his glasses to the top of his head and pinched the bridge of his nose where they had sat. "My great uncle doesn't have a high opinion of Zook either. I'll take you to him if you want. But I'm going to tell the truth to him about you not being Amish."

It wasn't much, but it was a start.

"All right." I took the scissors and, leaning over a trashcan, started to cut along the edges of the bowl.

"*Ay, Dios mio.*" Consuelo grabbed the scissors from me. "If you're going to get a good Amish bowl cut, I will show you." She took out her phone. "Me and some good video tutorials, anyway."

FORBIDDEN GIFT

JOHANNA

I must have drifted off to sleep because, when I awoke, rich golden rays of sunlight gave the outcropping a warm look despite the chill air. And somehow, I didn't feel so alone. A soft comfort had entered my heart where just earlier there'd been only waves of despair. I felt an odd kind of hope I hadn't experienced in a very long time.

The hope gave me courage to speak my thoughts to *Gott* out loud, just like Mammi had taught me. Not many of the People prayed aloud about personal things like Mammi did, at least none that I knew. She had something special.

"Hullo, *Gott*." Miracle lifted her head at the sound of my voice and one ear twitched. "I'm sorry for all the trouble I've caused."

I was truly sorry for the suffering my writing had caused my family. Although I still didn't think I could stop it on my own nor, to be honest, did I want to.

"I'm sorry for hiding my gift and publishing in the newspaper against the rules of the *Ordnung*."

Despite what Lizzie told me yesterday about the bishop's rules, I knew the deceit had been wrong. I lived under the covering of this bishop and the *Ordnung*, and the sooner I faced that, the better off we would all be. I knew that now.

But still something inside me wasn't done. I pressed on, ready to be rid of the burden.

Suddenly, it seemed fitting the top of the rock was flat, an altar of sorts. Whether I agreed with the bishop or not, for the sake of my family, there was something I had to do.

Sliding down off the rock, I searched for something to write with. Finding some burnt wood next to an old campfire, I slid it into my pocket and returned to my perch. Miracle still lay there flicking her tail. She seemed glad to have me back and leaned her head on my hand as I stroked under her ears.

Retrieving the wood from my pocket, I crudely penned a declaration into the stone beneath me. Surprisingly, my etching was darker than I had expected and the words easily readable from where I sat. When I finished, I had a list of all things I decided to give to *Gott*.

My love for words was there—writing and reading them, along with Mammi's journal and the secrets it held. A host of other things, including my pride, were included on the list. The very last thing was a vow. If *Gott* wanted to use me to help our family out of this trouble with the bishop, then so be it.

I would do what Mamm had asked and marry Mordecai— no matter how I felt about it.

When I finished, I threw the stick deep into the woods, sending Miracle bolting for what she thought was a trailside nibble, I'm sure.

I then told *Gott* that all the things on the list were his, including my heart if he wanted it. I knew that Mammi was smiling somewhere in heaven.

I lingered for a few more minutes after that. The air had grown colder, but my spirit felt warm and new. Whatever came into my life from that point on, I would trust that *Gott* would turn it for *gut*. There was a Scripture in that somewhere, I was sure of it. Mammi would have quoted it to me.

She also would have told me to come in from the cold.

Obediently, I slid down from the rock, but my ankle caught on a clump of moss. I crumpled for a moment in the thick grass at the bottom and waited for the pain to stop. Looking up, I could see Miracle's head peering down at me, a mouse tail hanging limply from the side of her mouth. I shook my head and smiled. She'd gotten her snack after all.

I moved my ankle in slow circles until I felt like I could walk on it. Grabbing at some nearby goldenrod to pull myself up, my eyes were drawn to the patch of moss that I had disturbed in my fall. It now stood on end, tiny roots in the air. I went to press the moss back down, but something etched in the rock beneath caught my attention.

In the late afternoon sun, I pushed more of the goldenrod aside and moved quickly to scrape off more and more of the moss until I discovered two sets of letters or initials joined together with the plus sign. Surrounding them was a roughly hewn heart.

Since this side of the rock sat in the shade, the letters were difficult to read. I tried to follow their engraving with my fingers, but I wasn't sure where one letter began, and the other ended.

Remembering the campfire, I snatched another piece of burnt wood and checked Mammi's pocket for the white handkerchief she was always known to carry. I thanked *Gott* when I felt it. Odd that she had somehow prepared me for this moment. Unfolding the cloth, I placed it over the heart, rubbed it with the blackened wood for an image and hoped for the best.

Carefully, I folded Mammi's handkerchief and returned it to her pocket. I pulled myself up onto the rock to rest my ankle for just a bit more before heading home.

CHAPTER 18

JOHANNA

The engraving I'd found on the rock held my attention so much I ignored my injured ankle for most of the way back home. As I neared the house, I saw Dat silently rocking on the porch, probably waiting for Mamm to finish cooking dinner.

Dat would know what the letters meant. This house had been in Mamm's family forever.

Forgetting myself and the *Bann*, I marched right up to Dat, pulled the cloth and the stick of burnt wood out of my pocket and showed him my rubbing.

"What do these letters mean?" I waved the cloth in front of him and explained where I got it. Somehow, I expected him to understand. To be whole. And to be the father who loved me more than anything.

Instead, Dat just sat and stared straight ahead out to the field behind me and beyond. I remembered the *Bann* then and bowed my head with the weight of it.

Even if Dat could speak to me, he wouldn't. The bishop said our conversation had to be limited. *Ach*! Here I was disobeying the bishop again and in plain sight of anyone who might be traveling down the road. And I was putting my father in danger while I was at it.

I snatched the cloth from Dat's lap, but not before he had gotten a *gut* hold of it first.

I stood there holding my end in a stupor, not sure what he'd do. His eyes went to the charred stick still in my other hand. He grabbed it and started writing something on my handkerchief. When he was done, he folded the handkerchief and placed it carefully back in Mammi's apron pocket.

His look went back to the fields.

I turned to go back into the loneliness of the *Dawdi Haus* when Dat grabbed my hand. His thick, callused fingers covered mine, and for just a moment, there was no stroke and no *Bann*. Just Dat and me, like we used to be.

I was a little girl again, holding tight to Dat's hand while together we walked through the fields, measuring the progress of the corn. We were walking out to the mailbox surrounded by tiger lilies to get the mail for Mamm. And then, together, we were feeding the brand-new steers their bottles.

I couldn't stop the tears. It had been so long since I felt a connection with my father like I had now.

Too long.

Dat's hand grew clammy then and almost all at once his grip loosened. Alarm rushed through me when I saw his face droop.

"Dat, are ya okay?"

But the sudden slouch to one side and the uneven smile told me he was far from being okay. As Dat slowly slid from the chair onto the porch floor, I did my best to break his landing.

Frantic, I screamed for my mother.

Mamm came flying through the door. Then she just stood there, stuck in time it seemed, as she took in her husband lying prone on the porch floor. An almost silent, "Oh no," escaped her lips.

I didn't know what to expect from her, considering the *Bann* and the gravity of the situation. But I wasn't prepared for her sudden accusations.

"What have you done?"

Breathing hard, she shoved me aside. Her focus tunneled in on Dat, unconscious on the rough wooden floor slats. As she gathered him in her arms, words—mean and hateful words—sprung from her tongue and lashed out at me.

"Why don't you *ever* listen?" she seethed. "You don't care about our family. You know what the bishop would do to us if he saw you out here with your father. And yet here you are and look now what you have done."

I recoiled as if I'd been slapped. Surely, she knew I would never do anything to purposely harm my father. But Mamm didn't seem care. I could tell she was just getting started.

Dat would have been upset to hear her. He would have told her to stop. Made her take back her words.

But something inside me knew Dat wasn't listening. Not in this world anyway.

Silently, I watched as her tears poured out onto Dat's work jacket.

And then Mamm did what she did best. She shut me out.

CHAPTER 19

JOHANNA

Hot tears streamed down my face, and I wiped them away with my dirty shirt sleeve. After helping Mamm and David move Dat, I ran all the way to Mose's house. I found him in the barn feeding his own new steers. I buried my face in his strong arms.

Mose, careful to obey the *Bann*, did not speak. But ever mindful of my feelings, he placed his hand on the top of my head to smooth my hair.

Tears sprang afresh as I shared the news with him. I got out what I could about what happened. Mose hugged me quickly and broke the bishop's rule to tell me he was sure it wasn't my fault. Then he hitched his horse, gathered his family, and started off down the road to my parents' home.

Later that night, while in the *Dawdi Haus*, I put my hands over my ears to shut out the sound of my mother's cries. No, not just cries—keening. Mamm had started as soon as I entered the *Dawdi Haus* for the night, and she was still at it.

I had heard other women do this when they had lost loved ones. But hearing my own mother keen put a nail through my heart.

Even with both hands over my ears, I could still hear her laments coming through the walls all the way to Mammi's room while I prepared for bed. My heart wanted to be right there with my mother, to comfort her and to tell her I understood her pain. That I hurt too.

But the *Bann* made that next to impossible.

I tried to be present in the house earlier with all of my brothers and their families who had come as soon as they'd heard about Dat. But as soon as they left, Mamm took one look at me and left the kitchen where we had all been gathered.

There was nothing left for me to do but follow suit. I often wondered why people do what they do when they lose a loved one. I found out the hard way when we lost *Dawdi* and then, a few years later, Mammi Miriam. The Amish way was to keep "doing."

But I couldn't imagine that "doing" would ever be the same without my father.

As I undressed for bed, I saw Mammi's handkerchief drop onto the hardwood.

Dat.

In all the events that followed his passing this evening, I had forgotten the handkerchief, or I would have been more careful. Gingerly, I unfolded the cloth and placed it on the nightstand under the oil lamp. No matter how I looked, I couldn't decipher what my father wrote.

He'd known something about the letters, or he wouldn't have written anything. But whatever it was had died along with him.

I clutched Mammi's handkerchief to my chest. So much had been taken away from me in the last few days, and I had no idea how *Gott* was going to fix things. My father's last message would have been a comfort to me, and now it would never be found out.

Between my mother's keening and my pain, sleep wouldn't come for me. Way before light, I rose from bed.

Perhaps I could help by getting Dat's coffin ordered. If I beat my *Bruders* to the task and helped in some way, it might lighten the load that weighed me down.

I had just put on my black sneakers and sat down to eat a bowl of granola when I heard voices on the other side of the *Dawdi Haus* door. Someone was visiting Mamm mighty early.

I recognized Susanna's voice. The wife of the bishop.

After speaking comforting words to Mamm, Susanna spoke my name, and my ears perked up. *Ach*, how could a body help but eavesdrop in a house this small?

"Dorcas, I know you are hurting right now, but I need to talk to you about your plan for Johanna before things get out of hand."

I heard Mamm's chair slide out and back in. I was glad she'd sat to listen. Susanna's life as Amos Zook's wife was a hard one. She never spoke in my hearing of her suffering, but I saw the pain in her eyes nonetheless.

From what I'd gathered listening at frolics, Susanna had been new to the community long ago when she met Amos Zook, a preacher then who had come to our district from the Nebraska Amish settlement in Mifflin County. They'd been married shortly afterward.

"Is there anyone in the house, Dorcas?"

Mamm must have forgotten me in her distress because Susanna continued.

"What I say can't be repeated. And I'll most likely never speak about it to you again. But I'm going to share some things with you, Dorcas, for the sake of your daughter and your family." She paused a moment and then said, "Your daughter cannot, should not, marry my grandson."

I sucked in my breath and then quickly clasped my hand over my mouth.

Susanna didn't seem to hear me because she went on. And on. She shared with Mamm how difficult it was for her being married to the bishop. And how sometimes she questioned whether she knew him at all.

"Deep down inside my husband, something is festering. Something I can't explain. And lately, things have gotten worse, if that's even possible. He barely holds my gaze now. Like he was afraid if he did, the truth might come spilling out. And to be honest, Dorcas, I'm praying that it will. I don't care what holds Amos Zook in his self-made trap. I would gladly face it straight on to see my husband free. We've raised twelve hearty children together and have grandchildren and great-grandchildren.

"After all that, I should be close to this man. But there's a wall that he always puts up between himself and the People. The same one he often puts up between the two of us. And so far, no one's been able to break through it. Not even *Gott*. Not unless you count what happens in Amos's sleep sometimes." Susanna's voice lowered.

"More than once I've heard the name Ernst plain as day cross my husband's lips, and it's given me a lot to wonder about. Maybe somehow it's a clue. The name doesn't sound like any Amish I know here in Willow Brook or some of the other communities. And I wonder if maybe it was someone in his old community. The one he never talks about."

There was a pause in the conversation, like Susanna needed a minute to come back from her memories.

I knew Mamm was probably about as shocked as I was that Susanna had shared so much. It was not like her or any bishop's wife to do so. I had a feeling she had carefully calculated all her risks before coming over this morning.

And still she came. I smiled at that, and she started speaking again.

"I tell you all of this to say that Mordecai ... he's cut from the same cloth as his grandfather and twice as harsh. I would hate to see your daughter ..."

Susanna stopped then and both mothers remained quiet, except for some soft weeping from Mamm.

Susanna's chair screeched back.

"*Ach*, someone's buggy just rolled up. I thought I might get here long before your family, but your boys love you, Dorcas. And so does Johanna. Don't you forget that."

Mamm's weeping grew a little louder.

"I'm real sorry about Jakob, Dorcas. But you know what's right when it comes to that daughter of yours. After all I've said, you understand that making her marry Mordecai isn't a *gut* thing, *jah*?"

Mamm must have nodded yes, because Susanna gave her some pretty direct instructions on what to say to the bishop when he chose to come. After a soft goodbye, the back door snapped shut.

I cried with Mamm on the other side of the door and soon the house was filled with my siblings and their families. Tomorrow, there would be time to check on the coffin. Today, even if in the shadows, I needed to be with my family.

CHAPTER 20

JUDAH

Bertram showed up in the early morning and seemed a little shocked to be greeted at the door by a young Amish man. He got over his surprise, though, and even managed a little scowl.

"I told you, Judah, I'm not going to lie for you. No matter if it costs me my job."

"I'm not asking you to, Bert. Just get me into the community to speak to your uncle. Maybe he could use an Amish-looking hand in his shop for a week or two. What did you say he does?"

"I don't suppose you know anything about woodworking?" Bertram looked around my apartment as if scanning my shelves for a carved duck or something.

"A little," I offered.

Bertram took a seat on my couch and just sat there for a few minutes. "I'll take you there then."

On the drive, I tried to look straight ahead and not wring my hands, but I was unsuccessful at both.

"Maybe we should have called, Bert. I mean, are we supposed to just barge in?"

"My uncle doesn't have a phone."

"Oh, that's right. But don't some Amish get special privileges with phones or electricity, if they need it for their business?"

"Not Uncle Gideon. He's got sort of a strained relationship with the bishop. No special favors."

Why couldn't Bertram's uncle have worked with metal or leather? Entering his shop brought back a flood of memories that I had successfully shoved to the back of my mind for ten long years.

And the smell of the sawdust made my eyes water.

Dad.

Kelly woke with a start at the sound of pounding on her kitchen door. She stood up and looked at herself in the living room mirror. She had worked on a story late into the night and fallen asleep on her couch somewhere around 4:30 a.m. Dark circles and bags stood out under her eyes. Whoever it was had better not take her picture. She peeked through the eyelet curtain.

Sam.

Maybe she would scare her neighbor away with the way she looked.

"Hello, there!" he exclaimed when she opened the door.

"Oh, hi, Sam." She let out a yawn to let him know she wasn't up for a long visit.

"Wow, I can tell you're glad to see me."

She smiled. You never had to guess what Sam was thinking.

"Do you have anything good for breakfast? I'm half starved."

Kelly looked at her watch. It was only 9:30 a.m. She'd thought it was later. "I don't have anything made, Sam. I had a busy night."

"Well, let me take care of that, Kelly. Have you ever had crepes?"

She really shouldn't encourage Sam, but her stomach grumbled, and she let him in.

"I don't know if I have what you need."

"Oh, that's okay." Sam was already in her fridge, his hand in the air. "As long as you have eggs, milk, and flour, I can add almost any filling to these little wonders."

Soon her house began to fill with incredible smells. Sam had all but chased her out of the kitchen, so she went back into her study to do a little more research on publishing companies and small-town newspapers.

Kelly got lost in her work and didn't even hear Sam until he stood at her study door with the latest issue of the *Star* in his hands.

"Can you believe this?"

"I know. I've been looking into it the last few days."

"Oh?" Sam came up behind her so he could see her second monitor where she had opened an article titled "Anyone Can Publish a Newspaper."

"And you're thinking of doing something drastic?"

Kelly looked up at her monitor and smiled. "Oh, no, not really. At least I don't think so."

What was she saying? Of course, she wasn't going to buy a newspaper. That life was behind her. The article just gave some insight on the topic, so she thought she would save it.

"Well, I think you should." Sam went back into the kitchen and brought out a tray with the most delicious-smelling crepes. He had found a can of cherry pie filling in her pantry, and whether he knew it or not, he'd made her favorite.

She decided to eat a bit and let his words settle before she responded.

After she'd eaten about half her crepe, she swallowed and said, "Why, Sam? Why do you think I should be the *Star*'s publisher?"

"Well, I don't know."

Sam had been a high school English teacher before he retired, so he knew a thing or two about writing. She surprised herself by really wanting his opinion.

"I can see you doing it, that's all. You said you and Jack ran a paper before you moved here. And I think what this town needs is someone who really cares about the paper to own it. Not some big shot New York City house that doesn't give a darn."

Kelly let his words sit a bit as she finished her crepe. Without her having to ask, Sam slid another onto her plate.

"But I can't even call over there to get more information. I don't know what Judah would do if he found out his mom was considering this. Not with the way our relationship is right now."

When she'd finished the crepe, Sam took her dishes into the kitchen. "Well, I could call and ask a few questions for you. What do you want to know?"

Kelly smiled. "I guess I *could* call them myself. I just wouldn't have to use my real name."

"Exactly!" Sam came back into her study and smiled.

"But I'm not really sure—"

Sam handed her his phone. "I've got them on the line."

Kelly cringed. What was she doing?

"*Mountain Laurel Star.* Hello?"

Kelly took a few minutes to talk with a young woman at the *Star.* When the woman asked her name, Kelly forgot and almost gave her real one. Drawing a blank, she panicked.

"Tell them it's Dixie Divine." Sam had his hands cupped over his mouth.

"I ... I'm Dixie Divine."

The woman quickly made a phone appointment for Kelly with the editor for the next morning.

Kelly hung up and glared at Sam. "Really? Dixie Divine? You couldn't have come up with something better than that?"

Sam shrugged. "I cave under pressure."

Kelly wasn't so sure about any of this. There were still too many risks with Judah.

She looked more at her research and brought the publishing article down from her second monitor onto her laptop.

"How much money do you have?"

"What?" Kelly looked at Sam to see if he was serious.

"Buying a newspaper is more expensive than I thought." Sam was doing his own research on his phone.

Kelly hadn't gotten that far. She was only a half hour in to this whole idea, after all.

"How much is it?"

The price made Kelly almost tip in her office chair.

"That would take all of my ..." She caught herself before revealing more than she wanted to. She cleared her throat. "Thanks, Sam. Thanks for everything."

She started to get up to help him clean the kitchen, but when she entered, she saw the cleanup had already been done.

Sam smiled at her from the front door. "At least think about it."

Kelly nodded, her arms crossed in front of her chest.

"Well, see you later, Dixie."

Sam gave a little wave and then ducked out the door and slipped through his hedge. Good thing, because she had grabbed her rolling pin.

FORBIDDEN GIFT

JUDAH

Bertram really surprised me sometimes.

When we arrived at his uncle Gideon's, Bert's introduction sounded so smooth that when I asked Gideon to hire me on as a temporary apprentice, he readily agreed. Bertram made it clear I wasn't Amish, but needed to quietly observe the community—undercover. Gideon seemed to be okay with that, and he even gave me a back-of-the-shop bunk where I could sleep.

Apparently, the Willow Brook bishop had pretty much left Gideon alone while other carpenters in the community were limited to the number of customers they could take on. With nearly half the community coming to his door for carpentry work, Gideon felt so overrun he didn't even take the time to question me about what or who I planned on observing. He seemed pleased, though, when I showed I knew a thing or two about woodworking. And I think Bertram's jaw even dropped a bit when he found out I knew what a sliding bevel was.

When I walked Bert to his car, I told him what I could about my father and his passion for the craft. I surprised myself with being open about things with him. Normally, I didn't talk about Dad with anyone.

Quickly, I found out how Gideon kept up with his large workload without the use of electricity. Most of his tools ran on pneumatics and used a system of pressurized air for power. I could see all the piping along the ceiling and air hookups seemed to be everywhere across the workbenches.

I had a hard time keeping up with Gideon at first, despite his age. But soon, I became almost as fast and efficient. Before I knew it, the day was over.

Gideon had hung up his shop apron when the bells above the door jingled.

DEBRA TORRES

Looking up, I saw an Amish man wringing his hands and looking more at the floor than at either of us.

"What's the trouble, Abe?"

Abe shot me a quick look and brought his gaze back to Gideon.

"Can we, uh, talk private?"

I raised a wave to Gideon as he turned to address me and then headed to the back room where I found my bunk. I hadn't counted on the walls being so thin, though, and I could hear everything, including Abe's boots shuffling in the sawdust.

"I know I owe ya, Gideon. And I know it's a lot."

Gideon remained quiet, letting Abe say his piece.

"I said I'd pay ya after the crops came in. But I can't. It hasn't been a *gut* year and what with the horse going lame …"

A long pause followed, making even me uncomfortable. I didn't know how the Amish handled debt, but there was something about Abe's story I didn't trust.

Bert had recently written an article on local crop production. "Best in years," I think was in the headline. I was sure Gideon must have known it as well.

Gideon cleared his throat. "You owe me nothing, Abe. Consider it a clean slate."

I heard the ripping of paper. Footsteps. And the door clicking shut.

Gideon was cleaning his bandsaw when I came out and grabbed the broom.

"I know we only met just today." I needed to start slow with this Amish guy. Maybe he needed to learn a thing or two about getting taken. "But I think there was something wrong with that guy's story."

"There's always something wrong with Abe's stories."

"So why do you let him take you like that?"

159

Gideon sat down, and his shoulders sagged a little.

"Abe is a member of this community." He sighed. "And I serve where I am able."

"But—"

Gideon held out his hand, stopping me. "Abe has a wife and fourteen children and a brand new *Bobbeli*. He comes from time to time asking me to fix a broken chair leg, a cracked dresser drawer. This time it was a new table for his *Dawdi Haus*. He tells me he'll pay, but never does."

Glad there were no more customers in the shop, I gave Gideon all I had learned from College Finance 101.

"Do all your customers treat you this way?"

"Some."

"And what about your bishop? Isn't he the guy in charge here? Why doesn't he do something about it?"

A cloud came over Gideon's eyes then. He turned and took the broom from where I had left it. Sweeping hard at the floor I'd already cleaned, he told me it was time for dinner and pointed to where I could wash up.

Dinner at Gideon's table started in silence, but soon he began to answer my questions, which I kept focused on mundane things for now. He was a widower and had a sister who brought him meals. Tonight, she had left something called Dutch Goose, and I ate more than my share. This beat fast food any day.

Halfway through dinner, Gideon surprised me by bringing back up the conversation we had in his shop. "The bishop and I haven't been on very *gut* terms for a long time." He moved beets around on his plate with his fork while he talked. "Actually, it's a story that goes back more than forty years."

My ears perked up. This was information I knew I didn't deserve, having only met Gideon earlier today. I wondered if being Bertram's friend had anything to do with his openness now.

"What happened with the bishop?" I tried to sound casual while I pretended to be interested in my beets. But I hated beets.

Gideon stared out the window toward his dark fields and started to tell me his story. I had the feeling it was a tale he didn't often tell, if ever.

He told me how bishops were chosen randomly from a group of eligible men who were already serving as ministers like he had been. I could feel my eyes getting big at some parts. In the selection, an elder passed each man a hymn book, and the one who had the Scripture verse slipped into it got to lead the whole community. The process sounded like a child's birthday game to me.

"That's it? That's all there is to it?" I tried not to raise my voice, but I couldn't help it. I grew up in church. Our pastor had gone to seminary, he'd received a degree, and even had a "calling." Or so he said.

Gideon's hand went out trying to calm me down.

"I know it must sound odd to you. But it's actually in the Bible. In Acts one verses twenty-three through twenty-six the disciples drew lots when they chose who was to replace Judas. The lot landed on a man named Matthias. Among the Amish, though ... things aren't always as perfect."

Gideon circled back to his own story. "I was among the eligible ministers, but Amos Zook used a disruption at the back of the room to knock my book to the floor and switch mine for his."

As he spoke, I felt my temperature rise.

"You had the slip of paper?"

Gideon slowly nodded. "In my *Ausbund, jah*."

"Why did you let that happen?"

"I thought ya might ask that." The lines around Gideon's eyes deepened, his eyes glazed, and he looked out the window again into the night. "Can ya guess?"

I couldn't really. I mean, how can a man who knows that he should rightfully be leading the Willow Brook community sit back and watch while an imposter lives out what should be his life?

"No." It was an honest answer.

"Well, I guess I just figured that if Amos wanted to be bishop so badly and was willing to lie and cheat to get there, who was I to stand in his way?"

"Sort of like what you did for Abe back there? Letting him have what belonged to you just because, well, just because he needed it?"

"It's like that a little bit. But deep down, I don't think Amos is happy with what he did. A woman he had been engaged to saw the switch happen as well. I think the threat of being found out has bothered him all these years."

"Is there anyone else who knows?"

"Actually, you're the only one I've ever told." Gideon gave me a crooked smile that made me feel a little funny inside. It had been a long time since anyone had trusted me like that.

I got up and started scraping my dinner plate.

"And I don't think the woman told anyone either, or else the community would have had him step down ... and slapped the *Bann* on him."

I sat back down.

"He certainly did his part in keeping her quiet, though." Gideon served me a slice of his sister's chocolatey ho-ho cake and shook his head.

My mind went to extremes, but Gideon wasn't done yet, so I kept quiet.

"She had quite a talent for writing, but when Amos became bishop, he worked hard to convince the community to ban it to get back at her for breaking things off with him—even though a few years had passed. I think he was also afraid that somehow she would use her writing to expose him."

My ears perked up. Bertram had been right. "*Banned* it?"

"Mmmhmm." Gideon had taken a big bite of cake. He chewed slowly and then swallowed. "Said writing for self-expression—poetry, journaling, fiction, even song writing—was a vain pursuit that led to pride. I was at the Sunday service when he announced that one. He'd got the backing of most of the ministers and no one else seemed to mind. Or care. But Miriam, well, I saw her face fall when Amos said that. I think he appeared even holier to the rest of the community. Like he was finding a hidden sin that most of them hadn't thought about. But his former betrothed knew the truth behind his new rule, and his arrow had hit its mark."

"Is this woman still alive?"

"*Nee*, she died a few years back. Took her talent with her to the grave, as far as I know. Bishop never let her use it."

Chapter 21

Johanna

I rose to a dark and silent house. A full day had passed since Dat's death, and David would be coming soon to feed the herd and to bottle-feed the new baby steers that had arrived this week. I could hear some of their bawls from Mammi's bedroom window.

Just like them, I longed for my mother. I'd stayed clear of her and everyone else yesterday, remaining in the *Dawdi Haus* or in the shadows most of the time. I wanted to give her space and to let what the bishop's wife said yesterday settle. If she wouldn't receive me, maybe knowing I'd taken care of the coffin arrangements would bring her comfort and show her I cared.

Noticing the chill in the air, I realized I'd let the fire go out again. I quickly slipped into my cape dress and sneakers. I simply didn't care about life's details right now. Fighting off a shiver, I grabbed Mammi's heavy cape as well before heading out the door.

I gazed at the sun just now peeking through the trees and stepped out into the grass. It crunched with frost, and I felt glad to be wearing shoes. I'd just turned the corner of the *Dawdi Haus* when I saw the bishop's buggy roll up.

All I could think of was my mother and what she'd soon be facing if she heeded Susanna's words and told the bishop she'd changed her mind.

I turned on my heel and headed back into the *Dawdi Haus* and shut the door.

I paced the floor and fought the urge to open the door that divided us. How I longed to rush to Mamm's side. She needed someone to support her in what could be the hardest thing she'd ever done. She'd just lost her husband, and now, here she was, alone with the one man who had the power to turn her family's lives upside down.

And she was about to make him very, very angry.

A shiver ran through my spine when I heard the bishop knock.

I nearly had my hand on the knob before my sense returned. My presence in the kitchen would do Mamm more harm than *gut*, I was sure of it. With my back to the door, I silently slid to a sitting position and waited.

Gott, be with Mamm. Give her the strength she needs right now.

A minute or two passed and I could hear the bishop shuffling on the porch, anxious to be let in. But Mamm did not answer. I thought maybe she had decided not to let him in when suddenly a chair scraped against the hardwood, and I heard her get up from the table. With measured steps, she walked to the door and, finally, I heard the click of the latch.

"Dorcas." The bishop's voice sounded raspy, and I wondered if he had caught a cold.

"Bishop." Mamm sounded a little shaky but strong. I decided to keep praying.

A short, awkward silence passed and I wondered if Mamm was trying to think of what to do or say.

Food, Mamm. Offer the bishop some food.

Our bishop enjoyed a *gut* meal more than anyone I knew, and he had quite a sweet tooth. I hoped Mamm had some of the chicken pot pie and hot milk sponge left that my sister-in-law Emily had brought into the *Dawdi Haus* yesterday. That should put him in the right frame of mind, no matter how early the hour.

"Would you like something to eat?"

I smiled.

"Don't mind if I do. Susanna's breakfast was mighty light this morning." The bishop chuckled softly as if he had told her an inside joke and probably patted his belly. "I think she's trying to tell me something."

While Mamm prepared the food, the bishop said he was sorry to hear about Dat. I thought it kind of the bishop to say, but wondered if that was the real reason for his visit. I imagined Mamm was probably thinking the same.

The meal took a little time to warm, and then came the serving, and the silent prayer.

My back grew sore as I leaned against the door, but didn't dare move lest it give a creak.

The bishop asked for more, and Mamm's chair scraped against the floorboards again. I hoped, for her sake, that she had poured herself a cup of tea for comfort.

After serving him again and waiting for him to finish, Mamm rose to clear his dishes.

My heart started to race as I considered what conversation would come next.

Speak, Mamm. Speak.

"I have to admit, Dorcas, you surprised me a bit the other day with your idea about your daughter and my grandson."

"Oh, Amos. That's just what I want to talk with you about. You see—"

"Now, Dorcas, I just came to tell ya that the more I think about it, the more I like your idea. I wanted to let ya know that I told Mordecai about your, ah, suggestion the other night and he has accepted. Said he'd be glad to help your daughter out of her ... ah, situation."

"Well, that's just the thing, Amos. With Jakob passing and all—"

"Jakob's death does put you and your family on shaky ground in the community, doesn't it, Dorcas?"

The bishop's words skittered down the strings of my prayer *Kapp* and pressed in on the stress points in my shoulders. I cringed. Bishop Amos didn't care one bit about the state of our family. I could tell by the way he was not listening to Mamm out there.

"A union between our two families would strengthen the bond between us, don't you think? It would let the community know there isn't something wrong that might drive one of us out."

I wanted to scream. He was driving a spike right into Mamm's heart with all that talk. She feared this very thing and the bishop knew it.

"Mordecai agrees that the sooner, the better for this event. Especially since we're nearing wedding season anyway. Johanna can do a public confession this Thursday, and then we'll have the wedding right after."

I had to physically hold my hand over my mouth so as not to scream. Mamm must have protested in some way, because the bishop repeated himself.

"Thursday, Dorcas."

My mind raced. There was so much I wanted to say. Should I go ahead and risk my whole family's standing in the community with the words that were ready to burst out of me?

Gott?

A light rap sounded on the outside door. With a shaky voice, Mamm excused herself and stumbled on her way to open it. I heard the voice of David's wife, Mary. Not my favorite sister-in-law by a long shot, but my heart rose with hope that she had come in on this conversation nonetheless.

The bishop quickly thanked Mamm for the meal and left. I waited for the door to bang shut and his buggy to roll away before I left to see about the coffin.

I needed air. Physically, I felt a little better from my sickness and a long walk would do me *gut*. Mammi had always insisted our family use Gideon for all our woodworking, so I started out the two miles to his shop on foot. The sun had risen to the treetops now, and I tried to focus on the beauty around me instead of the worries whirling in my head.

JUDAH

I woke to the repetitive sound of a hand plane and pushed the dark green shade aside. What kind of person even functioned at this hour?

Still groggy, I pulled on my clothes and made my way out to the front of the shop.

It should not have surprised me, really, that Gideon rose this early to start his day. With the number of orders he let me see on his list yesterday, it was a wonder he went to bed at all.

I shivered against the cool of the shop, and briefly considered returning to the warmth of my bed. Instead, I coughed to get his attention and asked how I could help.

Gideon had set me up to work on a table and a set of chairs he had started for a new family somewhere east of Willow Brook when the bell above the door jingled.

Didn't anyone in this community sleep past dawn?

I peeked through the chair legs I was working on to see what other old geezer had come in search of free furniture when a knot formed in the pit of my empty stomach.

Ima.

The minute Johanna walked through the door, Gideon's pneumatic drill stopped. Wiping the sawdust off his shop apron, he walked over to her.

I strained to hear their conversation from behind the chair, but their quiet tone made it difficult. Gideon gently squeezed her shoulder and gave a quick hug to Ima, er, Johanna. She hung her head and wiped her face with her sleeve a time or two as she listened to him. When their talk was over, Gideon pulled a clean handkerchief out of his pocket and gave it to her.

Another early-bird customer entered the shop. Johanna gave a quick wave to Gideon, said thank you, and turned to leave.

Glancing in my direction as she headed out, Johanna stopped in her tracks. Her face grew pale like the day I had seen her in the river. Then, she gathered her wits and made her way to the door.

JOHANNA

That face. It had to be him.

But how could he have gotten into Gideon's shop? And in Amish clothes no less. Didn't he get the blanket he'd shared with me on the riverbank from his car? He had talked about his cell phone then. Saying he wished it wasn't dead so he could call an ambulance for me.

The man wasn't Amish, and yet now he looked like one and was working for Gideon?

Who was he trying to fool?

I should turn right around and let Gideon know who he had working for him dressed in Amish clothes. But the man had saved my life. Complicated it, but saved it nonetheless.

Still tired from what just happened with the bishop, I walked through the door and made my choice.

JUDAH

I thought I could just sit there and let Johanna walk away from Gideon's shop before I had a chance to speak with her, but I was wrong.

I never thought I'd be glad that Gideon didn't have a toilet in the shop.

Making an excuse about needing to use the outhouse, I exited shortly after Johanna and scanned the empty road for a trace of her.

Where had she gone in such a short time?

As I turned to head back inside, I heard a small cough. The sound drew my eyes to the barn just as a slip of black cloth disappeared around its back corner. Shoving my hands into my pockets, I breathed white puffs into the frigid air as I made my way around back. I turned the corner and came face-to-face with Johanna. The morning sun glinted reddish-brown on a stray curl.

For the first time in probably forever, I couldn't think of what to say.

"Who are you?" she hissed.

I wasn't prepared for her question or to find her so quickly. Sure that I could probably come up with something better, I settled on the truth.

"My name is Judah Barton."

"You are *not* Amish."

She knew. Of course she knew. The day I'd rescued her, I'd looked anything but Amish.

"No."

She clenched her fists. Were the Amish allowed to hit people? I didn't think so and felt glad for that truth.

"Then why, Judah Barton, do you try to look like one of us? Gideon is a kindhearted man. If you are here to hurt him ..."

I smiled on the inside at the boldness of this young Amish woman. They might not be allowed to fight, but she certainly was anything but passive right now. I tried to come up with an answer that would satisfy her. Again, I surprised myself with the truth.

"I came looking for you."

Her green eyes widened and a dread started in the pit of my stomach. I could sense more truth coming.

"I work for the *Mountain Laurel Star*. I was sent to find you."

She clamped her mouth shut then and turned and walked away. I let her go and went back to Gideon's, the bell announcing my arrival as I walked through the door. I didn't get to say much to Johanna, but it had been a start.

Gideon was hard at work sanding a plank of wood and did not look up. I saw more planks leaning against the wall and picked one up and joined him. A long time passed, and I'd begun to work up a sweat before Gideon broke the silence.

"So, did you find her?"

I looked up at him and around the shop first to make sure he was talking to me.

I chuckled. "How did you figure that one out?"

"Johanna Yoder, as a *Maedel*, may be past her prime, but she's still a beautiful young woman."

"Past her prime?"

What was he talking about? Johanna had to be still in her twenties. Bertram had told me the Amish marry young, and even after Gideon explained the Amish custom to me, I still felt confused. Most of all, I wondered how all the Amish guys in the community had overlooked her.

"Sure am sorry about her Dat, though."

I tried to sound like I knew what he was talking about. We hadn't gotten to her family business.

"Uh, yes, I hope he'll be feeling better soon."

Gideon frowned at me and then dusted off the piece he had been working on and carefully leaned it against the wall. Without saying more, he laid another plank across the saw horses and started sanding again.

I helped sand a few more planks before I figured out we were making a coffin.

CHAPTER 22

Kelly finished her breakfast while Peaches gave herself a bath on the chair next to her. She had canceled her appointment with the newspaper shortly after she'd made it. What was she even thinking, letting Sam talk her into that? Buy the newspaper? Who was she kidding? She knew all that went into running a paper and wasn't sure she was up for it, again. Plus, it would take all but a few thousand of Jack's life insurance money. She felt crazy even considering it.

When she'd phoned the newspaper to cancel, she'd cringed but went ahead and called herself Dixie Divine. Where had Sam come up with that one? The young lady who took down her message yesterday didn't seem to care about her name, the cancellation, or life in general.

Kelly guessed life was pretty rough for everyone over at the paper. Her mind went to Judah. The paper, even though it wasn't huge, had been his dream job since he'd been a young boy. Big newspapers didn't seem to appeal to him. She could envision him moving up at the *Star* after he had been there longer.

Now he'd never have the chance.

Kelly shook her head. *Enough.*

She gave Peaches some of her whole-wheat pancake and decided it was time for a walk. She grabbed a thick hoodie, strapped on her old fanny pack, and shoved her phone, ID, and keys inside. As she had almost completed one lap around her neighborhood, her phone rang with an unknown number. Usually, she wouldn't pick up, but it was a local number, and she wondered if it could be a client she hadn't yet put into her contacts.

"Hello, this is K—"

"Is this Dixie Divine?" A man's voice came barreling over the phone.

Kelly's hesitation must have been too long, because the man started talking again before she had time to respond.

"This is Hilton Hughes. I was told you had some questions about the *Mountain Laurel Star*."

So much for canceling this call yesterday. The girl probably never even took down her message. Kelly opened her mouth to decline again when an odd feeling formed in her *gut*. Sort of like how she'd felt when she'd almost turned down Jack the first time he'd asked her out.

She spotted a nearby playground, empty now since the kids were all at school, and moved over to a swing and started asking questions. Just as she figured from her earlier research, the editor told her a sad tale and sounded pretty desperate. As he spoke, she detected a slur to his words and wondered if he had been drinking.

So, this was the great Hilton Hughes. Kelly had read his name on the masthead of the newspaper since they had first started their subscription years ago. On top of following in his father and grandfather's footsteps as editor-in-chief of the *Star*, he wrote a weekly column where he spewed political beliefs very different from her own.

She remembered committing to praying for Mr. Hughes a few years ago. She hadn't prayed for the man in a while, and she felt badly about that. Especially since it sounded like things had gone downhill fast for him.

"So, I've got a few of my best reporters searching right now for her, and once she's back working for the *Star*, we're sure subscriptions will soar."

Kelly had let her mind wander. She hated when she did that. "Um, I'm sorry, Mr. Hughes. Who are you searching for?"

"Ima Righter. Barton and Hochstetler tell me they're close to finding her."

Barton? Kelly's mouth went dry. Her son was out looking for Ima so that their paper wouldn't fold? She really didn't see how Ima's presence on their staff, good writer or not, would fix their financial woes. She guessed Hughes was grasping at straws by now.

"I'll discuss this with my lawyer and get back to you."

Kelly smacked her forehead after she hung up. Why had she said that? She got up off the swing and started a slow jog down her road.

Her head was spinning after her conversation with Hughes, but somehow the jogging helped despite how much she hated running. Kelly knew she stood in a precarious position. If she didn't buy the paper, it could sink, and her son would lose his job. If she did buy it, her son might never speak to her again. Talk about helicopter parenting!

She laughed at that.

Judah would be fine, with or without her help. She knew that. He had some growing up to do, and maybe losing his job was just the thing he needed to make some changes. But she didn't want to see an end to their town newspaper, not if she had anything to do with it. The *Star* had been an important part of her family's life here in Riverview, and their community needed it too. The way Hughes talked, it might not last another week.

Lord, what am I supposed to do?

If her relationship with Judah didn't change soon, she wondered how things would go if she were his boss's boss? Now *that* would be weird. Maybe she could remain elusive and keep her new pseudonym, Dixie Divine.

She dismissed that one. Like anything else, she'd eventually be found out for who she really was, and then she'd have to add lying to her list of transgressions.

Ugh.

Kelly slowed to a walk and made her way up her driveway, making sure to send a glare in the direction of Sam's house just in case he was looking out his window.

Bertram could sense Hilton's desperation. He shouted a lot more these days and didn't seem to care about his staff coming in later and later each morning—if they came in at all.

Bertram tried to stick to his normal schedule, which let him in on a lot of Hilton's morning phone calls that traveled through the vent. He'd given up trying not to listen. He couldn't help where his cube was located. And he was pretty sure that most of the sound also came through the walls.

Ugh.

The call with Ms. Divine, or whatever her name was, seemed to go well. But judging from what came out of Hilton's mouth after he had hung up, Bertram could tell Hilton wasn't convinced she was the answer to their problems. From what Bertram had heard since they'd printed the story on their potential shutdown, he knew this woman wasn't the first one who had inquired about the *Star*.

Bertram tried to concentrate on his story, but couldn't help overhear Hilton's latest conversation with Walker

Press. This would make the third time he'd spoken with them this week. Each time the threats of a shutdown seemed worse. Bertram knew they were running out of time.

Hilton's drinking had seemed to increase over the past week as well. Every day now, Bertram smelled liquor on his breath and saw the evidence in the red of his eyes. He prayed his boss would gain an understanding through all this trouble and realize a relationship with God was what he really needed.

The rest would work out somehow. Bertram believed God for that.

Judah had told Hilton he was close to finding Ima, but hadn't given him much more information. The not-knowing was probably eating Hilton alive. Bertram wished he could do something to help speed things up. Then maybe he could let his boss in on what was going on. But he knew timing was key here. If Hilton was in the know, much of the good that could come out of this setup would most likely be lost. For Ima—or Johanna—and for the paper. No, better stay quiet for now, even if it was tough to watch Hilton go through this situation.

"Hey, Bertram."

Bertram jumped a little. The smell of whiskey filled his cube before he even looked up. When he did look, he felt surprised to see the bottle in his boss's hand—as if he'd forgotten it was there.

"Yes, boss?"

"I need you to proofread the next issue's front-page story. It's a follow up to the one we just ran about shutting down. I came up with an idea just now that might help flush out Ima Righter, and I put it in there. I can't stand all this waiting. We don't have time for it." Hilton wavered on his feet.

"Are you okay, sir?"

His own boldness surprised him, but there were serious signs here that his boss needed help. He stiffened, expecting his boss to explode, stomp off, and maybe fire him on his way to his office. Instead, he just stood there a few moments without replying. Then, Bertram's words seemed to finally register.

"What do you mean, Hochstetler?" Hilton's eyes narrowed into slits.

Bertram wasn't sure where to go with this. He glanced at his Bible standing snug on his desk between his style guides and a few of his college textbooks.

Hilton followed his gaze and then sneered. "Don't give me your religion crap, Bertram. I get enough of that from my family."

"I was just—"

"The story, Hochstetler," Hilton called over his shoulder as he headed back to his office. "Open the story and let me know if you see any errors. It's going to print soon."

Bertram opened the attachment Hilton had emailed him. Grabbing several tissues, he mopped the sweat off his brow as he read the story's headline: *Finding Ima.*

JUDAH

"I thought maybe you had something going for Johanna Yoder."

I guess since Gideon owned the shop, he still considered my small room his. I squinted at the morning light streaming through the cracks in the green shade and then gazed at him sitting with his legs crossed on the ladderback chair next to my cot. The smell of his coffee breath reached my nose.

"I, uh, never said that I did. Why?"

"Well, in case you did, I thought I would let you know that time is running out. I just heard she's as *gut* as engaged to Mordecai Zook."

I tried to play it cool. "I hope she'll be happy, then."

The bell jingled and he turned to go, leaving me to deal with the mess in my head.

Strangely enough, after I let Gideon's news sink in, I felt glad for Johanna. I really did. No matter the issue of the *Star* folding, or that I would be out of a job. What was important was that Johanna would now stop being a maid, or whatever her people called a single Amish lady.

She didn't need the newsroom or any of that.

I felt pretty certain her life among the Amish was an all or nothing thing. I didn't think she would be allowed to stay Amish if she chose to leave and, in her community, the married life was better for a young woman.

So good for her.

And since there was no point in my being here any longer, I felt ready to gather my things and be on my merry way. Hilton wouldn't be happy about my news, but at least I'd tried. Throwing my things into my duffle bag, I thought about hitting a Goodwill bin on my way home to ditch my Amish get-up.

I really was glad. Except for one thing.

There had been this look in Gideon's eye that told me there was more to the story.

I couldn't put my finger on it, but something bugged me about the way Gideon spoke earlier when he'd told me about Johanna. Maybe it was the way his eyes had flitted from mine when I told him I hoped she'd be happy.

I dropped my duffle bag on the cot.

I heard Gideon sanding some dovetail joints he'd made for a dresser drawer, and I felt a twinge of guilt he was doing the task alone. Especially when I saw the pile of drawers next to him.

"What haven't you told me?"

He continued to sand as if I'd been there the whole time. "You don't know who Mordecai is, do you?"

To answer that question would have revealed more about myself than I cared to, so I just shrugged.

"Like I told you, Mordecai's last name is Zook."

Zook must be a common name around here.

When I didn't respond again, Gideon said, "He's the bishop's grandson and twice as ornery. He wore out his first wife. Last spring, we buried her."

"What? Why would Johanna agree—"

"I'm guessing this upcoming engagement has something to do with Miriam, the bishop's former fiancé."

"I thought you told me she was dead."

"She is, but the bishop is still hurt because she rejected him long ago. And because of his grudge, none of Miriam's family has ever been in *gut* grace with him. Jakob Yoder worked hard at making peace with the bishop. Now that he's gone, the family stands on shaky ground here in the community, and they know it." Gideon lifted the drawer he had been sanding off the workbench, blew off the sawdust, and rubbed his fingers over the joints. They must not have been smooth yet, because he brought the drawer back up to the bench for more sanding. "Thought maybe your arrival here had something to do with helping Johanna."

How did this guy know so much? I shook off my surprise —for now.

"There's got to be some kind of law against this, Gideon. The bishop can't just kick an entire family out of the community. Who does he think he is?"

"He thinks he's the bishop—appointed by *Gott* with the highest place of authority in the community to lead us in following the unwritten rules of the *Ordnung*."

Gideon's sanding continued, and a trickle of sweat made its way down his forehead. I waited for more, but Gideon was done talking.

He had said enough.

I took up some sandpaper and another drawer, and started helping him with the joints as my mind processed everything he'd said. About an hour passed before either of us spoke, and more than once I caught Gideon staring out the window at his wheat field. Odd, I thought, that a carpenter as busy as he would even care about planting crops.

I wanted to try another topic, in hopes of leading to the information I sought.

"What's with the wheat?"

Gideon turned to me, but didn't answer.

"I mean, why do you look out so much at that field? Why do you even plant one—busy as you are?"

He turned away then, and I thought, after the conversation we had just had, maybe I was pushing my luck.

I was about to let it rest when I heard him speaking low as he sanded the wood of his current drawer. I moved to the opposite side of him so I could hear and continued to work my own piece.

"Wheat is a crop I just can't seem to give up. This one is winter wheat. *Jah*, I don't have much time to farm, but I like to see their golden-brown seed heads bowing in the sunlight. And the fields, when they are white for harvest, give me a feeling I can't get from carpentry or anything else."

"Do you mean like in the Bible?" I hadn't meant to ask, but there it was.

"What?" Gideon let his hand rest on the drawer.

"Well, it's a distant memory for me, and I don't even know what I believe anymore, but isn't there a Bible verse about fields being white for harvest—wheat fields or some kind of grain?"

Gideon smiled. "Well, I guess there is."

"You said the other night that you were supposed to be bishop over this community, didn't you?"

Gideon just looked at me then, his smile faded a bit.

"Maybe you still are."

Gideon shook his head, blew his nose from all the sawdust, and stretched out to his full six-feet-three.

I figured I'd really done it now, but I was tired of hearing about Bishop Zook and how he ruined lives. Gideon could kick me out if he needed to. But if someone around here had to say what everyone else was thinking or feeling, I guess I was the one to have to do it.

Gideon gave me a piercing look. "This may sound odd, but I'm going to tell you it anyway, considering what Johanna Yoder is up against. If you *are* here to help her in some way. I want to be a part of it."

I was the one to get up now and stretch. I didn't know what to make of this man. He seemed so real. So genuine. His care for others felt even greater than his care for himself. It had been a long time since I'd known someone like him.

I had to get some fresh air.

My packed duffle bag lay on the cot just on the other side of the wall, and it called to me. This was getting way too complicated. Wasn't Amish life supposed to be simple? There was much more to all of this than I had come here for. It was time for me to hitch a ride back to my own life. Liza Lou and Consuelo had probably become fast friends, leaving me in the dust.

Soon, there would be no dog and no job to go home to. I kicked at the piles of sawdust on the floor a little. Until I figured out what to do, I decided I could do something about this floor at least. I told Gideon where I was headed as I strode out to the barn to grab his large push broom.

Outside the sky had turned a steel gray. I kicked at a frozen tuft of grass, hurt my foot, and gave a yelp.

"Judah, in here!" The muffled call came from a broken window in the barn. As my eyes adjusted to the darkness inside, I saw Bertram, smiling big.

"Judah!"

"Bert, what are you doing hanging out in Gideon's barn? It's freezing in here!"

"I just got in here when the bell over the door jingled. I didn't know who was coming out. Gideon could get in trouble with the bishop if he finds out he's spending too much time with"—he made air quote marks with his fingers—"*Englischers.*"

The bishop. I'd had just about enough of him.

I was glad to see Bertram, though. Gladder than I ever thought I would be to see the big lug.

"So, have you found her yet, Judah? We don't have much time."

"Time?" Time for me in Willow Brook consisted of sunrises and sunsets and plenty of work in between.

I sighed deeply as I remembered my real-world deadlines and my adrenaline started to flow again.

"I've seen her. Talked to her even."

"Great! I've got something more for you to tell her."

Bertram bounced a bit on his toes. I wondered if it was from cold or excitement.

"Well, it's not like I can just pick up the phone and call her. And besides that, she's got a lot on her mind right now."

"The paper is about to go under. Do you think she would have a little time to think about that?" Bert had taken on a snippy tone now. This was a new thing. He shook his head.

"I'm sorry. It's just that Hilton is under a lot of pressure. Since you're not there to share the load, he's unleashing everything on me."

Now I felt bad for the guy.

"But he's come up with a plan. One that I think might actually work." Bert grinned stupidly.

"Let me guess. It has even more to do with Johanna."

He clapped his hands. "He's offering her the senior writer position."

Suddenly I needed to sit down. Hilton had promised that position to me if I found Johanna.

"Hilton doesn't even know Johanna." Now, I sounded snippy, but I didn't care. "How does he know she can handle a position like that?"

Bert shrugged. "At this point, I don't think it matters to him. The subscribers and the advertisers want Ima Righter, and he's giving all he's got to reel her in."

"How does he even know what people want?"

Bert pulled a newspaper out of his coat and held it close to my face. I snatched the paper out of his hands and brought it over to a window covered in barn grit.

"The story went front page today. He's told everyone about our search for Ima and the position she'll get when she comes forward."

I let out a snort. "Half the people in Riverview will be calling to say they're Ima. I can't believe he didn't think of that."

"He told me he's got a way to vet them so he can find the right one. Something about her grandmother's name that she mistakenly added to one of her stories nearly a year ago. Hilton took it out before it was published after she wrote and asked him to. No one in Riverview knows the grandmother's name except for Hilton and the real Ima when she comes forward."

"Her name is Miriam."

Bertram cracked a smiled. "I don't think you'll pass as Ima."

"How long is he giving her?"

"Two weeks."

I let out a groan. "By then, Johanna will be married to an ogre who will probably abuse her and take away any ambition she ever had to use her gift."

I gave him back the newspaper, grabbed the push broom, and marched back into Gideon's workshop, leaving Bertram in the cold of the barn.

The thoughts swirling through my head seemed to be at war as I swept the floor for Gideon and helped him finish a few tasks, hoping he wasn't in the mood to talk. Because I sure wasn't. I wanted to keep quiet about what Bert told me in the barn. No one here even needed to know about that latest development. Not even Johanna. After things died down, and she moved on to her new life, it wouldn't matter anyway.

The paper would pull through this. It had to. And without Johanna taking the senior writer job.

I must have been lost in my thoughts because when I looked up, Gideon was staring at me and asking if I understood.

"What was that, Gideon?" I needed to get out of here and fast. I didn't need to see Johanna again. Her life would work out somehow, without any more of my help. She was Amish, after all. Nothing too complicated about that. I would just tell Bertram she wasn't interested and wash my hands of the whole thing.

"I need you to take this coffin over to the Yoder place," Gideon said. "You can take the team and the wagon I've got ready outside. The funeral will be starting soon. Johanna's brothers or cousins will help you with it once you get there."

I started to protest, but the door jingled, and soon Gideon was busy listening to an expectant mother with multiple children in tow while she explained her need for more beds. Through the window, I saw another buggy rolling up.

The sigh I let out was a little too loud and Gideon and his customer looked my way. I covered with a cough and told Gideon I would be back soon.

Back soon? The Yoder house was the last place I wanted to be. With any luck, I could catch Bert before he left. Maybe he knew how to drive a wagon. I used a dolly to pick up the simple pine box and rolled it outside.

JOHANNA

I sat and watched people buzz around me from the corner of the room. It felt like torture to just sit here, but since I was under the *Bann*, accepting help from me was forbidden.

Susanna passed me carrying a large plate of whoopie pies and gave me a sad smile. I returned it. She had tried and for that, I felt grateful. It was good to know she cared.

All our neighbors, family, and even distant relatives were showing up now to pay their respects.

But even though it was my father who had passed, and I was surrounded by people who had loved me since I was a child, I felt invisible. I figured the People must be wondering about me. They had heard of the *Bann*, but the grapevine had also told them I would soon marry Mordecai Zook.

I knew they were waiting for the "okay" from the bishop after my kneeling confession to include me in the community again. This would take place just before my wedding ceremony.

Although, I didn't know if I would ever feel truly accepted again.

I chose to disappear to the barn until the funeral began.

From my hidden perch in the hayloft, I stopped petting Miracle long enough to peek through the dirty window and saw a buggy carrying Dat's coffin pull up.

Now what was that newspaper man doing delivering the coffin?

Mose came out then and helped the man carry the coffin into the house. He left quickly, probably wanting to give my family privacy as they filled the coffin with my father in his *mutza* suit.

Fresh tears spilled out on my cheeks for Dat.

Sometimes I was glad to be under the *Bann*. Keeping to myself in the barn suited me just fine for a time like this. I peeked out again at the newspaper man to make sure he had gone, but he still sat there in Gideon's wagon. What on earth was he waiting for?

JUDAH

Before he headed back to the *Star*, I had flagged down Bert. He remembered some of what Gideon had taught him about horses long ago and tried to pass that small bit of knowledge onto me.

Quickly, I had learned how to drive the horses forward.

I had dropped Bertram off at the last bend in the road about a half hour ago, telling him I would come back for him as soon as I made the delivery. But after delivering the coffin to the Yoders just now, I realized that Bert had left out one important thing: how to go in reverse.

Frantically, I looked around and hoped he would somehow appear somewhere, but no luck. I swatted the horses with the reins and used whatever words I could think of that might get the horses to back out.

Still, they stood.

Feeling desperate, I feared Johanna's brothers would come back out and discover I wasn't as Amish as they thought.

Just then, Johanna hopped onto the bench and motioned for me to move over. Gladly, I handed the reins to her, and, clicking her tongue, she deftly maneuvered the horses backward and out of the path of the buggies that had begun to arrive.

I was amazed by her skill and told her so. The smile on her lips made my heart jump just a bit.

I had this odd urge to speak to her about the offer. Tell her ... tell her what? That the senior writer job that I had dreamed of for the past two years was being offered to her instead of me?

Thinking about her life and the options she had right now, I started to feel bad for her, and something moved inside of me. I thought of what Gideon would have done.

"Johanna, I—"

She turned to me, but a shadow quickly came over her face as a burly Amish man pulled into the drive with a batch of sour-faced children in his oversized buggy.

The children gawked at Johanna, and the big guy did not look happy.

She ducked her head and handed the reins off to me. As quietly as she had come, she disappeared into the barn.

I found Bert still making his way back to Gideon's. Pulling off the road in front of him, I waited for Bertram to climb up into the seat before telling him what I thought

about my future as an equestrian.

When his laughter had died down, I said, "I'm heading back after I drop you off at Gideon's. I might get a chance to talk with Johanna with so many Amish around her house today. Maybe, I'll just kind of blend in."

"I had planned to stop by Consuelo's and check on Liza Lou. Make sure your giant of a dog hasn't wrecked her place."

I nodded my thanks. "I can't believe those two hit it off so well."

"Maybe Consuelo just needed a friend." Bert smiled and hopped out of the wagon as I pulled into Gideon's barn. He waited for me to hop down also before saying, "You need to tell her today, Judah. If she marries that guy, it's all over for the paper. We may as well start looking for jobs on Monday."

I nodded, but I had the feeling that if Johanna married Mordecai Zook, more than our jobs would be in danger.

CHAPTER 23

Kelly gave Peaches a belly rub and then called her brother John, a lawyer with a large firm in Upstate New York. It would be cold this time of year, so she might just catch him in the office rather than out training for another one-hundred-mile race.

Ultrarunning was something Kelly didn't understand. Neither did John's wife, apparently, but that wasn't something she wanted to get into—again.

"Hey, Kel!" He sounded out of breath. Not a good sign.

"Are you running?"

"Yeah, took the week to train for the Grizzly Burn in Colorado. I'm doing the 100K. It's coming up soon. What's up?"

Despite the choices John had made in his life, her brother was a great lawyer and what he thought mattered to her. If he told her to forget about the newspaper, she would most likely follow his advice unless God had something else in mind for her.

But John surprised her by responding to her idea with excitement. He thought it would be a good way to invest her money and said he trusted in the current economy in small-town America to be able to sustain her investment. Especially if she capitalized on the rise of digital media.

"To be honest, Kel, I've been a little worried about you, living all by yourself and working from home. "

Kelly rolled her eyes. If their mother had been alive, she would have said the same thing.

"Okay, John, don't go all 'Mom' on me."

John laughed and then his breathing grew heavier. He must have hit a hill. Kelly learned not to ask deep questions when John was trudging upwards.

When his breathing evened out, Kelly ended the call after John promised to do some legal research on the *Star* for her.

JUDAH

Gideon surprised me by coming out the door dressed in what I guessed was Sunday best for an Amish man. It hadn't occurred to me that he would be attending the funeral, and he didn't seem to mind me heading back over there as well.

I let him drive, though.

As we made our way back to the Yoders, it seemed like the entire community had decided to show up. I had never seen so many buggies on the road before. It was like an Amish traffic jam, and I smiled a little as I compared it to a trip I'd made to New York City just a few months earlier.

Because I was with Gideon, I felt more comfortable joining the community in Johanna's house. I couldn't believe how they had transformed their home into an open space with benches that seated more people than I could count.

I saw Johanna in the front, sitting next to a woman I guessed was her mother. The woman sat rigidly and did not speak once with her daughter.

The funeral ran long with not one but two sermons. How did these people sit so long on these benches? I had a hard time not falling asleep. Twice, I looked over at Gideon and thought I saw him nodding off as well. I guessed he had mastered the art of sleeping sitting up after so many years of being Amish.

After the funeral, the people moved the benches around and added tables to serve an amazing Amish feast.

There was a corn soup with rivels I couldn't get enough of, and a sweet peanut butter spread someone called "peanut butter jelly" on homemade bread that kept my attention as well.

Studying the room while I ate, I was amazed at how many people came up to Gideon during the meal. People seemed drawn to him. Obviously, he was still more than a carpenter to them. I thought of his wheat field.

Later, I caught a few glimpses of Johanna. She seemed to stay off by herself, and I noticed the other Amish went out of their way to avoid her.

If that's how they treated their grieving, then you could count me out of this community.

What was I saying? Maybe my Amish bowl cut was getting to me.

But something seemed off because friends and family surrounded Johanna's mother while her daughter sat alone. What was wrong with these people?

When I finally gathered enough courage to go speak with Johanna, she was gone.

I left the house then, giving Gideon some excuse about needing air. He didn't seem to mind or even hear me as he participated in a deep conversation with an Amish couple. Again, I noted how people seemed drawn to him. The things I overheard them talking about weren't trivial—how to care for a sick parent, marriage issues, dealing with a son who was in something called his *Rumspringa*—whatever that was. Obviously, these people felt like they could trust him.

I guessed this trust was why they didn't seem to question my presence so much. If Gideon was okay with me being there, it seemed they were as well. But I kept my mouth shut as much as possible anyway since my knowledge of Pennsylvania Dutch was limited.

Stepping outside, I just missed getting run over by a few Amish kids playing tag.

For a funeral, there seemed to be still a lot of life going on. My mind drifted back to my own father's funeral. After Mom and I left the church that day, the house seemed so quiet. I couldn't stand it. That's when I started spending as much time away from the house and her as I could. Everything reminded me of him.

Johanna obviously needed some space, and it looked like Gideon was in it for the long haul down there, so I rambled into the barn and made my way up to the hayloft, feeling exhausted. These early Amish mornings were tough. I hadn't had this little sleep since college.

The barn straw smelled sweet. I shooed a barn cat off a soft spot and decided to shut my eyes for just a few minutes.

I woke with a start. The barn cat had made her bed on my chest and slept there, purring softly with every breath. Its fluffy gray tail flickered and tickled at my nose. I reached up and stroked her head.

"Liza Lou would eat you for lunch."

I missed my dog and my bed. Stretching my legs, I woke the cat, and she jumped down and arched her back in her own stretch.

"Sorry about that." I stepped over to a window and rubbed the glass with my shirtsleeve. The guests seemed to be leaving now. Gideon's buggy still sat where we had left it, but I wondered if he wanted to head back too.

Scanning the yard full of departing Amish from this view, I saw a sea of black felt hats and bonnets. Johanna could be anywhere by now. I regretted my nap. I'd missed my chance.

Why hadn't I gone after her when she disappeared from the house? A sense of urgency washed over me, and Bertram's news rushed back to my thoughts. I needed to find her and at least let her know she had options.

The gray cat rushed down the wooden steps in front of me, and I was about to follow when a voice came from below.

"Where have ya been, Miracle? Did ya find somewhere warm to nap this time?"

JOHANNA

I cradled the cat in my arms and enjoyed the closeness of her touch. Being shunned was taking its toll on me. With no one to talk to and no one to touch, I felt starved for human interaction. My eyes welled up. I missed the warmth of Dat's hugs. Even after his stroke, he still reached out for a hug from time to time.

I didn't think anyone understood what the *Bann* could do to an Amish *Maedel* who was short on experiencing human touch to begin with.

Or maybe they did.

I pulled the cat close and took in the smell of her. Usually, she holed up in between the hay bales in the loft upstairs. Most times, I could figure out where she had napped based on the smell of her fur.

The spicy, musky scent that met my nose was new to me. Curious, I pulled the cat in to inhale it again.

"In my barn, a cat like that won't last a week."

Miracle jumped from my arms and ran back upstairs. I looked up to meet Mordecai's jet black eyes. One wandered to the left while the other focused coldly in my direction.

I picked the hay off my dress and avoided his stare. "Why ... why's that?"

"A cat is only *gut* if it's mean and half starved. Let it work for its keep. You feed it and coddle it, and your barn is filled with mice."

"We don't have many—"

"Who was that you were driving with when I pulled in?"

"Gideon's hand. He needed—"

"Looked like a *Dummkopp* to me, having a woman drive his wagon."

"I was only—"

The slap came hard and fast, totally shocking me. I brought my hand to my cheek in horror.

"We might as well get this straight from the start. I don't take back talk from anyone. Especially my woman."

My world came crushing in then as I realized what my future held if I married this man. Struggling to breathe, I sat down hard on the bottom step.

Mordecai's eldest son came in then, telling him their buggy was ready. My future husband gave me another long look up and down and then turned to go.

"I'll see you on Thursday."

JUDAH

I wasn't quite sure what had happened down here, but I'd heard every word. The red handprint on Johanna's cheek told me the rest of the story. Her look told me she was upset to find out I had witnessed what had happened.

I'd read Johanna's writing. And I liked it more than I admitted. She wasn't the type of woman who would let herself be abused. Not by a long shot.

"I really need to talk to you." I sat down next to her.

She started to cry then and cautiously I reached to console her. She leaned into the hug as if starved for it. Miracle jumped into her lap.

Bertram's urgency and the timing of her Thursday wedding rang in my ears.

"There is something you need to hear. Something that could help."

I couldn't tell if she heard me. She had pulled away from me and was using the handkerchief I had offered.

"Not here." Johanna rose and peeked out the barn door, looking left and then right. "Let's talk out at the rock tomorrow morning at ten o'clock."

She wiped her tears with her apron, took a deep breath, stood up straight, and returned to the house.

I let a few minutes go by before I went to look for Gideon.

Kelly had six months. That's what John told her late that afternoon after his twenty-mile training run was over. Even with all the money from Jack's life insurance, she still just had six months to get the paper back on its feet before it would drop back into the red again. Unless it really started turning a profit.

She had plenty of ideas to help turn the paper around. Building a more robust website and enhancing online subscriptions, social media, and advertising were just a few.

Kelly surprised herself with the excitement she felt thinking about it. Maybe her brother was right. Maybe she had worked alone long enough.

John had also surprised her by saying that the paper was worth the risk. He had looked into the pros and cons for her and decided that, with a better digital advertising effort and social media reach, the only way for the paper to go was up.

"Think of it as an adventure." Her brother had always been the optimist. "Who knows, one day you might write a best seller about your journey."

Adventure. That about summed it up.

CHAPTER 24

JOHANNA

I sat down hard on the ladderback chair with my throbbing cheek to the wall. I'd sensed my mother breathe a sigh of relief as she'd watched me enter from the side door. I'm sure she'd wondered where I had been. Mamm would want to make sure her only daughter was present—shunned or not.

What had I done, telling the man in the barn I would meet with him? I didn't have anything to say to him, but I couldn't shake the feeling that maybe somehow he could help. Remembering what it felt like with his arm around me didn't help any either.

I held my hand to my cheek which still stung from Mordecai's slap.

I sat silently and watched the women put away what was left of the funeral meal. Lifelong family and friends surrounded me, but no one looked at me. I felt thankful for this now—at least no one would notice the welt on my cheek.

A loud crash came from the kitchen, and I turned toward the sound. I caught Mamm's gaze and realized the light from the propane lamp had revealed my secret.

A look of horror mixed with regret washed across her face. She sucked in her breath so much so that Susanna laid a hand on her shoulder and led her to a chair. I bowed my head low then and angled myself back into the shadows.

I would meet with the journalist tomorrow.

Entering Consuelo's apartment, Bertram greeted Liza Lou and noticed she'd put on a few pounds since just last week. The smell of rice and beans wafted to him from the kitchen.

"I don't blame you for eating, girl. Consuelo is a fantastic cook." He patted the dog on the head and then walked into the kitchen.

"Ahh! Your boots, Bertram! Take them off. Take them off!"

Bertram looked down at his mud-caked boots. He'd forgotten all about them in his quest for food.

Consuelo grabbed her broom and began to sweep like a mad woman until every last bit of mud had been swept up and deposited in the bin.

"I'm sorry, Sway," he said. "My mind was on your beans."

Consuelo smiled but still chided him a bit more before ladling out a huge bowl of black bean soup and covering it with a blanket of white rice. Bertram saw chunks of green pepper and chorizo, and his mouth watered.

"Where are you getting mud like that, Bertram?" Her eyes were sharp, and she sniffed the air between them. "Do I smell horses?"

Bertram, caught up in the scent of the beans, let it slip exactly where he had been.

Consuelo's warm eyes darkened. "Is *that* the Amish community where Judah is?"

Bert realized his mistake and tried to remember what he had said. Spoon in midair, he looked at her blankly.

"Willow Brook, Bert. Judah is *there*?"

Bertram shifted his eyes back to the soup. Now he'd blown it. What kind of undercover journalist was he anyway?

"Bertram, I'm not going to tell anyone. But I need to know if Judah has gone to Willow Brook to find the girl. There's something about that place ..."

There was no stopping Consuelo's rant, Bertram knew that much about her already. So, he told her everything.

Somehow it felt good to get the secrets off his chest. Or maybe it was a stomach full of Sway's rice and beans that made him feel so good. Picking up his empty bowl, he rinsed it in the sink and turned to give Liza Lou a good belly rub before he left.

"I'm worried about Judah." Consuelo continued to sweep at some invisible dirt as he headed for the door.

"He's fine, Sway. I just left him. The Amish woman, her father died a few days ago. When I left him earlier, he was going to her dad's funeral with what looked like the rest of the Amish in Pennsylvania."

"There's something about that community, Bert. I can't quite put my finger on it. My abuela was always telling me stuff to keep me out of trouble when I was a teenager. It's all kind of jumbled together. But there was something she said about Willow Brook." She paused and leaned on her broom. "Now, what was it?"

Liza Lou realized her belly rub was over and nuzzled at Bertram's hand for more. Bert bent down and began again while Consuelo took some time digging into her thoughts.

"It was about a convict, I think." She had her hand on her hip as she studied the crucifix on her wall. "An escaped convict who had disappeared in the woods here back when my abuela was a young woman. It had to have been a little over forty years ago. I remember her saying that she kept a gun in the kitchen drawer, just in case."

Consuelo laughed a bit and shook her head at the memory. Liza Lou had fallen asleep, and Bertram looked at his watch. It was getting late.

"Wow, that's some story, Sway. But I've got to head out now. There are a few things I need to do at the paper."

"*Uno momento.*" Consuelo held up her hand. From the look in her eyes, her mind was still back somewhere, remembering. She snapped her fingers. "That's it! My abuela heard the guy was rumored to be living somewhere with the Amish at Willow Brook."

"Well, it's a good place to hide. Slopping pigs and mucking stalls is a good way to cover your scent." Bertram edged toward the door. He'd been here too long already. What if there was something Hilton needed him to do? He grabbed his hat and thanked Consuelo again.

She shook her head again and then held one thick finger in the air. "Abuela said she'd heard he'd become a priest."

"A priest?" Bertram almost laughed at that. A priest among the Amish. Now that's someone who would certainly stick out. "Okay, thanks, Sway."

His phone began to vibrate. Hilton.

Consuelo followed him to the door. "Tell Judah to be careful. I don't know if that man is still alive."

Bertram nodded and left her standing on her back step, looking like a mother hen.

Just before he hit the call back button on his phone, it hit him.

The priest.

Quickly, he sent a text to Judah. Without revealing much, he asked for a photo of Zook. He knew the Amish didn't like to have their pictures taken, and he respected that, but he had a niggling feeling that Bishop Zook wasn't really who he said he was. And if that was the case, a photo might come in handy before this thing was over.

JOHANNA

Later that evening, as they buried Dat, I made sure to avoid Mamm's eyes. As the bishop spoke a final prayer over Dat's grave, I watched my family bow their heads in prayer. Tenderly, I let my eyes rest on each of my seven brothers, their wives, and children down to the last *Bobbeli* sleeping in her mother's arms. Little Grace had been born a month ago today.

If I married Mordecai, I would be doing this for them.

The bishop's words to Mamm still rang in my head: *It would let the community know there isn't something wrong that might drive one of us out.*

I knew exactly what his words meant. This wasn't the first time the bishop had threatened our family. I'd heard Mamm's stories about her own mother's drive to write that had caused so many problems with the bishop. She said she was often surprised they were allowed to stay.

And now I was under the *Bann* for the same thing.

I stole a quick glance at Mamm and saw her wipe away fresh tears. The heat on my cheek had lessoned. Hopefully the mark was no longer visible. There was no telling what Mose would do if he saw it.

I wondered if Mamm thought it odd that I had picked Mose to stand by at a time like this.

I should be over there next to her.

Little Grace sneezed. And the realization hit me.

I was going to have to go through with this wedding to save my family. I could see no other way around it. We'd all made sacrifices in this community. Marrying Mordecai would have to be my cross to bear.

Unchecked tears formed tiny streams down my cheeks as I watched each community member help cover Dat's grave with soft earth and then leave. The bishop and minister had been the first ones to go, my family had followed, and then the rest of the People.

Caught up in their own grief, no one seemed to notice when I stayed behind.

And that was fine by me. I needed to be alone with Dat.

I looked around at the cemetery, the resting place of all the People in Willow Brook. Identical, plain gravestones marked each grave.

I gazed at *Dawdi* and Mammi's stones and then looked out over the sea of other deceased relatives. Everyone from our earliest German immigrant ancestors to my Dat were buried here—almost two hundred years' worth of community.

A sharp wind rustled the trees overhead, and a single red leaf from a sugar maple landed on Dat's grave. The first of many to come. I sighed.

In the quiet, I heard a familiar *chica dee dee dee* sound come from thick branches of the blue spruce that spread out in the corner of the graveyard. There it was again, only closer now. I felt a smile spread slowly across my face.

I had forgotten about Dat's birds.

After his stroke, Dat had my brother Joshua build several feeders in the yard, and then set them up in front of every window of the house. When he wasn't trying to help his sons with the steers, he would sit in front of the feeders and watch the gold and raspberry finches make quick work of his black oil sunflower seeds. The dark-eyed juncos cleaned up whatever dropped to the ground.

And then there were the chickadees.

Dat had been slowly filling a feeder one day when the black-capped little gentleman lit on his shoulder. If I hadn't seen it with my own two eyes, I don't think I would have believed it.

Dat moved slowly anyway, just the right pace for his new feathered friend. The little bird seemed content to sit for quite some time on Dat's shoulder. Darting its head from side to side, the chickadee acted like it was sent there with a purpose.

Seeing Dat beam with pride as he watched the bird on his shoulder, I believed with all my heart that it was.

I looked up into the spruce to see if I could spot the little bird.

Chica dee dee dee.

I could see him now and, despite my sadness, managed another smile.

The events of the day rushed back at me then, and I knelt at the foot of the fresh soil on Dat's grave and pressed my hands into it.

"Dat, what am I supposed to do?"

I shook my head. Why did I even need to ask? I knew exactly what Dat would say to me if he were alive. Ever the stickler for the rules of the Willow Brook *Ordnung*, Dat would tell me to follow the ways of the bishop. To keep in step with the People.

It did not matter that an *Englischer* from the *Mountain Laurel Star* told me he had a better plan. Dat would want me to turn away from such foolish talk.

I looked up at the trees and remembered my time on the rock. I had already made a vow to *Gott*. What was I doing questioning it? Dat used to say that sometimes all we had was our word, and I had given mine.

Strengthening my resolve for what I must do, I let the earth fall through my fingers. I would die to the wishes of my heart and marry Mordecai.

JUDAH

What rock? Why hadn't I taken the time to ask her what rock she was talking about?

The buggy horse sauntered in front of us. It was getting late, but clearly, Gideon was in no rush to get back.

I cut the silence between us.

"You're good with your people."

Gideon didn't respond till a quarter mile later.

"What were ya doing in the barn with Johanna?"

There was no beating around the bush with this guy. I told him what had happened. No reason telling him anything different.

Gideon remained silent for several moments and then slowed the horse to a stop. I wasn't sure if he was going to kick me out or pat me on the back.

"You mean to say that he struck Johanna while you were just a few feet away?"

"I didn't know that he hit her, Gideon. I was upstairs, remember? I wasn't supposed to be there, wasn't supposed to hear all that. I came downstairs when I heard him leave. She was sitting on the last step with her hand over her cheek. It wasn't until she looked up at me that I saw the welt."

"Why are ya here, Judah?"

I told him then. Told him about Ima, the *Star*, Hilton's offer ... everything. I even told him about how I had found Johanna in the river. And the rock that I had to find. I figured if there was anyone Johanna could trust with her secret in this community, it would be Gideon.

Gideon picked up the reins then and let the horse take us back home.

We rode the rest of the way in silence.

CHAPTER 25

The sun was just starting to set and the air growing colder by the time Bertram arrived at the *Star*'s empty office. Glad for the privacy, he turned on just a few lights, wanting to draw as little attention to himself from the outside as possible. Bertram cupped his hands in front of his mouth and breathed into them, hoping to warm them up before opening his laptop.

Sitting down in his office chair, he wheeled himself over to the thermostat and was about to turn up the temperature when he remembered Hilton's tirade about keeping it low to save money.

Looking around at the empty newsroom which normally buzzed with activity, he couldn't see how bringing up the temperature would make much of a difference.

Fingers stiff, he punched the buttons of the thermostat until it reached seventy then rubbed his hands together. Adrenaline rushed through his veins. Finally, he had something he could do to help Judah and the paper. This lead could end up being a big deal. A really big deal.

Back in his cubical, Bertram slipped off his chair and onto his knees.

God knew how many lives were involved here, and Bertram thought it high time he asked for help. After he had finished his prayer, Bertram got back in his chair, wiped his eyes and began researching whatever he could find on the life of the so-called bishop, Amos Zook. Zook was a common name among the Amish. Perfect for someone who wanted to "blend in."

Okay, Amos, what were you trying to pull with these people?

Bertram's excitement rose. The more he dug into the story, the more he wanted to know. He felt like a journalist now, a real journalist. This is what he went to school for and why he put up with a salary that barely paid the bills. And also how he endured an editor who seemed to like nothing more than to tear his work apart.

Finally, he was using his gifts to help uncover injustice and expose it to the world.

As Bertram researched on his second monitor, he opened a fresh document on his laptop to paste important information he found. Then, he opened a second document and began to write his story. He hadn't planned on writing a story. Not yet anyway. But the words seemed to flow without really even trying. Most likely, this would never get in the paper, not yet, anyway. But it was good to get the truth out all the same.

As he continued his research, he came to a roadblock when he discovered that the only documents with photos were in print or stored in the microfilm room at the public library. The building was only open for another hour and it'd take about ten minutes to get there.

He grabbed his keys and paper and pen for notes and decided to leave everything on. He'd come back later and work on the story a little more here before heading home.

As Bertram stepped outside, he was surprised to see it had grown completely dark. He'd been too focused on his research to realize the time. On the drive over to the library, he tried to rein in his thoughts. There were so many possibilities here—so many options. No need to let himself get carried away, he just needed to find the truth.

The library was quiet this time of night. Bertram greeted an older woman in large red-rimmed glasses who sat behind the desk but she didn't look up from her book. He followed the signs down the empty hall toward the microfilm room. It had been a long time since he had used a microfilm reader, and his hands fumbled as he loaded the film. He tried to slow down, but felt pressed for time. There were so many reels to look through.

Looking through old archived newspapers for a fugitive from the seventies on microfilms was tedious work, and his eyes soon grew tired of the dim light.

"Someone really needs to transfer all of these old records to the internet," he grumbled as he rubbed his eyes. The woman with the red glasses shushed him. The shape of her frames made her look like a bug.

"We close at ten," said the bug.

"Oh, okay, I just need a little more time."

"There is no more time. We close at ten."

Bertram looked at his phone and sighed. How had it gotten so late? He was no closer to finding anything than when he'd left the office.

The woman gathered her keys and began locking doors, glancing back at him with the same scowl as before. Bertram slapped down his pen little too loudly and the woman jumped.

"Sorry, I'm just a little frustrated."

She sighed and nodded, her scowl now faded. "What are you looking for this late?"

"I'm looking for information about something that may have happened in Mercer County in the early seventies."

The woman cocked her head, and then laughed. "Things were different then, I'll tell you that much."

Bertram sniffed a source. "Did you live around here?"

"I did. I worked at The Muffin Top, a bakery on 5th and Main. It's a pizza place now."

"Do you mind if I ask you a few questions about something that may have happened during that time?"

She gestured around the room. "I have to close up. Run the vacuum. Sweep the front."

"What if I help you?" Her scowl returned and Bertram sweetened the offer. "I'll vacuum and sweep. And afterward, I'll buy you something at the coffee shop across the street."

"It closes at eleven thirty."

"I'm a fast worker."

A smile crept across her face, and she stuck out her hand. "I'm Nora."

Bertram learned a lot about Nora over four caramel macchiatos and a few frosted maple scones. It was always best to build some trust in an informant before digging in deep.

As Nora munched on a scone and shared her story, he realized she was full of opinions. She'd grown up in Mercer County and knew everything about its history, its economy, and even its politics.

After he had listened for a while and the shop began to clear out, Bertram asked the real questions.

"Nora, I couldn't find any information tonight on what I was looking for in the microfilms. The story should have made headlines back when you were, well ... younger. But I can't find anything. Maybe I've got the wrong county or something."

"When did it happen?"

"If I'm right, I think it would have been in the early seventies."

Nora smiled as she sipped her macchiato.

"What?"

"That was when Ernst Fisher was mayor."

Bertram shrugged. "And?"

"Ernst was the richest man in Mercer County at the time. You combine money and power, and you can keep reporters quiet. Especially around here in the early seventies. There was no social media around at that time, you know, Bertram." Nora took another bite of her scone and then glanced around. "Seems like we're the only ones left. Perhaps we should head out."

"We've still got another ten minutes." Bertram had to move fast. Chances were slim that Nora would agree to hang around in the parking lot for more questions.

Nora nodded, but began to clean up their table.

"Was there ever any news that may have gotten covered up about an escaped convict hiding in the area?"

Nora frowned. "I really should be charging you for this."

Bertram started to pray. He'd already spent most of what he had on his debit card until payday. If there even was a payday.

Nora smiled then and batted a hand at him. "Nah, just kidding. It's not often I get treated. What I've got in here," Nora tapped on the side of her head, "it's all yours."

Bertram took out his pen and notepad. "What was his name?"

FORBIDDEN GIFT

By the time Bertram pulled into the newsroom parking lot at midnight, he felt he had what he needed to blow the lid off the forty-year-old court case. He might even be able to save the paper with what he'd found out about Ernst Fisher's brother, Matthias. The mayor's brother had escaped from prison about the same time Amos Zook showed up in Willow Brook. As Bertram took the steps up to his office two at a time, he whispered a prayer of thanks.

Bertram noticed the chilly office air right away. Checking, he saw that the thermostat had been turned back down to fifty-eight degrees. He hadn't noticed anyone in the office when he left, but he could have been wrong.

Without turning on the harsh overhead lights, he made his way back to his cube, where he'd left his laptop open. But now, the computer lid was shut.

He shrugged. Maybe he was too tired to remember. He had to have shut it before he left. Bertram sat down at his cube to transcribe his notes and flicked on his desk lamp. A few moments later, as he began to make a little headway, the fluorescent lights flickered on.

He squinted against the cold blue of the overhead lights, their buzz grating instantly on his nerves.

He leaned around his cube wall to address whomever had turned on the lights. "Is it okay if we leave those—"

Hilton still had his hand on the light switch. "You're back."

"Yeah, umm, just finishing up a few things." Bertram could hear his own words fall flat. He'd never been a good liar.

Hilton sneered. "That's funny, from the looks of what you were researching on your computer, it seemed like you were just starting something."

Bertram swallowed hard. How would he get out of this? His eyes fell to the corner of his cube where his Scripture-of-the-day calendar sat.

God is our refuge and strength, an ever-present help in trouble.

Seeing the verse gave him the peace he needed. So what if Hilton knew? He had more invested in this paper than any of them did.

"I'm sorry. You're right. I was at the beginning of something." Hilton's sneer faded, and he flicked the lights back off. Slowly, he walked toward Bertram's desk.

As he neared, Bertram had to keep his mouth from gaping open. His boss seemed more disheveled than usual— as if he hadn't slept or showered in days.

"Are ... are you okay?"

"What, me?" Hilton placed a hand over his chest and smiled. "Yeah. Sure, I'm just fine."

Bertram sat a little longer, waiting for the truth. He'd learned recently that letting people know you care about them was key in sharing the gospel. He wanted Hilton to know he was all ears if he wanted to talk.

Hilton pulled a silver ring off his finger and took his time inspecting it under Bertram's desk lamp. "Have I ever told you that my dad was editor of the *Star* before I was? This is his college ring. He got a degree in journalism from Penn State." Hilton let out an uncharacteristic sniffle as he wheeled another desk chair up beside Bertram. "Losing the paper has me a little down if that's what you meant before."

"Have you been you drinking?"

Hilton bristled. "So what if I have?"

"It's just that, well, it doesn't look like it's helping any."

Hilton's shoulders slumped. Then, he put his head on his arms on Bertram's desk and was quiet for a long time. Bertram thought maybe he had fallen asleep.

Come to me, all you who are weary and burdened, and I will give you rest.

"Hilton, I know you told me not to tell you about Jesus, but I only see one way to help get you the peace you need."

As the words of salvation flowed so easily from his lips, Bertram felt God's power. He knew he'd never be able to take credit for what he'd said no matter the outcome.

When he'd finished, Hilton wiped some tears from his face and said, "I feel brand new."

Bertram had never introduced anyone to Christ before, so Hilton wasn't the only one drying his eyes on his sleeve.

JUDAH

The smell of bacon and eggs woke me late the next morning—the first morning I'd gotten to sleep in since joining this community. Gideon had set up a little table next to my cot and had left a steaming plate piled high along with a cup of hot coffee.

I didn't see him so I dug into the meal and ate heartily, cleaning my plate. Concerned about the time then, I slipped on my broadfall trousers which were still cold from the night. I did a little crazy dance to warm them up.

Gideon was not anywhere in the shop either. I grabbed my coat and walked to the barn where I found Gideon preparing the horse to hitch up to the buggy. I thanked him for breakfast and looked around to see what I could do to help, feeling a little sheepish about sleeping so late.

"Are you going out?" I handed him some straps that were hanging from a large rusty nail, hoping they were what he needed. Gideon took the straps and started buckling them around the horse.

"We both are."

Gideon told me he'd been up early that morning having a talk with *Gott* about Johanna. His eyes filled with tears as he told me about the control Amos had over Johanna and her family that now had them trapped.

"I'm taking you to that rock, Judah, because I think *Gott* may be inviting you to help them."

A weird warm feeling came into my chest and I smiled. It had been a long time since God used me to help with anything.

The buggy now prepared, we got in and Gideon clicked his tongue signaling the horse to start. We rode for a few minutes before he spoke again.

"What I'd really like to do is leave you off at Hal's Rivermart and send you on your way."

My smile faded.

He stopped the buggy for a few minutes and stared at the empty road ahead. The horse swished its tail.

"But I can't do that, can I, Judah? You have something Johanna may need, even if it means she leaves the People. And I can't stand in the way of that."

Gideon paused for a minute, letting his thoughts come together, I guess.

"I'm sorry if I put this on you yesterday—trying to set you up with Johanna. I just thought I saw something between the two of ya when she was in the shop. There are rules among the Amish who are baptized into the church. They can't marry *Englischers*. But I couldn't help but think that, somehow, you might be *Gott's* way out for Johanna. If she has to leave the community because of an *Englischer*, then so be it." He shook his head. "And I sure can't stand back and let that sweet girl marry someone like Mordecai just so her family can stay out from under the thumb of the bishop. There has to be another way. Amos has blinded the eyes of the People for far too long."

Gideon took out his handkerchief. I could tell his heart was broken over the burden Amos had laid on the Yoder family, for all of the Amish here, really.

"I had no idea my silence over Amos's cheating the lot over forty years ago would come to this. This morning, I was completely honest with myself and *Gott*, and discovered there was a bit more involved that day."

Gideon's eyes took on a distant kind of look, and I remained silent, letting him say what he needed to.

"I'd always told myself I'd given up the lot to be bishop because I was giving Amos a chance. After all, he was a fairly new minister in the community. It just seemed like he needed the position more than I did. But now I wonder if that was the real reason I did it. Maybe there was more to it. Maybe what I thought was humility was really just fear."

I understood that. Fear had gotten in the way enough in my life, as well. Gideon made the sound with his mouth that got the horse moving again.

"When it comes right down to it, Judah, I have been just as wrong as Amos. *Gott* was the one who did the picking. If he had wanted Amos to be bishop, the lot would have fallen to him. But it didn't. And all this time the both of us have been living out a lie."

Gideon clammed up then and, after a few minutes in silence, he stopped the buggy once more. I looked around and noticed a trail leading into the woods. Gideon pointed to the path and said it led to a small outcrop of rocks on the Yoder's land. He winked when he told me that Amish courting couples would sometimes meet at the rocks for a quick visit.

I wasn't sure how I felt about that information but decided to let it go. I gave him what I hoped was a confident smile and headed toward the path.

Despite what Gideon had said, I couldn't help the selfish ambition mixed with fierce jealousy that rose up from nowhere inside of me and told me to go back. After everything I'd done to become senior writer at the *Star*, was I really going to give it all away to someone I had considered to be my biggest rival just over a week ago?

I didn't have to do this. If I walked away, no one would ever know. Gideon would get over it, and maybe I could pay Bertram to keep his mouth shut.

My feet kept moving forward though, and eventually, the path led to a clearing where a large outcropping of rocks stood. I didn't see Johanna anywhere. Maybe I had the wrong outcrop. Or maybe she'd simply decided not to come.

Surprised by a sudden feeling of disappointment, I started to climb the rock but slipped. The movement set something slithering off into the undergrowth, and I eased back up giving whatever it was a few minutes to clear the area.

Then I laid back on the rock and looked up into the oranges and yellows of the trees above. They swayed gently and the breeze released a flurry of leaves into the clearing. I could probably catch one if I tried, but the sense of heaviness around me stopped me from doing so. I shut my eyes.

I need some help here.

The prayer felt odd but somehow right. A soft flick of fur swept my cheek, and I sat up. Miracle quickly found a place in my lap and rested her head on my thigh like she'd known me all her life.

I stroked her long gray fur and told her all my troubles.

FORBIDDEN GIFT

JOHANNA

I don't know how long I watched the newspaper man through the leaves of a sugar maple sapling. Feelings stirred inside of me that shouldn't. Couldn't. I did my best to pretend they weren't there—to turn my body back down the trail that brought me here.

But still I lingered, drawn toward this man even though all the rules in my community told me to flee.

I shook my head. These feelings were best forgotten. Besides, there wasn't anything he could tell me about the newspaper that could change my mind about my marriage to Mordecai. What's done was done and would get sealed for eternity tomorrow. Mamm had a plan for our family's safety, and it was up to me to carry it out. I had promised her, and I'd promised *Gott*. End of story.

And most likely, the end of me.

I turned to leave and had gone a few silent steps when I allowed myself a quick look back.

David and his boys had headed over to New Wilmington for an auction and Mamm had left early to help Mary and my other sisters-in-law can pumpkin puree for winter pies. Usually, I was expected to help, but the *Bann* gave me the out I'd needed. Staying for a few more minutes seemed okay.

I thought he would have given up on me coming by now. But he still sat, one arm behind him for support. He seemed to be talking to himself. Curious, I took a few steps closer and saw a familiar flick of a tail.

Ach, Miri, ya crazy cat!

I inched a little closer wondering what was so important that the newspaper man needed my cat as an audience. Miracle must have heard me then because she got up and turned, giving me away. The man carefully slid himself down from the rock and walked toward me.

JUDAH

"Hello, Johanna." She'd surprised me, but I tried not to show it.

"Hullo."

"I like it here. Do you come out here a lot?"

"Just to think. And before the *Bann*, to write."

"The *Bann*?"

She shook her head, not ready to share more.

"Well, it beats my cube any day." She stared, and I hurried to explain. "It's a small desk space with walls where I write at the newspaper."

"A cube?"

"Well, it's a square, see?" How did you explain a cubical workspace to the Amish? I used my fingers to form a square and then spread my arms wide to indicate the space. "It's about so big. Not quite an office, but not a desk out in the open either." I'd always been a little embarrassed about my cube. I longed for that senior writer's office with the windows that sat next to Hilton's. I swallowed hard. I looked around like I might offer her a chair and then motioned toward the rock. "Would you like to sit down?"

She walked over to the rock and easily pulled herself up.

I looked down at the forest floor then, studying the leaves. I couldn't say what I'd come to say. The job was mine. Not hers. But somehow, I had to tell her. I opened my mouth to speak, but she beat me to the punch.

"I don't want it."

"What?"

"Whatever it is you're going to offer me, I don't want it."

My arms crossed. "How do you know you don't want it? You don't even know what it is."

She shrugged and stroked her cat who had curled up in her lap. "Whatever it is, I don't want it. I need to stay here. To be here."

I wasn't prepared for this answer. She was supposed to jump at the offer. Sweat began to trail down my back.

"Here? Do you even know what kind of life is waiting for you after tomorrow?"

She nodded. "I know."

"The man you're going to marry, he probably killed his last wife through abuse and neglect and you're willing to walk right into that?"

She stared out into the woods for what seemed like a really long time. "I have ... responsibilities."

She seemed planted right there in that spot. Rooted right to the ground. I hadn't even said what I'd came to say and didn't even know if I could say it. On top of that, odd feelings began to rise up in me, catching me off guard. I felt confused.

Miracle rolled onto her back then and Johanna stroked her belly. "If I don't do this, my family will have to leave."

"Your family? What does you marrying the bishop's grandson have to do with them?"

I knew, but I'd asked anyway.

She stared off in the distance again, rubbing the cat between the ears. Miracle closed her eyes and pressed into her.

I needed a new angle to get her attention. I'd make the offer. Maybe she'd throw me a bone now and then when we were at the *Star*. At least we'd have a paper if she came on board. And better yet, she'd still be alive.

"You know, I wasn't even going to tell you about it." I folded my arms for emphasis.

She looked up from petting the cat, her bonnet hat thing slightly askew.

"I was going to keep the offer to myself. Tell my editor you had refused. Find a way to save the paper on my own."

"Why don't ya, then?"

This was going to be harder than I thought.

"Because I can't. Not knowing you're slaving over that beast and getting beat up in the process."

She winced and then let out a slow sigh. "I've made a promise. It's the only way."

"You have seven adult brothers and the only way to save their families and their farms is for *you* to do this? Don't they have a say in this?"

"Mamm chose me. They may not even know exactly why I'm doing this."

They needed to know. The wedding was tomorrow.

This was definitely not going the way I'd envisioned it. I grew quiet.

She turned to me then, her green eyes full with tears.

"*Denki* for trying to save my life a second time, Judah."

She slipped down the rock and started making her way through the tall fern. Miracle jumped down to follow.

What could I say that would make a difference?

It's a story that goes back more than forty years. Gideon's words came at just the right time.

"I know why the bishop wants your family out."

She stopped and turned back to me. Miracle lay in the weeds at her feet once again exposing her furry belly hoping to get in one more rub.

CHAPTER 26

JOHANNA

How would this man know anything about my family? Especially this—the thing that has been such a burden for as long as I could remember. How did he know?

I walked back over to the rock and hefted myself up next to him. "What do you know?" I knew my tone sounded suspicious, but I didn't care.

As he told me all he knew, I couldn't believe it. Wouldn't. The bishop cheated his way through God's election? That explained a lot if it were true. But Mammi engaged to the bishop a few years before that? I wasn't going to believe that. He had his facts wrong. How could Mammi ever love such a horrible man? Even if she were young at the time.

And why had Gideon told this newspaper man and no one else? He knew how much we suffered. Maybe Gideon was upset because he hadn't been chosen so long ago. Maybe his information was twisted because he felt hurt, or jealous even.

But I knew Gideon, and I knew that couldn't be true.

A butterfly rested its wings on the edge of the rock. Miracle assumed her pounce position, and I rolled my eyes.

"Not now, Miri."

I waved my hand at the butterfly, and it took flight, but not before the cat was already in motion. The orange-and-black wings flitted into the woods, and Miracle made an unsuccessful leap into the fern below. Peering over the side of the rock to see if she was okay, I remembered the rubbing.

It still stung not being able to read the letters, not to mention whatever it was Dat had written on Mammi's handkerchief that day.

I slid off the rock and began to circle it. Perhaps the engraving was nothing. But I had to see it again.

JUDAH

Something spooked the cat, and she ran off quicker than I thought she could. When Johanna finally stopped circling the rock and started pulling brush away from the side of it in random places, I started to wonder about her mental health. But then I saw what she must be searching for.

The heart looked almost like part of the rock. Squinting, I made out a gouged A. Z. + M. S. Johanna let out a little gasp and sank to her knees in front of the engraving.

"Who are they?"

Johanna looked up at me. She remained quiet for a little while and then found her words.

"The bishop and my grandmother. It makes sense now. She had been a Stoltzfus before she married *Dawdi*."

I opened my mouth to speak when Johanna's expression suddenly changed. She tilted her head away from the rock and breathed in deeply through her nose. Gathering her dress, she left the woods the way she came only this time moving even quicker than Miracle.

Confused, I knelt down and brushed the rest of the weeds away from the heart. The engraving seemed very old. Patches of moss filled in some of the heart, giving it a greenish outline. Lichen grew in many places below it. The pale green fungus would provide a feast for the deer in the dead of winter.

I found a sharp stone and absently started to scrape some of the lichen away. What was I doing here anyway? I hadn't come any closer to "recruiting" Johanna for her new position. The newspaper would probably tank by the beginning of next week and I'd be looking for a new job.

My scraping eventually exposed a light pitting in the rock below the heart that had been hidden by the lichen. I called for Johanna but got no response. Miracle returned and sat on my lap while I scraped. The marking seemed to be a line joined by two others.

An arrow?

What was that smell? I stood and sniffed at the air. Again, Miracle bolted down the path.

JOHANNA

The smoke thickened as I left the woods.

Flames licked the roof of the *Dawdi Haus*. My thoughts raced to Mammi's journal hidden somewhere inside. I knew it was there and now I would never find it. I felt sure Mammi had written the answer to what Judah had said out at the rock—and maybe even more than that—in that journal.

I cried out and fell to my knees in the yard. David and his sons would still be at the auction and Mamm at the frolic. By the time anyone got here, everything would be lost. The heat of the flames made me dizzy and reminded me of my fever just last week.

Where did ya hide it this time?

Dawdi's words pierced my thoughts. I jumped a little and even looked around the yard to see if I was still alone. Something crashed inside the *Dawdi Haus*, and my mind raced back to *Dawdi* and the hidden journal.

In my dream, he had come into the kitchen and Mammi had seemed afraid. She had glanced around the room like she was trying to remember something. Her eyes went somewhere before she looked at me. Her eyes went ... where?

The drawer? The drawer!

I rose to my feet. The journal was in the utensil drawer in the kitchen. I had already searched there, but maybe I hadn't looked hard enough. Gideon made custom drawers all the time. Maybe there was a special way to make them so that they only appeared empty.

The flames hovered just above the front door, and its molding hung precariously off to one side. I didn't let myself think as I ran for the back door. If I had, I would have second guessed my decision to run inside.

A veil of smoke hovered around the patches of live fires throughout the room and ceiling, but I noticed a clear path to the kitchen counter and the utensil drawer.

"Let it burn, Johanna. Let it all burn."

The voice came from the door I had just run through. Squinting, I saw the outline of an Amish man.

"Bishop?" My voice sounded hollow. Crouching down low where the smoke was thinner, I held my apron to my mouth and called between breaths. "We need to put it out."

"There's no putting out this one. Everything is going to burn."

Why wasn't the bishop going to get help? I could find the journal while he let others know about the fire.

"There's something I need to find, Bishop. It's Mammi's journal. I know it will help." Violently, I flung the drawer open. I didn't have a good feeling about the bishop being here. Something felt odd about it. I probably shouldn't have mentioned the journal to him either. Why did I tell him about the journal? Moving quickly, I started flinging utensils everywhere till I reached the bottom.

"What's inside that journal has haunted me for forty years. It's time for it to burn. To let the past stay put."

The bishop's voice sounded louder this time. Slowly, he moved toward me.

Why wasn't he panicking like I was. There wasn't much time!

I turned around. He held something in his hand. Coughing threatened to overtake me, but I felt my way around the drawer bottom until I found a slight indentation on one side of the wood. I clawed at the depression desperately until it finally popped open. Reaching down in, I explored every spot possible, ready to feel the journal's cool leather on my now blistery hands.

But there was nothing.

A pain greater than I'd ever had exploded in my head.

JUDAH

As I made my way along the well-beaten trail to Johanna's home, the smell of smoke increased with each step. A few of the Amish had already arrived and were beginning a bucket chain from the creek. I heard sirens in the far distance.

Looking at how the flames lapped the house, I didn't know why they bothered.

Men were moving livestock out of the barn and out to pasture. The wind changed, and I did my best to scan the property. I didn't see Johanna anywhere.

A sense of urgency filled me, and I began to call her, not worrying about what the Amish around me might think. Circling the house, I saw the back door to a small addition was ajar.

Looking to my right and left, most of the Amish seemed busy with the main part of the house. Johanna would have been here helping.

Unless she was inside.

Something in my stomach sank.

In a few strides, I was inside the small home. An open drawer hit me in the *gut*, and I practically tore it off its hinges. I coughed. The smoke was bad in here, very bad.

An old fire safety song started playing in my head, and I sank to my knees as the song told me to go.

Why was I here? Of course, she wouldn't have come into a blazing house. What would she have come back to get? From what I knew of the Amish, they didn't put a lot of stock in their material possessions.

As I crawled on the hardwood, my hand scattered a pile of wooden spoons, a wire whisk, and even a rolling pin or two. What were all these things doing on the floor?

I made my way into a bedroom and then on into a small bathroom. Even down on the floor, the smoke began to burn my lungs. I grabbed a towel and tied it around my nose. I had to get out. Maybe Johanna wasn't in here, after all.

Back in the kitchen, I touched something smooth and hard. A rock. I pushed it aside with a little effort and set my hand down into a pool of liquid, sticky and warm. I brought my hand to my nose. It smelled of iron.

Blood.

I flailed my arms across the floor until I found Johanna and gathered her to me.

"Help! Someone help!" My words felt strangled as the smoke closed in on us and I coughed. "God, help!"

I noticed a fuzzy light somewhere ahead, and I pulled Johanna across some charred hardwood as hundred-year-old beams fell deeper into the room. I carried her in my arms for the last few steps to the open door as the final bit of breath left my lungs.

CHAPTER 27

Kelly had fasted most of the day, repeatedly giving the idea of buying the paper to God and then taking it back again. She fought anxiety more times in one day than she could count. She even called her pastor for counsel. He listened and helped her consider all the different paths and he'd prayed to God, asking for clear direction.

Kelly stopped at the local grocery store on her way home from Wednesday night church to get some gas in her car. As she stood at the tank pumping gas, she noticed a bright red car filled with young men a little younger than Judah in the parking lot.

She watched while two of the men left the car and headed toward the grocery store. Instead of walking to the store together, however, they separated and entered the store from different sides of the building.

Another young man left the car and started coming toward the gas pumps. When he was just a few feet from her, he tripped and fell flat on his face.

A surge of alarm ran through her.

"Lord Jesus! Are you okay?"

The man looked up at her. "Yes, ma'am. Just tripped over my own feet."

Kelly noticed his slow movements and unsteadiness as his friend rushed over to help.

Once the man had placed his obviously drugged friend in the car, he ran around to the driver's seat and drove the car to the front of the store where both of the other men were now running out. The vehicle sped out of the parking lot, taking any doubts about her involvement with the paper with it.

The people in Riverview needed to keep communicating with each other and reading news from a larger paper in Mercer County wouldn't be the same. Those larger papers wouldn't report on the small things that really mattered here in their town—things like the spread of drugs and local robberies. People needed to know what was going on in their neighborhoods, and they needed to be given clear direction on what they could do to help.

If that had to start with her, then so be it.

JOHANNA

I heard someone keening soft and low and then I didn't. And there it was again.

There were other sounds too. Beeps and footsteps. Whispering. Curtains being pulled this way and that. But when all fell quiet, the keening would start again. Soft at first, and then building. A woman crying for someone or something she'd lost, maybe. It was a lonely sound, making my heart ache.

I struggled to rise in order to find the woman in all this darkness. I reached out so I wouldn't trip. The keening stopped and the woman was gone.

Hours later, the woman was in the room again and there were two voices now.

"You have to stop this, Mamm. The bishop says they'll be wed as soon as she's better."

"I can't. What's been done is done with the bishop. And besides Johanna agreed to the wedding."

"How could she have agreed to this?"

"Mose, it's the *only* way. I know Mordecai is a hard man, but they'll make it work. It has to work."

"Mamm, he nearly raped her when she was sixteen."

"That never happened. I would've known." A chair creaked and the woman spoke again, her voice now cold. "She would've told me. She's my daughter."

"She barely told me. It was after one of the first Singings ya made her go to. She saw that I wanted to take Linda home, and somehow ended up in Mordecai's buggy."

"I'm not going to listen to this." The woman's voice wavered.

Whoever they were talking about, she needed to listen. I could feel it.

"You should've seen her when she came to me in the barn that night asking me to get her other dress. Telling me not to say anything. I think she was afraid even then of what the bishop could do to our family. It's not right. It's not right at all. Mamm, ya need to stop this."

There were footsteps, and the door softly shut.

Time passed. People came in and left. My eyes felt too heavy to open.

And here they were back again talking in my room. The voices seemed slightly familiar now, but still, I wasn't sure.

"It's been days, Mose. When is she going to wake up?"

The room was quiet.

The woman tried again. "*Denki* for letting me ... us, when Johanna is better, stay with you until ..."

"Until what, Mamm?"

Could they argue somewhere else?

"Mose, in just over a week I've lost both my husband and the home where we raised our children. I was born in that house, and it had been in my family for generations." There was silence and then a little sob. "But never mind my home, now I could lose my daughter as well."

The chair squeaked.

"Mamm?" The son's voice had grown soft now.

"I'm sorry." The woman wailed her words. "What have I done wrong? It's too much for anyone to bear. That's what it is. I've lost everything."

"Not everything, Mamm."

"I wouldn't be able to speak with my daughter even if she were able."

"Why is that?"

"You know why."

"You would let the bishop get in the way of your relationship with your daughter, hurt as she is?"

"Mose, you know as well as I do, even before all this, I've never been a very *gut* ... I've never been able to ... You know what I'm saying."

"*Nee*, Mamm, I can't say that I do."

The two felt silent then, and I was glad. Their drama seemed too heavy a burden and my head hurt.

Bertram drove up behind Gideon's barn on Monday morning. Hilton had taken to the story right away, but they hadn't gotten very far on it. Still, Bertram felt like they could be really on to something, and he wanted to share it with both Gideon and Judah. When he opened the shop's door, he was surprised to see a stranger at the carpenter's bench.

"Can I help ya?"

"I'm looking for Gideon ... and also Judah. Are either of them here?"

"Judah was taken to the hospital after the fire, he's been there a few days now and Gideon's gone to check up on him this morning."

Fire? What fire? And what did it have to do with Judah?

Bertram rushed back to his car and then on to the hospital over twenty miles away. When he entered the hospital, he felt as if he was walking in slow motion. The man had said it'd been a few days since the accident, but Amish men and women still filled the small waiting room. As Bertram sought out an empty corner, he caught sight of Gideon making his way down a hallway.

He did his best not to push the Amish woman who blocked the way between him and his great uncle. Bertram looked at him over her shoulder and read what was in Gideon's eyes before he spoke. Bertram had to swallow and look away.

"He's in a bad way, Bertram." Gideon laid a hand on his shoulder and gently led him away from the others. "He took in a lot of smoke."

"How did the fire start?"

"Fires start, Bertram. And the Amish rebuild."

He opened his mouth to ask more questions but then Gideon stopped in front of a patient's room.

"He's in there. I need to get some air." Gideon gave him a nod and turned back down the hallway.

Nothing could have prepared Bertram for the sight of his friend hooked to a ventilator.

Quietly, he knelt on the floor beside the bed and prayed.

It didn't take long for Kelly's brother to review the contract for the purchase of the *Star*. Before she could talk herself out of it, Kelly signed the forms and overnighted them back to him so he could get the signed copies to the lawyers over at Walker Press.

Kelly thought she'd feel anxious and filled with fear after what she'd done, but she found herself a little relieved. When the paper hit her window this time instead of the door, she actually felt a little excited to dig through her nasturtiums to find it.

Shaking off the dirt and a few petals, she looked up to find Sam watching her.

"There's something different about you." He pointed his finger at her and squinted.

Kelly smoothed her messy hair. Had she put on makeup before her morning walk? She didn't even care. The surprises seemed endless living next door to a man as spontaneous as Sam, and he'd definitely seen her at her worst.

She gave a loud sigh and let her guard down for once. "Well, I did it."

"Did what?" Sam looked at her more intently now, maybe wondering if she'd dyed her hair a different color.

"You'll never guess, Sam. So, I'll go ahead and—"

"No, give me a chance on this one, Kel."

She sat down on her stoop and waited, holding the newspaper in her lap.

He spun around and pointed at her again. "You bought the *Star*."

"What? How did you ... who told you?"

"Well, Kelly, it would seem that some of us read our papers more quickly than others."

"It's in the paper?" Kelly opened the *Star* to see her news plastered over the front page. They had kept her name out of the story, thank goodness, but the fact that there was a story made it all seem so real. Her commitment was now public, and expectations would soon start rolling her way.

Kelly took a deep breath. "Well, at least they kept Dixie's name out of it." She smiled a little at Sam. "I don't think that the editor-in-chief knows my real name yet. I'm glad he decided to respect my privacy like I asked through their lawyer."

Sam sat down on the other side of the stoop. "I'm sorry if I got a little excited the other day when I ... you called the *Star*. I just knew it was something you *could* do and be great at."

"Thanks, Sam." She got a mental image of the young man face down at the gas station. "I just couldn't bear to see our town without a newspaper."

Sam winked. "And maybe a little had to do with Judah?"

"Maybe, but not all, Sam. And I think that's what's so good about it. I'm not doing it to rescue my son. There are a lot of other reasons."

Kelly stopped talking then, struck by the hugeness of how her life was about to change.

JOHANNA

Someone was in my room, and they took hold of my hand.

"I saw your cat, Miracle, today."

My cat?

"I went to the house, well, what remains of the house, to see what I could gather from the ruins before David clears it all to rebuild. Something happened to me there, Johanna, that's hard for me to explain. It's helped me to start thinking straight. And I don't want to just tell you about it. I want to read ya what I wrote about it in a small journal Mose gave me."

Her journal?

"But first, I want to tell you that I'm sorry." The woman gently caressed my hand. "So sorry."

A day later, Bertram felt a little disappointed that his friend didn't look any better. After arriving, he'd gotten out his New Testament and read Judah a few chapters before praying again. As he prayed, the door opened, but Bertram kept his eyes closed and head bowed until a nurse asked him to move so she could switch out Judah's IV bag.

The ID around her neck said her name was Alfreda. Bertram stood and asked if he could help. She shook her head.

"We're just working on his lungs, sugar."

Bertram nodded.

"You're not Amish, are you?" She looked him over from head to foot.

"No, ma'am." He realized the nurse probably assumed Judah was Amish, like the rest of Willow Brook. "I'm just a friend."

"Well, it looks like your friend could use a little good news about now. I hope you have some for him." She busied herself checking Judah's pulse and temperature. "He deserves to hear something good after what he did for that girl next door."

"Girl?" He'd only seen Gideon for a few minutes yesterday. Apparently, he'd left out some details.

"The other Amish that was injured. She's not come to yet, but doctors are saying any day now."

"Was she in the fire too?"

"Wow. You need to read a newspaper or something." The nurse shook her head and chuckled at her own joke.

Bertram hadn't read a paper in a while. It's like the world had stopped for him and Judah for now.

The vinyl chair squeaked as he sat down.

"Look, this is probably none of my business, and I know it breaks all kinds of privacy rules for me to talk about it, but I think the young Amish woman over there doesn't want to wake up from her coma."

"Doesn't want to?"

The nurse gave him a knowing look and pursed her lips. "Just because I try to be invisible when people are visiting my patients doesn't mean I'm not listening. I think if I were her, I wouldn't want to wake up either, not with what she's got coming."

"What ... what exactly is that?" Bertram tried to play it cool but knew he was failing big time.

The nurse didn't seem to notice. "She was supposed to be married last week."

Bertram slowly nodded. Judah had mentioned that.

"Her fiancé has been in several times trying to get her to wake up. One time I had to stop him." She gave a small grunt and bent to smooth a wrinkle on Judah's blanket. "Nobody's rough with my patients." Slowly, she shook her head. "I would never marry a man like that."

Bertram shook his head too.

The nurse started pulling away her cart.

"So ... so why do you think any of that has to do with Judah?" Bertram knew he was speaking too fast. He had to play it cool. Trying to appear casual, he stood and leaned one hand on the wall.

"Ah, Judah here." Her smile brought warmth from her eyes. "I've got him pegged as her knight in shining armor. Do you know he saved her from dying in that fire?"

Bertram hadn't heard that either. He looked over at his friend whose skin had taken on a dusky gray color.

"I think that somebody besides me ought to tell her who's in the room next to her. And that's all I'm going to say." Alfreda left then, and the door clicked shut behind her.

A few minutes later, Gideon arrived and told him the whole story. The parts he knew, anyway. How the fire started and why Johanna ran inside the burning *Dawdi Haus* remained unclear.

"Her cousin Ben said that he saw someone go in after Johanna even before Judah arrived. That person came out without Johanna and slunk into the woods."

"What are the Amish going to do about that?"

"We're pacifists, Bertram. God is judge. Not us."

"But what about the bishop? Is he at least asking some questions? If that person started the fire, they could start others."

"I have a feeling that the Yoder home was a one-time thing."

Bertram had more questions, but he could tell by the look on Gideon's face that he was done talking, at least for now. He'd have to do a little investigating on his own.

And soon, he had to pay a visit next door.

JOHANNA

The woman's voice shook as she read, but I didn't care. She reminded me of someone, and I liked listening to her. I could tell she was being careful not to read in front of anyone else but me. When the nurse came, she would stop and when the nurse left, she would start again.

The door had just clicked shut from the nurse's latest visit. The woman cleared her throat and began where she had left off.

"Just before dawn, I quietly left Mose's house. I'd had another sleepless night and didn't see the sense in taking up space at his breakfast table. They had barely enough room for themselves. Besides, Mose was always looking at me with those 'knowing' eyes of his. He'd had them since he was a boy. And he'd been his sister's advocate forever.

"I let my feet take me along the worn path from Mose's home to where my house once stood. I could see the rubble of it in the distance. Thin lines of smoke still rose up out of the ash. Mose had told me that the men of the community were already planning on helping my sons rebuild. Since the house was to go to David, he had been heading up the efforts to get a rebuilding plan started. A *Dawdi Haus* addition would be my new home. Me and Johanna would live there if Johanna …"

The woman fell silent for a minute. And then she went on.

"As I came up to what had been my home, I made my way through the burnt wood, avoiding the parts that were still smoking. Little by little, I figured out where the rooms of the house had been. With a sad heart, I said goodbye to where I had spent most of my life.

"Poking my way through what had been our kitchen, I was so glad to see our old cast iron cookstove still standing under smoking beams. From what I could see, it looked okay, except for some charring that I might be able to clean off with a little elbow grease. Digging through the still-warm ashes, I found a few more treasures. My Mamm's glass pie plate glinted in the sun after just a bit of rubbing with the edge of my cape dress.

"And I found Jakob's slate.

"I held the pie plate and slate close to my chest and slowly raised my head to the sky. And I thanked *Gott*."

The woman stopped again, and I waited with her to get through the emotion.

"It's no secret that I hadn't been 'walking close to *Gott*' for a good time now. My mother would tell me that right to my face if she were alive. Right about now, she would chasten me for following my own will instead of seeking out *Gott's* plan.

"Looking out across our land, I found a few more things to be grateful for. The barn had been untouched by the fire. The silos were full, and I could hear the gentle bawl of the young calves in their small, white hutches. Their bellies still full of the milk replacer that David and his boys fed them before dawn.

"Heading into the barn, I was met by Johanna's cat, Miracle. She looked hungry, so after patting her, I pulled the heavy lid off of the barrel where Johanna kept the cat food and filled her bowl. Although the creek ran full nearby, I also found a small saucer and filled it from the water pump. Miracle seemed grateful for both.

"I was about to turn back to what was left of my house when I heard soft mews somewhere in the rafters above me. Miracle heard it too and swiftly padded her way to the source of the sound. Amazed at how quickly she'd found the kittens, I realized they were hers.

"I walked up the wooden steps to the second floor of the barn and searched for the place Miracle had chosen to hide her brood from the danger of the tomcats and other animals that might want to hurt them.

"Kneeling by a good-sized hole in the barn floor, I could see the cat's hiding place in a small, squared-out space in one of the rafters. The spot was cozy with little piles of fallen straw, but I noticed that Miracle's eyes weren't at rest. I followed her gaze to one of the smaller kittens, maybe the runt of the litter, who seemed to have wandered off. The kitten was missing its chance to squeeze in next to its brothers and sisters and find its teat.

"Trying to balance on wobbly legs, the kitten mewed softly from her precarious perch. Miracle's body was taut and, even though she was nursing, I had the feeling that if the kitten moved any closer to the edge of the rafter, she would do whatever it took to snatch her baby before it moved to the point of no return. Even if it meant her own death.

"That's when I had an idea. Flattening my body out on the dirty floor, I reached my arm into the hole and carefully felt for the kitten. A small bit of warm fluff filled my hand and, resisting the urge to bring the kitten toward myself, I gently lifted it toward its mother. Bringing my arm back through the hole, I peeked through just in time to see Miracle guide the kitten in to feed. The mother cat rested then, and her eyes closed.

"Miracle was a wonderful mother, as I figured she would be. I watched long enough to see some of the other kittens finish nursing and get licked cleaned from top to bottom. Not one of her kittens was left to fend for itself. Miracle cared for each equally."

The woman gave a small, nervous laugh then and took my hand again. "I wish I could say the same for myself. I guess that's why I chose to write my story down. Part of me wanted to show ya that come what may with the bishop, you are more important to me than whatever happens to us."

The woman seemed so sad, and I longed to reach out and comfort her.

"Please wake up, Johanna."

Kelly walked straight past the *Star*'s building and went up and down Main Street three or four times before building up the courage to go in. Her meeting with Hughes started in just a few minutes, and she probably couldn't afford to pass the building another time—although she wanted to.

She could do this. It was just like meeting a client, she told herself. Hold your head up high. Shoulders straight. Shake hands with a firm grip, but not too firm.

Lord, please calm my nerves.

She swallowed and willed her feet to enter. Hilton had told her that his top reporters were still on assignment, and she was fairly certain there wasn't a chance she would run into Judah. So seeing her son wasn't her concern. This just seemed like such a big career move for her, the biggest since before Judah was born.

But she'd felt God leading her this way.

The girl at the reception desk must have been the same one who answered the phone for her a few weeks ago. She had the dull look Kelly had envisioned over the phone and barely looked up when Kelly entered. With a crack of her gum, she motioned to a lone chair set against the wall.

The waiting area smelled musty, and there were sun-bleached stacks of newspapers lining the wall under the windows—not a very inviting experience for possible advertisers. Kelly took out her notepad and starting writing down changes, including evaluating the staff. She needed enthusiastic, energetic people to turn this paper around.

Hilton Hughes came out then and shook her hand.

"Ms. Divine, I'm so glad to see you. Please, come this way."

He led her back to his office and began to tell her the story of the paper along with its rise and fall over the past few years. Although Walker Press had mismanaged itself, Hughes admitted that the *Star* could have done better with what it had.

After listening to him talk for a little while, she decided she needed to level with him about who she really was.

"I appreciate your honesty, Mr. Hughes."

"Hilton, please."

"Hilton. But now I need to be honest with you. My name isn't Dixie Divine."

He cracked a smile and let out a sigh. "Well, that's good to know, because I didn't know how I was going to announce you to the staff with a straight face." He sat forward at his desk and his smile faded. "What about the papers you signed?"

"I had my lawyer use my real name on the actual documents that you didn't get to see. I stayed quiet about my name because"—Kelly stifled a sigh—"I'm Judah Barton's mother."

Hilton sat back in his chair as Kelly told him her whole story—everything including losing her husband and Judah moving out. After that, she felt fairly certain Hilton understood why she avoided using her real name and why, at least for the time being, she wanted to keep it quiet. At least until Judah was off assignment and back in the office and after she had a chance to tell him what she had done.

Then, Hilton took some time to get Kelly up to speed on how things were going with the paper. He had a few spreadsheets that clearly mapped out the last five years for her.

Kelly's jaw almost dropped at the significant jump that happened just two years ago. "What's that spike in subscriptions?"

"That's when Ima started writing for the paper and that"—he pointed his pen at the most recent downward dip—"is when she stopped." He pointed to the second spreadsheet. "And the readers aren't the half of it. Advertisers were behind this as well. When they saw that subscriptions were up, they came in droves. Many got personally attached to Ima's writing too. Harper, Inc. was one of them."

Kelly really couldn't believe one writer could make that much of a difference. But the charts didn't lie.

"Why did she stop?"

"That's just the thing." Hilton shook his head. "I've never really met her. Our communication was always through the mail and handwritten."

"You mean her stories were handwritten?"

"Yep. I had one of our writers transcribe them, and then we would pretty much print them 'as is.' She never needed much editing."

"Wow. That was some risk you took on Ima, to allow her to write for the paper before really knowing who she was." Kelly didn't mean to be condescending, but there it was.

"It was a risk, I know." Hilton's shoulders slumped a little. "But I thought it was one worth taking. Just look at where we were before I found her."

Kelly agreed that the *Star* had been in a tight spot like they were in now.

"I think it was a good decision you made to make it more attractive for Ima to write for the paper again."

Hilton looked up. "You do?"

"It's perfect. If this Ima is local and if she's got the writing experience we think she has, it would be hard for her to turn down an offer like that."

"Sounds like you've changed your mind on taking risks." Hilton smiled.

Kelly smiled back. They agreed she would work from home to help keep her identity hidden until she had a chance to tell her son in person.

As she walked back down Main Street, she felt pretty good about their first meeting.

CHAPTER 28

JOHANNA

Things had begun to clear in my head. Although some sketchy spots remained in my memory about the fire, I knew who I was now and that was a comfort.

The touch of skin on my hand now felt strangely familiar. Who was it?

The person gave my hand a nervous pat, a gentle rub, and then started to sing.

I had forgotten the song, but from somewhere deep inside, I started to remember. Mammi Miriam had taught me the song. The one that had gotten me into so much trouble that day Mamm heard me sing it.

A chair screeched across the floor, and both the song and the touch stopped. I was alone again.

Gott, help.

Opening my eyes was the last thing I wanted to do. So, I wouldn't. Not yet. I'd lost everything in that fire. My home. And everything that reminded me of Mammi and brought me comfort. I'd also lost the hope of finding her journal so all my questions could be answered.

I needed answers now more than ever. Especially after what Judah told me at the rock.

I didn't know why the journal wasn't in that drawer. I had been so sure. Thinking about it now made my head hurt. All I wanted to do was sleep.

FORBIDDEN GIFT

Two Amish men were arguing in Johanna's room when Bertram finally got up the courage to visit her. One, he recognized as Gideon's bishop. The other was younger with a lazy eye. The look he gave Bertram with his good eye seemed anything but friendly.

"Um, I'll come back later." Bertram pushed his glasses up his nose and headed back across the hall.

Hours later, the rhythmic sound of the heart monitor and continual hiss of the oxygen machine felt strangely soothing. Before he knew it, he'd fallen asleep in the vinyl chair next to the bed.

He awoke to the sound of Alfreda making her rounds. Bertram didn't want to disturb her, plus he felt strangely guilty about not carrying out the mission she had for him yet, so he kept his eyes shut.

After what seemed like forever, Alfreda left the room and Bertram got up and stretched his legs.

How am I going to do this, Lord?

As he moved around the room, trying to become more alert, he noticed a piece of white paper sticking out from under Judah's fingers. Carefully, Bertram picked up Judah's heavy and unresponsive hand. Choking back his emotion, he lifted out the note.

The princess is alone. Tell her that the prince needs to hear her voice.

Bertram rolled his eyes. Alfreda was such a romantic.

Still, he had to try. He knew that. Folding the note and putting it in his pocket, he told Judah he would see him later, but for now, he had a job to do.

Bertram tried and failed to play the part of a super sleuth as he pulled up his collar and put on his dark prescription shades on his way across the hallway to Johanna's room.

Inside was more of the same that he saw in Judah's room minus the ventilator.

Why did all hospitals have to smell this way?

He felt a little embarrassed as he walked up to Johanna's bedside. He'd never met her formally. He stuck his hands in his pants' pockets and felt Alfreda's note. A fresh wave of courage rolled over him.

"Uh, hello, Miss Righter, or ... ah, Miss Yoder."

JOHANNA

I was drowning. The water was deep, and the shock of the cold numbed my body. My thoughts slowed, but I didn't feel afraid. I was stuck. So stuck. I reached upward to where I saw the sun shining. My hand hung in the air for just a moment, but there was nothing to hold on to.

Then his arm around my waist pulled me. He was always pulling me out of things. I had suffered from so much loss and sank, alone, in it.

I didn't know how much more of this I could take. I could stay asleep forever. If I were dead, there would be no more pain.

... but those who hope in the LORD will renew their strength.

My skin grew warm and tingled all the way to my toes. I felt the softness of the blanket. Smelled the antiseptic of the room.

Someone was speaking.

"And so, I just wanted to tell you, in case you really do hear me, that Judah is in really rough shape in the room next door."

Judah?

"He was the one who pulled you out of the fire."

Fire? No, it was water. He had pulled me out of the water.

"And while he was in the house looking for you, he took in a lot of smoke. They've got him hooked up to a lot of machines—cleaning his lungs, the nurse says. And maybe, when you're feeling better, you could go over to Judah's room and visit him. Judah's nurse seems to think that he's waiting to hear from you."

Me?

"And that's about it. Except that maybe I could pray for you."

And then he spoke the sweetest prayer I'd ever heard. How could he talk so easily to *Gott* like that? Like a friend really, but more. The man's faith reminded me of Mammi. After a prayer like that, how could I wish myself dead?

The door clicked when the man left, and after a few minutes, it opened again. The chair scraped against the floor and my mother's familiar voice began to fill the room.

"I know I haven't given ya much to live for in the last couple of weeks. If I'm honest with myself, most of your young life."

Mamm's voice sounded different today. Softer.

"And burdening you with the responsibility of this marriage doesn't help any." Mamm took a deep breath. "Johanna, you need to know that I've changed my mind about the whole thing. Mose is right—you shouldn't marry Mordecai. Your father wouldn't have wanted it. And I ... I don't want it either."

The song came again then. Clear and sweet, Mamm belted out my grandmother's song like her life depended on it.

I opened my eyes then. Things remained a little fuzzy but I felt thankful to *Gott* for the sight in front of me.

Mamm had her eyes shut as she sang and tears streamed

down her cheeks. The strings of her prayer *Kapp* grew damp. I couldn't help but smile at the picture, though.

My mother loved me. And come what may, that was enough for me.

Mamm helped me through the rest of my recovery, even staying in the hospital room with me each night so I wouldn't have to be alone. Soon, the nurses' visits finally slowed, and there was talk of me going home. I knew it was time. A few days later, when Mamm stepped out to get some air, I grabbed my IV pole and slowly wheeled it over to Judah's room.

I closed the door softly behind me and walked toward his bed. I felt embarrassed at first. Here I was in a hospital gown without my cape dress and alone with a man. But Judah had his eyes closed. And from the looks of him, I didn't think he was going to open them anytime soon.

Oh, Gott.

I watched as the ventilator helped him with every breath. Flashbacks of water and then fire played in my mind as I kept my eyes on the machine, the tubes, and the rise and fall of Judah's chest.

While I sat there watching him, I felt a shift take place in my heart. Something rumbled inside of me like the sound of furniture being moved across the hardwood as if I was getting swept clean and rearranged. A feeling of love came then, unexpected and sweet. I let myself forget, if just for this visit, Mordecai and all of my promises.

I started to speak, really speak, as a friend and maybe a little more to this man who had done so much for me.

Maybe somehow, he could still hear me.

I had heard people when I wanted to in my coma. Some I had shut out, but others had held my attention. And as far as I knew, Judah wasn't in a coma. The doctors just had him on medication while the machine helped heal his respiratory system.

With the change that had taken place in my relationship with my mother and all that I had been through in the fire, I felt ready to let him know more about who I was. He could decide for himself how he felt about me.

When I'd entered the room, I had no idea what I was going to say. Now I had so much. The words bubbled up even before I opened my mouth.

I sat up straighter in my chair. Feeling just a little bit taller, I began.

"Judah, it's me, Johanna. I'm here in your hospital room."

I looked him over closely, searching for even a slight twitch of a finger, but I couldn't see anything. I decided to plow forward regardless of his response.

"So, I'm feeling better, and I wanted to come over to tell ya that. I've been in the hospital for over a week and ..."

I told him everything, probably a little more than he needed to know. But finally, I finished. Emotionally and physically drained, I had just enough energy to cap off my words with something I hoped would impact Judah as much as it had me.

I sang Mammi's song.

As the final note still hung in the air, Alfreda came into the room to check Judah's vitals. Smiling, she took to humming my melody as I prepared to leave.

"That should do it, miss."

I looked at her. "Do what?"

"Bring what his soul was longing for."

"Oh, well, I hope it will. I did my best."

"And it was all he needed."

As I left the room, Alfreda gave me a wink. I locked eyes with her and smiled.

CHAPTER 29

Bertram entered Judah's hospital room early and was surprised to see Gideon already sitting in the chair next to the bed.

He smiled broadly, glad to have his great uncle in the room. Judah's coloring looked a little better today, and Gideon filled him in on the latest news from the doctor. Soon, they would ease him off his medication and the mechanical ventilation machine so he could begin breathing again on his own.

"Glad to hear it, Uncle. Thank you." Bertram grabbed a tissue from the small table next to Gideon's chair. Good news had been hard to come by these days. The search for information on Amos Zook had been difficult as well and had weighed heavily on his shoulders. He and Hilton needed a breakthrough, something that told them they were on the right path, but the pieces just weren't coming together.

Together, he and Gideon sat for a few minutes just listening to the rhythmic beats of the ventilator.

"We're bringing home Johanna today."

More good news. Bertram felt glad for that, but immediately pictured the Zooks arguing in her room a few days ago. Her future concerned him, and he could do little to help.

Bertram started to pace.

"You know, Bertram. I told Judah I would be willing to help wherever I can when it comes to Johanna's future. He's told me what he's after."

Bertram stopped pacing. He hadn't expected this. Willow Brook was a tight-knit community. Sharing inside information with "English" like himself was not a common thing. Maybe this was the help he and Hilton were looking for.

He took the opportunity to share with his great uncle where they were with their suspicions regarding Amos Zook. From the look on Gideon's face, Bertram could tell he was only a little surprised.

He held his hand over his forehead for a few moments as he took in the information. "If what you say is true, it would answer so many of my questions about our bishop." Gideon looked up. "What do you need?"

"Is there anything, anything at all that you've seen or heard that would let us know we're headed in the right direction?"

While Gideon sat thinking, Bertram paced some more. Only this time, he put his thoughts to action and started praying. God knew where all this was headed. He could help Gideon remember something, anything, that would let them know how this search should continue.

Gideon sat in his chair for a good long time with his eyes shut. Bertram thought maybe he had fallen asleep when the name "Ernst" passed through his lips.

A thrill ran through Bertram's heart. Nora had mentioned an "Ernst." A brother to Matthias Fisher.

"Did you say 'Ernst'?"

"Yes. As our bishop has aged, he's been known to nod off at times at church meetings. A few summers ago, the minister's sermon had ended and the room was clearing.

For some reason I was still there when the bishop started to stir. I think he was still asleep, but he looked right at me and called me 'Ernst.' His voice had changed as well—sounded more like an *Englischer* than Amish to me. I didn't know what to make of it, at first. The bishop, well, he doesn't speak much to me. After he came to, he scowled at me and brushed off the event like it'd never happened."

Gideon shifted in his chair. "Normally, I wouldn't think much of something like that. Except there is no Ernst among the People. And even if there was one in another district, why would the bishop, in his sleep, talk about someone he barely knew? I have to think that this Ernst meant a lot to our bishop at some point in his life and that's why he repeats his name in his sleep. I tried to talk about it to his wife, once. She didn't say much, but seemed to know exactly what I was talking about."

An Amish woman knocked softly on the door then letting them know the nurse was ready to wheel Johanna to the waiting van.

Gideon stood quickly and had almost made it out the door when he turned back to give another long look at Judah.

"I hope that helps."

Bertram smiled. "It just may be the piece we were looking for."

JOHANNA

As I left the hospital with Mamm and our driver, I realized nothing had really changed regarding my circumstances. I was still engaged to the bishop's grandson. My house had still burned down. My father was still dead.

But I had Mamm now, and that meant a lot. And the bishop had allowed my family to talk freely with me again because of the upcoming kneeling confession and wedding. I reached out and squeezed Mamm's hand as we rode in the van. Her eyes looked sad when they met mine.

She didn't want me to marry Mordecai anymore. Earlier, she had told me that come what may with the bishop, I was free to marry who I wanted.

But there was something deep inside of me that couldn't let it all go. I remembered my declaration before *Gott* out there on the rock that day. No matter if Mamm had lifted her request that I marry Mordecai, I had agreed to it. And so, the wedding was still on.

As we settled into my brother's house back in Willow Brook, Mordecai drove up in his buggy. He'd brought his whole pale-faced brood over with him. They waited in his large buggy while he came into the house to speak with Mose and Mamm, not bothering to address me personally. He shared our new wedding date.

Both Mose and Mamm started to protest at his demand for such an early date while I was still recovering, but I found myself putting up my hand.

They stared at me until I spoke.

"I will marry ya this coming Tuesday, Mordecai."

Mordecai nodded, spun on his heel, and headed for the door causing Mamm and me to rush to the porch to politely wave goodbye.

As he rode off, I noticed I hadn't heard a peep from his six children the entire time.

Things remained quiet between Mamm and me for the rest of the week, and I caught her watching me a lot. She and I shared the bedroom that belonged to Mose's boys, while they slept on mats in the living room. One night, I was lying next to her on the double bed while my thoughts ran rampant through my mind.

"Daughter, this is all my fault."

"Mamm, what's done is done."

"But it's not done, not yet. You don't have to do this."

"If I don't, who knows what will happen to our family. Nothing *gut*, I imagine."

"Then let it happen." Mamm rolled over on her side to face me. I could feel her warm breath on my face.

"I can't. I agreed to this."

"Mordecai can find another wife."

"I'm not doing this for Mordecai."

Mamm grew silent then. Although she crossed her arms over her chest, I could feel her resolve lessening.

"Besides, Mamm, with our house gone, there is no room, no place for me now. David will rebuild, but I don't want to spend my days living in a *Dawdi Haus*. It seems that marrying Mordecai is the solution that *Gott* has provided for us all."

Mamm rolled away from me then and faced the wall.

"*Gut Nacht*, Mamm." I sighed and prayed for sleep to come quickly.

"How's it going, Chief?"

Hilton cringed and let out a low growl. Bertram couldn't blame him, really. The search had been tough on both of them. He set two Americanos, no cream or sugar, on Hilton's desk. His boss took one and sipped.

"Finding information on this has been harder than I thought it would be." Hilton stared at his computer and drank the coffee until it was half gone. "Being a newspaper editor, I figured it would be easy to find information on a guy in the 1970s, but your source had been right. Someone covered his trail well, and here we are, over two weeks into the search with nothing to show for it. It was good thing your uncle gave us that information. Without that ..."

Bertram sat down next to his boss and stared with him at the blank computer screen.

"You've got nothing."

Bertram almost felt the need to duck, but then Hilton gained some control. His boss had been doing better, Bertram thought. He'd joined a recovery group that met at Bertram's church. Hilton told him the people there were teaching him a lot about letting go. Bertram was glad he had some good news to share.

"We have a lead on a picture. Well, kind of."

His boss spun to face him. "A what?"

"Nora texted me this morning. She said that late last night she remembered seeing a picture of the Fisher brothers in an old box of newspapers in the library attic. She said the brothers weren't the subject of the photo, so she figures that's why it was overlooked and printed."

Hilton pushed his office chair away from the desk. "How long ago did she see it?"

"Well, that's the tricky part."

"How long ago, Bert?"

"Five or six years, she says." Bertram left Hilton's office and headed to his cube to grab his stuff.

He peeked over the side of the cube wall as Hilton came out of his office. "But she said that no one ever goes up there, so it all should be intact. And she gave me the key."

Bertram let the key sway side to side on its chain in front of Hilton, who grabbed it.

"Well, searching the internet has gotten us nowhere. I'm up for searching through some old newspapers."

Bertram had to rush to keep up with his boss.

Nora wasn't kidding when she'd said no one had been up in the library's attic for a while. The air was thick with the smell of old newspapers and black mold. Bertram used the flathead screwdriver in his pocketknife to crack open a few windows that had been painted shut.

The cool, fresh air helped make the search bearable, and they divided up the roomful of boxes into manageable sections.

"Do you have that picture of the bishop that Judah sent us? You'll need it to compare to anything you find."

Hilton nodded and they each set out to search.

Over an hour later, Bertram had about enough of the stale air and musty newspapers when Hilton gave a shout from the other end of the room.

"Well, I'll be a—" Bertram gave Hilton a look that made his face flush. He shrugged. "Some habits are hard to break, Bert. Check this out. I think we may have a full house here."

The story was dated November 17, 1970, and was about a bar that had just opened in the area. Some churches had expressed discontent about the addition, saying the establishment would add to the corruption of their town. But it looked like the mayor supported the new business as much as he did the local nightlife. The front-page story included an interview with the mayor as well as several local pastors. Bertram tried not to give his "so what" look to Hilton who seemed excited about the piece. Nowhere did the article mention the mayor's brother, though. He looked up at Hilton and offered a half smile.

Hilton motioned for Bertram to flip through some more pages. "Keep reading."

Bertram used his sleeve to dust off an old card catalog and laid the paper out flat. Hilton stood to peer over his shoulder. Flipping through articles on local effects of the oil crisis and neighborhood factory strikes, he found a center photo spread of opening night at the bar. There were plenty of pictures of people in flamboyant clothing typical of the early 70s, flashing peace signs and holding up bottles of beer.

Bertram thought about the pastors and wondered what they'd thought of the spread. Crime had increased in Riverview in the seventies. Nora had told him that. A corrupt mayor and a community that moved away from its morals would do that to a place, he figured.

He looked at each picture until a large one in the corner caught his eye. The focal point of the image was the owner of the bar, Bill Downy, as he poured a shot of dark liquid for someone who, from the dazed look on his face, seemed like he had already had one too many. In the background, the mayor smiled as he stood side-by-side with someone who looked a lot like a younger version of Willow Brook's bishop.

Bertram used the magnifier app on his cell phone to see the image better. He looked up at Hilton.

"You think this is Bishop Zook?"

Hilton already had his phone out and had pulled up the image Judah had sent.

The man in the newspaper certainly looked like the bishop. Besides being older, the man hadn't changed much. Bertram began to feel like Nora's help was worth all the coffee and scones money could buy.

Bertram took the paper and descended to the library's main level to show Nora.

"You nailed it!" Nora surprised Bertram by offering him a fist pump, but he pumped back and smiled widely.

"Now we just have to find out if Zook, or I mean Fisher, really had a criminal record."

"Oh, let me take care of that one. I know a couple of the guys over at the station." Nora checked her watch and grabbed her coat. "I've got a break coming up."

Bertram's heart raced at the possibilities. He had to let Judah know what was going on.

JUDAH

"There you go, honey. How does that feel?"

It hurt to breathe, that's how it felt. And now that I was awake and breathing on my own, I got to enjoy all the discomfort that went along with it. I let my breath out slowly and thought of how I had been able to get Johanna out of that fire and decided to stop complaining.

I knew I would do it again if I had to.

Bertram had been by yesterday to tell me that Johanna had been released to go home. It had been touch and go with her as well, he'd said. He'd made sure to add that it seemed like *someone* wanted us both here on earth for a little while longer.

I'd rolled my eyes at that but kept my opinion to myself. Let Bertram believe what he wanted to believe about God. I was done trying to get in the way of other people's faith.

I'd spent way too much time doing that, Mom would be sure to say.

Mom.

Where was she anyway? Hadn't anyone called her? Things were rough between us, but I didn't think they were that rough. She normally would have been the first one here. I cradled my head in my hands and willed myself to take it slow.

When Bertram entered the room with Hilton at his side, I thought about asking if she had been by, but decided not to. If she didn't want to come, that was her business. I was surprised how much her absence hurt, though. Quickly, I pushed the feeling away.

Whatever.

Bertram smiled when he saw I was breathing on my own. I smiled too and let out a few coughs.

"It's good to see you awake." Bertram smiled again.

"Thanks, I appreciate the two of you coming by."

"Coming by?" Hilton jabbed a thumb in Bertram's direction. "This one here has practically lived here all this time."

Bertram stuck his hands in his pockets and looked at the floor.

"Wow." I gave a little cough to cover a strange stir of emotion.

Hilton had a gleam in his eye. "When can you get out?"

"I think they said I would go home midweek."

Hilton was shaking his head. "Has to be sooner than that. And you can't go home. Not yet."

I laid my head back on the pillow. What did he have planned now? I looked to Bertram for some clarification.

"It's a little complicated, Judah." Bertram talked softly now trying to create the calm before the storm, I gathered. "We—"

"We found some evidence that can indict Willow Brook's bishop," Hilton said.

"What? I mean, I know he cheated his way into being bishop. Gideon told me that, but that's not enough to send him to jail."

Hilton's eyes grew large. "Oh, he's done way more than that."

The two of them spent the next half hour filling me in on what they had discovered at the library and what someone named Nora might get at the police station. I had a hard time believing what they said, but if they were right, things over at Willow Brook were about to explode.

Johanna's whole life would turn around.

"This could really shake things up over there." My heart rate starting picking up, which we could all hear through the monitor by the bed.

Bert paced the room. There was something he wasn't saying.

"We don't have a lot of time, do we, Bert?"

"I spoke with Gideon recently, Judah. He told me that Johanna is moving forward with the wedding this coming Tuesday."

"In two days?"

"Yep. He said he tried to talk Johanna out of it. So have a lot of people, including her mother."

"He'll end up killing her, doesn't she know that?" I pulled the buzzer for the nurse. I needed out of here.

"That's just it, I guess. Gideon says she knows, but she's told God she'd do it and is determined to keep her word."

I began stripping the medical tape off my IV. "She's crazy. It's crazy. God wouldn't want her to marry a man like that."

"Whoa, Judah." Hilton had his hand on my shoulder. "We want you to get out of here as much as you do, but I don't think that—"

"What's going on in here?" Alfreda entered, and she didn't look happy.

"I have to go now. I'm ready." I tried to sit up and look healthy while Alfreda gave me a once-over.

"That's for the doctor to decide. He'll be here in the morning."

"I can't wait—" I jumped from the bed and the room began to spin.

It was Bertram this time who got me to sit back down. "Judah, we have a little time. The wedding isn't until Tuesday."

"Wedding? What wedding?" Alfreda was busy taping my IV back into place. Weren't nurses supposed to be seen and not heard, or something like that?

Bertram apparently hadn't heard that. "Johanna is marrying a potentially abusive man on Tuesday."

Alfreda looked from Bertram to me and back to Bertram again. "But she's in love with him." Alfreda pointed a thick finger at me.

I did not see that coming.

"In love? With *me*?"

"Mmmhmmm." Alfreda finished tucking a warm blanket in around me as if she hadn't just dropped the biggest bomb.

Bertram shook his head. "Um, okay. Alfreda, was there another patient you needed to see?"

She looked at her watch. "Sure do. We'll see you boys later." Before leaving the room, she looked over at Bertram. "And don't think I don't know that you're trying to get rid of me." She jutted her chin at me. "He needs to know the truth about that sweet girl. That's all I'm saying."

Kelly let the phone slide into her lap. What in the world? Her son had been in the hospital for over two weeks, and no one had notified her?

She'd given the editor of the *Mountain Laurel Star* a good piece of her mind before she hung up. He'd said that something big was going on, and he couldn't blow Judah's cover. The hospital, he said, had Judah pegged as an Amish man belonging to the Willow Brook community since that's where he'd been working undercover.

Kelly pressed her fingers to her temples. Why would he run into a burning building?

She hated having such limited information. Hilton just said her boy was recovering, would be let out of the hospital soon, and brought back to the community.

The community? Why not bring him home?

She'd almost said it over the phone but didn't. Judah probably wouldn't like coming home like that. He would feel weak and vulnerable. And Kelly knew herself. She would brood over him like a mother hen, which probably wasn't the best way to heal their broken relationship. As soon as he got on his feet, he would be out the door, filled with even more resentment.

So, after letting loose on Hilton at the beginning of their conversation, Kelly fell quiet and let him share with her all he knew.

Never before had she felt so empty. She was done with this feud. Her son needed her whether he knew it or not. She walked into his old room and fell to her knees at her usual spot by his bed. She laid her hand on his pillow.

Oh God, please.

JUDAH

The doctor who visited me the next morning was either a little too young for his own good or just needed to empty out a few beds. Regardless, getting released seemed way easier than I thought it would be. With a list of instructions on my care and a bottle of painkillers in hand, I headed back to Gideon's.

FORBIDDEN GIFT

A Mennonite driver had been sent for me since Bertram and Hilton were still wrapping things up at the paper. Bertram texted yesterday to tell me a huge story was in the works.

Hilton wanted me to be the one to share with Johanna what they had discovered. With the bishop out of the way, I'm sure my boss had hopes that somehow Johanna would write for the *Star* again, whether she stayed in the community or not. He and Bert were ready to involve law enforcement as well.

And besides all that, I had a wedding to stop.

When the driver dropped me off at the carpentry shop, I got out of the car slowly. Leaving the hospital as early as I did maybe would prove not to be such a good idea, but I could think of no other way. Johanna couldn't marry Mordecai. That was plain to me. Why it wasn't for her, I didn't understand.

The shop door's bells announced my arrival, and Gideon looked up from the work he'd been doing and smiled.

"Hullo. Aren't ya a sight for sore eyes."

"Thanks. It feels good to be out. Is it okay if I hang around here for a few more days?" I started to cough then and Gideon grabbed me a glass of water.

"You stay as long as you'd like, just take *gut* care of yourself." He looked a little worried about all my coughing and offered me a chair.

I waved him away. "I'm okay. I am a little tired, though. I think I'll go take a little nap."

I thought about telling Gideon what Bertram and Hilton had discovered, but then decided I wanted Johanna to hear it first, and I wanted her to hear it from me—not from the Amish grapevine.

But before I slept, I needed Gideon to do me a favor.

Peaches cocked her head to one side as Kelly reached for her keys after breakfast.

"Yeah, I know, girl, I don't get it either."

She'd been pacing all morning, wondering what to do. Her head told her to stay, but her heart said go. So she'd decided to go.

In her car, she connected to her worship playlist and let the music soothe her while she raced to the hospital. She had to wait as a silver twelve-passenger van pulled out before pulling into the parking lot. The Mennonite driver offered her a friendly wave. Her stomach jerked as she wondered if Judah was in that van. She knew the Amish paid Mennonites to taxi them here and there. She pushed the thought aside. Probably just visitors, she reasoned. Besides, she shook her head, the son she knew wouldn't be caught dead in a van like that.

Kelly breathed a sigh of relief when the senior volunteer at the front desk checked her clipboard and gave her Judah's room number. Quickly she strode down the hallway. Her hands were too sweaty to turn the knob, so she gave a gentle knock. A woman's voice inside told her to enter.

Once inside, Kelly's hopes tanked. The bed stood empty and a nurse gathered up tubes and equipment.

"Can I help you find someone?"

"I was just looking for Judah Barton." Kelly's words stuck in her throat. "I guess I'm too late to catch him. I'm … I'm his mother. The woman at the front told me he was still here."

The nurse scanned her from head to toe. "You don't look like an Amish man's mother." Her tone sounded sharp, but there was warmth in her eyes. Kelly smiled and started to explain but then thought better of it. She didn't want to blow Judah's cover.

"It ... it's a little complicated."

The nurse didn't give her the look Kelly felt she deserved. Instead, she offered her a seat. The hospital room's vinyl chair squeaked when Kelly sat. She opened her mouth to try to explain, but nothing came out. What was she supposed to say to this woman? A question made its way to her brain.

"Was he doing okay? When he left, I mean."

The nurse smiled. "He has some good friends."

Kelly was glad for that, but a little surprised. Last she knew, Judah had been isolating himself from his friends. "I'm really glad to hear that."

The woman smiled and turned toward the open door. A sense of alarm ran through Kelly. She needed this woman to fill her in on what had happened with Judah.

"Please don't go. I should have come sooner. I was only told he was here last night."

The nurse shook her head. "Him being Amish, it's hard to track down that kind of relative. Besides, there were so many here the day after the fire and even a few days after that."

Kelly nodded, taking in the information. It felt good to know that Judah hadn't been alone.

"I'm glad to know they came to support him."

"Oh, he wasn't the only one." The woman pointed across the hall. "The little lady, the one he saved, was here as well."

Kelly raised her eyebrows. "The one he saved?"

The nurse closed the door gently. "Here, let me sit down for just a few minutes and get you up to speed."

She introduced herself as Alfreda and told Kelly about how Judah had pulled a young woman from the fire at her home. She seemed certain the two were in love, but, apparently, the young girl was about to marry someone else.

When she'd finished her story, Kelly hugged Alfreda and left the room. As she walked down the wide hallway, she tried to identify the floating feeling inside her. When the answer came to her, she stopped walking. Something she'd hated about Judah's rebellion during his teenage years and on into college was the negative feeling that came with parenting a child who consistently made wrong choices. But this feeling—pride—was something she hadn't felt in an awfully long time. Her heart hurt because of that, but also felt glad.

Kelly smiled as she headed to her car.

CHAPTER 30

JOHANNA

My heart skipped a beat as Gideon's tan buggy rolled into Mose's drive. The chill air made me feel a little dizzy, and I sat down to rest on the double-seated glider hoping Gideon would have a few minutes to chat with me on the porch. He always had such good advice, and I needed some about now.

More than I liked to admit, I hoped Gideon had news of Judah. I felt a stab of guilt at that feeling. My wedding was tomorrow. To another man. But if nothing else, Judah had been a good friend to me. And now that I felt stronger, I wanted to thank him personally.

What was I thinking? Gideon was probably here to see Mamm. And as far as I knew, Judah still lay out cold in his hospital bed. On top of that, he would probably head back to his old life once released. No reason for him to hang around here anymore. Especially not after I was wed and in the bishop's family.

There would be no more writing for me. Definitely no more Ima Righter. And no more trying to convince me to work for the *Star*. My heart took a dip then, and I had to work to give Gideon a smile. Even so, I hoped he had brought good news regarding Judah's health.

Gideon tipped his hat as he walked up the porch steps. *"Wie gehts?"*

I wasn't feeling very well but responded with a *Wunderbar, gut* anyway. I could tell from the look Gideon gave me that he saw right through my fib. His shaggy gray brows sunk into a furrow.

"Since when did ya start telling lies?"

"I'm sorry, Gideon. Half the time, I don't know how I'm feeling these days. I know how I should feel, and I figure that somehow saying it out loud will make it true."

"Well, it doesn't."

"Yeah, I've pretty much figured that out." I looked down and studied my black sneakers. Anything to break his knowing gaze.

Gideon looked to the spread of Mose's acreage all the way out to the long rows of dent corn still drying in his fields and then sat beside me. A few tan buggies traveled the road in front of the house. The autumn air held a little bite, but other than that, the day was picture perfect. I felt a twinge of guilt in feeling so awful on *Gott's* beautiful day.

"I know I shouldn't feel so horrible." I hadn't meant to say that. I had to be careful around Gideon. There was such an easiness about him, I nearly always ended up saying things I thought were hidden deep down. I was so tired of hiding things.

"I think I know why you do." Gideon took off his felt hat and held it in his lap, slowly turning it in his hands.

"How can ya know, Gideon? I don't even know."

"Well." He stretched his long legs out in front of him. "You've got a pretty big event happening tomorrow."

"But I'm doing *Gott's* will. I should be happy about that."

"Do ya feel peace?"

"I do ... I mean, I did. Now lately, I just feel confused."

"What made you tell *Gott* you'd marry Mordecai in the first place?"

I stared out at the expanse of Mose's property for a good long time. A few hawks soared above. "I don't know. I guess it was a lot of things. Really, it's the only way I know that I'll be able to stop writing for good. And my family can be safe. I know Mordecai wouldn't stand for it, and probably just the fear of getting caught would be enough to keep me on the straight and narrow."

"You know what I think?" Gideon put his hat back on his head and stood.

With all my heart I wanted to know what Gideon thought, but I was also afraid. So many people I loved seemed against this marriage now, but I felt like I had to stand fast and hold my ground. My will had driven me all these years to write, but I'd found that sometimes you have to sacrifice the thing you love for the people you love. With Mordecai's thumb pressed down on me, I was sure I would be able to quit. Finally then, maybe I could be free of the gift and even maybe feel closer to *Gott* because I wouldn't be violating Willow Brook's *Ordnung* all the time.

I sighed. "What do ya think, Gideon?"

"I think you need to know that the bishop's rules are not always *Gott's* rules."

With those words, he left the porch and headed back to his buggy. My eyes followed him down the path. About midway, he turned on his heel and faced me again.

"Oh, I almost forgot the reason I came." He walked back up the porch and handed me a small note. With a wink, he turned and said, "Judah's back."

I stared at the envelope a good long time before gathering the courage to open it. Unchecked feelings swirled within me. I was engaged to be married. How could I justify opening a note from another man? My breathing quickened, and I tried some slow breaths to calm it down. Thoughts that an engaged woman should never have came to mind. What was happening to me?

Mamm called me from somewhere inside the house. If I didn't open it now, there wouldn't be another chance I'd be alone until morning.

I blocked out the guilt I was sure to feel later and opened the note.

Meet me at the rock at dawn.

There were a million things I wanted to read on that little fold of paper, but somehow those seven words would have to do.

"There ya are!" Mamm walked out onto the porch just as I slipped the note into the pocket of my long black apron.

"I'm here, Mamm." I gave her a small smile.

"Mose has churned some ice cream at the back of the house." Mamm smiled slyly. "I brought ya some."

Thanking her, I took the ice cream and sat with her out on the porch for a long while.

Later, when it was time for the two of us to go up to bed, it struck me a little odd that Mamm hadn't said a word about my wedding the whole time we were on the porch and even when we were getting ready for bed.

"*Gut Nacht,* daughter."

A few minutes later, she started snoring softly.

If the room weren't pitch dark, I would have taken the note out again and read its seven words. I still had no idea what I would do in the morning. But I had a pretty good idea I would regret whatever decision I made.

Was I dreaming? I had to be. There lay Mamm and me in the bed, but here I was in front of the washbowl in the corner of the room.

For some reason, I couldn't stop cleaning my face. Over and over again I gently rubbed my cheek—the one Mordecai had slapped that day in the barn—with a small wet towel. It hurt. And this time, the pain felt greater than before—even piercing.

I dipped the cloth into the cool water, brought it up to my cheek, and then back down into the water again. If I were an Englischer, I would have a mirror like the one I had in the hospital. Then maybe I'd have a clue what was going on. Quietly, I pulled up the green shade and carried the bowl over to the window. Holding it up at just the right angle into the moonlight, I tried to catch a glimpse of my reflection in the glass. I gasped and nearly dropped the bowl. With trembling hands, I set it back down.

The water in the bowl was dark. Filled with blood. My blood.

Waking in a sweat, I crept out of bed. Still shaking, it took me a few tries to grip the shade well enough to open it. Moonlight poured in filling the room and me.

Kneeling on the floor with my forehead touching the cold hardwood, I cried out to *Gott*. Afterward, I felt such an incredible peace. Whatever his plans were for me in all this, I knew I could trust him. Come what may.

JUDAH

I tossed and turned on Gideon's cot. With Bertram and Hilton's news fresh on my mind, I could hardly wait to see Johanna. Although all the pieces concerning Zook weren't completely put together yet with the law, I hoped that it would be enough to bring change.

The two wanted me to be the one to tell Johanna, so they decided to wait to have anyone confront the bishop until after I'd had a chance to meet with her.

Lying there, I realized something. It didn't matter anymore where all this would get me with the *Star*—or with any other paper for that matter. It felt odd to have the thing that had consumed so many of my thoughts not matter so much anymore.

It was similar to what had happened earlier today, when I watched Gideon put the finishing touches on a special table—a gift for his sister's family. Using the level, he noticed the balance was slightly off. When he tried to fix it, part of the wood had split in two.

Cringing, I waited for his response, expecting him to throw something or curse. But he just shrugged and said he would start on an even better one tomorrow.

That's what the plain life will do to you, I guess.

I waited through the night, hoping for a text from Bertram with more information. When morning light started seeping through the cracks in the dark green shade, however, I decided what information I had would have to be enough.

Without making too much noise, I dressed in my broadfall trousers. I was actually starting to like them. They were much more comfortable than my skinny jeans. I snapped my suspenders into place. Dad would have liked this look. It surprised me the thought about Dad came and went with only a pinch of its usual pain.

I left the shop quietly and headed for the barn. I had asked Gideon the night before if I could borrow his buggy and figured he would be up by now, but everything looked dark.

I had gotten pretty good at hitching up the horse to the buggy, but I hurried across the yard even so, knowing that I could still get tripped up with all those straps.

Today was Johanna's wedding day, and I wanted to make sure I would have as much time as possible with her before her family would expect her to start preparing.

Gideon was in the barn getting the buggy ready when I entered. I smiled. This man was starting to mean a lot to me, and there was something deep down inside that made me want to let him know.

"Thanks for letting me borrow your buggy, Gideon." I coughed a little. "I really appreciate it."

Gideon nodded and started to hand me the reins. But before I took them, I surprised myself by saying what was on my heart.

"I know you don't know a ton about me, Gideon, but I just wanted to thank you for taking a risk on letting me work with you." Again, he nodded and offered the reins. But I couldn't take them yet. I had more to say.

"I've never told you this, but my dad died when I was just thirteen. I guess, since then, I've made a lot of bad decisions—before he died even." My voice trailed off, and I wasn't sure I could say anything else, so I just stood there feeling stupid.

Gideon brushed the hay off a couple of old crates, tied the reins around a post, and gestured for me to sit.

Finally, he spoke. "How'd he die?"

I had avoided that question since Dad's death. I had even prepared a long list of lies just in case I was ever asked. But when I searched my brain for one, I couldn't think of anything but the truth.

"I killed him."

Gideon's eyebrows raised up an inch, but he just sat there waiting for more. So, I gave him the whole story. Might as well let him hear it all, I figured. He could kick me out if he wanted to. When I was done, I sat sobbing. It was an ugly cry, and there was no controlling it.

Gideon handed me his handkerchief. He put his long arm around my shoulders and let me sob until I thought I had nothing left.

"I think it's time you heard something, Judah. Really heard it."

I raised my head to face him, wiping more tears on the soaked handkerchief.

"Your Dat's death was not your fault."

My eyes blurred again.

"You were a stupid, rebellious boy when it came to those swimming lessons, Judah. And maybe you were a lot of other things too. But you loved your father, and in no way did you plan his death."

The truth hit me square in the face. Although my head still wrestled some with doubt and accusation, I felt a lifting despite all of that mess. The heaviness fled, and I didn't know what to do with the lightness I felt, but Gideon did. And for the first time in my life, the gospel of grace he shared with me made perfect sense.

It felt like hours had passed before I finally took the reins from Gideon and led the horse out to the road. Checking my cell phone, I was surprised to see that only a half hour had gone by. If I moved at a fast trot, I should get to the rock about the same time as Johanna.

Now, I had an even stronger desire to see Johanna free from the bondage she was about to enter. I didn't know how that would happen, nor how anything I would say could make a difference.

But maybe God could. And that would have to be enough.

Once at the Yoder's property, I tied the horse to a tree in a spot filled with clover still untouched by the frost.

What if she doesn't come?

She had to come. That was that. I wasn't even sure what I was going to say. There was the part about the bishop, but what Alfreda had said still swam around in my head, and I was still trying to make sense of it.

Bertram had explained that Alfreda was a bit of a romantic. But what if what she said was true? Her opinion made me feel a little different inside.

When I got to the rock, Johanna wasn't there, so I climbed up and waited. The canopy of red and yellow leaves over me was even more beautiful this time, and I lay down watching them, thinking about life and where it had taken me in the past few weeks. For some reason, I started thinking about Mom, and, whenever she came to mind, thoughts of God seemed to come right along with her.

God, please don't let Johanna marry Mordecai.

I must have dozed off because I woke to the sound of a soft giggle.

Sitting up quickly, I nearly fell off the rock. Alarmed, Johanna helped me right myself.

"*Ach*! Judah, I'm so sorry!"

I laughed. "I'm fine, really. You just surprised me."

Johanna laughed again. It was good to hear that after all she'd been through.

"Thanks for coming."

"*Jah*." Her green eyes were beautiful. "So *gut* to see ya feeling better."

I smiled and coughed a little. If she only knew. "Can you sit for a few minutes?"

She pulled herself up on the rock, and I took a few minutes to collect my thoughts. I felt peace all around us. I hoped that Johanna could feel it too.

"I know that today is a big day for you."

She nodded and looked down at her hands.

"But before you make your wedding vows, I want to share with you some things that my editor and a friend have discovered about your bishop."

After telling her all that I thought I knew, I could tell she didn't believe me. And if I was honest with myself, I don't know if I would have believed me either. There were some holes left in this story. And she'd grown up under this bishop her whole life as did her mother before her. And her grandmother had almost married the man.

That was a lot of history to compete with.

"Thanks for telling me, Judah. But the bishop is the authority of the People, and we have to trust him—even if we don't understand him." She shrugged her shoulders, gave me a sad smile, and placed a warm hand over mine.

"I'm glad to be your friend. And I need to thank ya for saving my life—twice. I hope you will come to my wedding today. It would mean a lot."

As Johanna slid down from the rock, I grasped for something else to say. Something that would make her change her mind. But I had nothing.

She was halfway down the trail when I remembered the heart.

JOHANNA

"Johanna!" Judah called to me from the rock. I don't think he understood I was dying inside. I took a few steps forward, but he caught up with me. I turned around and faced him, looking deep into his eyes.

"*Jah?*"

He cleared his throat. "There's something more. I had forgotten. Would you come back—just for a few minutes? I need to show you something."

I almost said no. Mamm would be wondering where I was. My purple wedding dress was waiting.

"Okay."

Together, we walked back. Judah led me around the rock, over to the heart. Mammi's heart.

I squatted down to trace it.

"With all that happened in the fire, I forgot about this. I found it right before I started smelling the smoke."

Judah pushed back some goldenrod growing at the base of the rock.

A tingle went up my spine.

An arrow had been carved in the rock under the heart. Less prominent and not as deep, but still an arrow, pointing straight into the ground.

I took a deep breath. My hands trembled. "Judah, do you know why I ran into the *Dawdi Haus* when it was on fire?"

He smiled and shook his head. I could tell he had wondered about it more times than once.

"I was looking for my grandmother's journal. After you showed me the heart that day, I had to find out why she had agreed to marry Bishop Amos in the first place. How someone I loved and respected could ever pledge her love to a man like that."

"This is sounding familiar."

Judah looked away after saying that. I knew he didn't mean for it to hurt me, but it stung none the less.

"I'm sorry, Johanna, that just slipped out."

I smiled weakly. I guess he was right in a way. At least from his point of view, my path looked pretty similar to Mammi's before she called off her wedding.

I cleared my throat. "I was so sure that the journal was hidden under a fake bottom in one of the kitchen drawers."

"So sure you were willing to go into a burning building to find it?" Judah cracked a smile.

"Something like that." I smiled too. "But it wasn't there, Judah. When I reached the kitchen and pulled open the drawer, the false bottom was there, but the journal wasn't underneath. I don't remember much about the fire, but I remember that. After that, something must have come down from the roof and hit me."

Judah and I looked at the arrow and then at each other. "Ya don't think?"

I smiled and shrugged. "It's worth a try."

Together we went to the barn to find some shovels.

JUDAH

The dirt was hard, and even with shovels, it took the two of us some time before we heard the clunk of metal on metal. We put aside our shovels then and began digging away the rock and clay with our hands.

Slowly, a rectangular box emerged. I grabbed one of the shovels for leverage and shimmied the box out of the ground. Once out, I let Johanna have the honor of discovering whatever was inside. Two clasps, almost rusted out, was all that stood now between her and her questions about her grandmother.

Secretly, I hoped there was enough in there to further incriminate the bishop. Most likely, an old journal written by someone many years ago wouldn't be enough evidence for a judge, but it sure would be for Johanna.

She got one clasp open but was having a rough time with the other.

I took the box from her. "Here, maybe we can knock it open with a rock."

Looking around, I found a thin piece of limestone shale and wedged it between the clasp and the box, forcing it open with a click.

Johanna sat there for a few seconds hugging the box. I looked away, wanting to let her have her moment. Slowly, she began to open it. Clods of clay fell to the ground as she peered inside.

I couldn't tell if she was laughing or crying until she reached in and pulled out the journal.

"Oh, Judah!" She gave my hand a squeeze.

I smiled. Whatever she found written there, I was truly happy that Johanna had this connection with her grandmother.

She started to open it, but I put my hand on the cover.

"Wait. Why don't you go somewhere that you can be alone and, you know, kind of just soak it in all by yourself."

Johanna nodded her thanks, gave me an unexpected kiss on the cheek, and was gone before I could say you're welcome.

CHAPTER 31

JOHANNA

I could hear the bawls of the baby steers. Those that had the chance to know their mothers had probably been separated from them just this week. Although they usually took a few days to adjust, most ended up being fairly content.

I sighed. Maybe my experience would be the same with my new marriage.

A hot, prickly feeling swept over my skin. The calves' lives were good, for a little while. But being raised on a veal farm, things always ended the same way. I tried not to think about that part.

Finding a warm spot in the hay, I gingerly opened Mammi Miriam's journal. Although my time was limited, I wanted to find the part that mattered most to me right now. Then, I'd savor the rest later.

I scanned the pages for dates. About twenty pages in, I found what I looked for. In her beautiful penmanship, Mammi had described what it was like to be pursued by the newest male member of the community.

> August 17, 1974
>
> Preacher Amos came to us quite suddenly at Bishop Obadiah's bidding a few weeks ago. And even more

sudden was his interest in me. I didn't know what to think of the young widower, but I did know the community had been fairly desperate for new blood. Willow Brook has grown so quickly, and while this is a good thing, it means a lot of the People are now kin.

Some babies are being born with genetic diseases. They say it is because we are marrying our close relatives.

Bishop Obadiah in Hickory Ridge has told us we are not to marry first cousins and even second cousins are considered a risk. Since we lost our bishop to the flu last winter, Obadiah has taken on our community in addition to his own.

So when Amos showed interest in me, Dat was more than happy about it. It was funny how he pursued me out in the open, instead of our traditional courting ways of Singings and late-night buggy rides home. I wonder if that's the way they did things in his community. He says he's from the Nebraska Amish community in Mifflin County. I don't know anyone from that region, so I'm guessing they just do things differently.

I heard a soft purring at my feet, and I smiled at Miracle rubbing into my stockings. I picked her up and scratched her fluffy belly. Wherever I ended up after today, I wanted to somehow take her with me when things got settled and her kittens were weaned. I'd do my best to hide the cat from Mordecai.

I stood and gave Miracle some food in her bowl, making sure to add a bit more for her kittens to find after they woke up from their nap. Knowing I only had a few more minutes, I flipped through the pages of the journal until I found the part about their breakup. My eyes grew large as I read about the secrets my grandmother had kept.

September 1, 1974

How could I have been so blind? Amos is not who he says he is. He's not Amish at all, and he's lied to me and to our community. He told me he had switched identities with a preacher of the Mifflin County Amish who was headed our way. His name is really Matthias Fisher. I think he told me everything to show off—he's sensed that I've been pulling away from him.

But I've broken off our engagement. I can't marry a man who isn't honest. I just can't. Dat is furious, but I have sworn to hold Amos's secret to my grave. I'm not sure the People would believe me anyway—me being a woman and Amos a preacher. Also, I'm a little afraid at what he would do if I tell.

I flipped through until I came to a page that crinkled as I turned to it. The page was rippled, as if once wet.

November 7, 1976

My heart is broken. Amos has been appointed bishop even though—with my own eyes—I saw him cheat his way into the ordination. And he is now wielding his new power in ways that the community is unaccustomed to. Just today, he has announced that there will be no more writing for pleasure in the community. He says this is a prideful endeavor that can easily become an idol in a person's life. I'm sure this new rule is targeted at me.

Amos wants my journal. He knows I share my heart on these pages, and he's fearful his secrets will be discovered.

This entry ended, and I looked carefully at the date of the next. Six months had passed before Mammi had gathered enough courage to write again. Somehow, I could see her curled up in this very spot etching out the words on her heart.

"Johanna?"

I slid the journal into my apron pocket and looked up at David.

"Hullo, I—"

"Mamm's been lookin' for ya, Johanna. She sent me over to look for ya here. Said she thought maybe you'd come to see your cat and her brood."

I was glad Miracle still lay curled up on my lap. I smiled and rubbed my hand across her soft fur one more time.

"I'll be heading back now." I rose to leave and David touched my shoulder.

"You don't have to do this, Johanna." His eyes pierced my own. *Ach*, why was everyone trying to get me to go back on my promise?

I sighed. "Do you remember when Dat used to say that sometimes all we had was our word?"

David looked down and kicked at the hay on the barn floor.

"That's all I have right now."

David rose his eyes back to mine. "Dat also used to say that we all make mistakes."

I left then, wishing more than ever that Dat was here to help me figure out what to do.

JUDAH

After Johanna had left, I stayed to fill the hole. There wasn't anything else I could do now. Oddly enough, somehow, I felt like helping Johanna find the journal had been enough. Maybe her grandmother had a thing or two to say in that book that would help change her mind.

"Gideon!" The voice sounded rough and boomed at the end of the trail leading out toward the road.

Why was someone calling Gideon?

"Gideon!" The voice sounded like Mordecai. He must have seen the buggy. I pushed the goldenrod back over the heart and stood.

He walked into the clearing now but stopped when he noticed me. I figured I'd use his shock to my advantage.

"Oh, hullo, Mordecai."

He squinted and gave me a sneer. "What are ya doing here?"

"Just thinking."

"There are plenty of other places to think."

He wasn't as dumb as I thought. But my college education against his eight grades had to count for something.

Botany. I had taken that as an elective.

I stooped and broke off some goldenrod. "Have you heard of this genus?"

Mordecai gave me a sneer. "What?"

"This species of plant, we don't have it in my community. I wanted to bring some back to our bishop."

"It's all over the road, Judah."

I could tell he didn't seem convinced. I felt like prey being sniffed out by a predator and kept the rock between us. After hearing him slap Johanna, I didn't think the Amish pacifist thing applied to this guy.

"*Den ... Denki*! I was told that some grew here, so I thought I'd come by before I left."

"You're leaving?" He took a more relaxed stance now. Glad, I'm sure, that I wouldn't be around to talk sense into his future wife.

"Umm, *jah*! Gideon seems to have things under control now in the shop, so I'll be heading back to my apart... er, community very soon."

"Well, that's *gut* to hear."

"*Jah*, I'm anxious to get back to my ..." Suddenly I felt a rock in the pit of my stomach. What was I anxious to get back to? I had a feeling the things that were once important to me wouldn't matter so much now. Liza Lou would be glad to see me. But most likely, I'd be out of work and looking for a new job. Maybe I'd even have to move to another location. One without friends and family. With the paper out of business, there wasn't much need for writers in this area.

I sighed, laid the goldenrod down, and rested my elbows on the rock.

My pause must have been too long because, when I looked back up, Mordecai had moved closer to the rock without my noticing.

I didn't really care what he thought, or even what he did to me. He was about to take something important away from me. And somehow, I needed to let him know that.

"Do you even love her?"

There, I said it.

Mordecai gave me a blank look. "Love who?"

Really? "Really?"

Mordecai frowned and crossed his arms over his chest.

"Today is your wedding day." I widened my eyes and said the words slowly, thinking he would make the connection, and maybe hoping just a little that he wouldn't.

A dim light seemed to click on in his brain and Mordecai smirked. "Well, *jah*, it is, isn't it? Too bad you'll be on your way."

"Well, I might not be clearing out quite so soon."

Whatever light Mordecai had smoldered and he sneered. "I'll thank ya to steer clear of the ceremony."

I decided that now wasn't a good time to tell him that the bride had given me a personal invitation. Let him think what he wants.

Now, I smirked. "Sure, Mordecai, whatever you say."

Slowly, I inched my way around the rock. Mordecai had moved enough to the side now where, if he made a lunge for me, there was a good chance I could outrun him—if I could run. I hadn't quite figured out my buggy getaway yet, though.

Mordecai stayed put.

"Well, best of luck to you."

He grunted something in return, and I had made it a few steps down the path and out to the road when I heard him right behind me.

"Oh, hey."

I spun around and flinched. Ugh. No way he could have missed that.

He tossed something at me, and I was showered with weeds.

"Don't forget your goldenrod." He offered me another smirk and left.

As I returned to the buggy, my heart pumped a little too fast. I took in some slow breaths to calm it down.

I wasn't sure how things were going to go down that afternoon, but I knew one thing, I wouldn't miss it for the world.

Bertram looked again at his watch.

Finding the last bit of information they needed to help incriminate Amos was taking longer than both of them had expected.

They had the image they were looking for, but the news Nora just texted him about the criminal records wasn't good. She had done her best, but unfortunately, the records were squeaky clean of any mention of Matthias Fisher and his arrest. With Nora's persistence, the station had consulted a retired police chief now living in Florida who remembered the arrest, but without the documents, they were up against a mountain of red tape. And after talking to Judah, they knew they didn't have much time as far as Ima was concerned.

The police had said if they could find a notice of arrest in the newspaper, and a story of Fisher's escape, they would be willing to investigate. So, they just needed to find a story, any story, written about his arrest. Surely there was a rogue journalist even in the early seventies who was willing to risk it all to tell the truth.

But even if there was, there had to be an editor under the power of the great Ernst Fisher who allowed it to be published.

And that was the tricky part.

Bertram and Hilton had come up blank searching in the library, so they had headed over to the *Star*. Since Hilton's father had been the editor of the *Star* as his grandfather was before him, they had quite a collection of printed newspapers in their own attic. But Hilton warned Bertram before they even started their search that both men had been "rule followers."

Bertram had a hard time believing that, knowing Hilton's style. But his boss assured him he had been somewhat of a black sheep in the family. Bertram was glad that Hilton had turned a different direction in the places that mattered.

Together they searched through musty boxes of old newspapers until their fingers were dried and starting to crack.

Bertram checked his watch again. Johanna would be getting married in a little under two hours, and they were no closer to throwing the book at Amos Zook than they were two days ago.

He took a minute to rub a clean spot on the dusty window with the edge of his shirt. The sky was blue, and the clouds puffy. A perfect day for a wedding, if the groom wasn't Mordecai Zook.

God?

"Wait a minute." Hilton looked up from his spot knee deep in old papers.

Bertram shook his head at his mess. Good thing he owned the place. Hilton obviously was following a "search and destroy" mentality.

"There was another editor before my grandfather passed the paper on to my dad." Newspaper ink had stained Hilton's fingers and smudges streaked across his face—making him look ready for a game of tackle football.

"Elmer Brown. He didn't last long."

Bertram didn't understand why this fact seemed important to Hilton. So what if another editor had held the paper for a few months before Hilton's father had taken the position?

When he didn't move or respond, Hilton turned to him and scowled. "Don't you get it? Elmer was fired for lettings things get printed in the paper that the mayor didn't like."

"Okay. When was he the editor?"

"Let me think. Let me think." Hilton tapped his forehead, adding a new ink smudge with each tap. "My grandfather had a stroke, and my dad was still in college. He wasn't ready yet to come home and take on the paper. In fact, if I remember correctly, he wasn't even sure he wanted the job."

"When was your father in college?"

"Oh, man." Hilton tapped his head this time with the silver school ring.

"That's it!"

His boss turned to him and frowned. "What's it?"

"The ring. You told me it was your dad's college ring. Does it have his graduation date on it?"

Hilton took off the ring and looked it over like he was seeing the inscriptions for the first time.

JOHANNA

Mamm watched me as I came out of our bedroom in my purple dress.

"You look beautiful."

I blushed at that. Focusing on appearances wasn't the Amish way. Plain people preferred the type of beauty that came from within—a sign of a good Christian life. But Mamm had been through a lot these last few weeks, and she'd grown a lot. New things seemed to be surfacing in her all the time.

"All set then?" Mamm also seemed determined to not comment on this wedding anymore. She had pleaded and begged with me, but now she had decided to leave it in *Gott's* hands.

She smiled at me as I approached her and clasped her hands to my own.

"Ready, Mamm." My pulse quickened. I still wasn't sure what to do with the news in my grandmother's journal. As I dressed earlier, I'd laid my fears and concerns all in *Gott's* hands just like my mother.

Mamm hugged me, and I could tell she was being strong for me. As we walked, I couldn't help but feel like we were walking some sort of death march out to Mose's living room where family and friends from the community stood packed into every corner.

She took hold of my hand again as we walked out to the room together. Most new brides chose friends for their side sitters, but I had chosen Mamm alone. The decision was a bit out of the ordinary, but the bishop didn't seem to care or even notice as we walked into the large living room space. Taking our seats together, Mamm tried to let go of my hand, probably thinking I might want my freedom, but I held fast.

The kneeling confession was quick and painless. I had done all the things I was confessing, and I had violated the *Ordnung*.

"I want to confess that I have failed ..." I kept my voice even and clear through the whole thing. The People needed to see me strong, I knew that now.

Bertram needed a break—just a few minutes to stretch his legs outside and get away from the smell of mold and newspaper ink. Good thing he didn't have any allergies, he found himself thinking often.

Once outside, he began to pray.

Johanna would be saying her vows in just over an hour. Willow Brook was a half hour away—if they sped. There was still time, but things were really looking bleak.

Bertram thought of the story of Abigail in the Bible. She had been married to a foolish man, one who nearly got his whole family killed by mouthing off to King David's men. Things turned out for Abigail, didn't they? She'd used her brain to fix things before her family had been destroyed

Her husband had died in his foolishness, and in the end, she married the king.

Bertram ran the story through his mind from start to finish. You never know how things are going to end up, he figured.

Coming back upstairs, he saw Hilton still hard at work. They'd found the boxes of papers printed under the leadership of Elmer Brown—the graduation date on Hilton's dad's ring had helped with that. Hilton had surrounded himself with the boxes and probably hadn't even noticed Bertram leave.

Bertram squatted down in front of a box now and shoved off the lid.

God, guide our hands, make our eyes sharp. We give all of this to you.

He grabbed a newspaper midway through the pile. In it, there was a story about The Muffin Top opening up—the bakery where Nora had worked. He thought maybe one of the young workers pictured behind the counter in the picture could have been her. He'd set the paper aside so he could make copies for her later. Even if it wasn't her, she probably knew the person in the photo.

He flipped the page and froze as he stared face to face with a mug shot of Matthias Fisher. The article stated that he'd been recorded as dead by the Eastern State Penitentiary, but his body had disappeared. The prison had gathered some evidence and later called it an escape.

The article very thoroughly covered the reason for Fisher's imprisonment—murdering three men—and even recapped his arrest information in the side column. The article included more information, but Bertram didn't take the time to read it all.

"Hilton?"

JOHANNA

My stomach churned and gurgled through the whole service. I felt embarrassed, as I was sure Mamm and most in the room heard. Yet, I thanked *Gott* they couldn't hear what was going through my mind as well.

Since finding the journal, I couldn't rein in my thoughts which seemed to run wild in my head. How could we respect a man who isn't who he says he is? A man who has lied and cheated his way into the leadership of our community?

My Mammi knew and never told.

She must have been afraid for her family. Just like Mamm had been her whole life. Bishop Amos had made it clear to Mammi Miriam that he would treat our family with a heavy hand if she let anyone know his secret.

Now I knew the truth. But I didn't know what to do with it, and the service seemed to be happening so fast.

If I was honest with myself, I had agreed to marry Mordecai because I felt like it was *Gott's* will for me to serve my family in this way. I could see no other way our family could stay in good graces with the bishop. My mother's plan had been a good one. Except for one thing. He wasn't really the bishop.

The preaching continued, and my thoughts rambled on. Somehow, I had to let the community know that the wrong person was leading them. They had been under the heavy hand of a liar and a cheat.

I looked around the room at the people I have loved all my life. All my *Bruders* were there with their wives and growing brood. And Mamm who was trying hard not to give me looks of despair throughout the preaching. I would die for my family, and I figured that marrying Mordecai was my way of doing it.

But now, I wasn't so sure if it was the right plan.

I didn't know how to prove it, but the wrong man would be reading me my wedding vows.

And then the thought struck me. If the bishop wasn't *Gott's* elect, there really wasn't any way he could perform this ceremony before *Gott*. And if Mordecai and I were to ever ... well, we would be sinning. Sure, the bishop had married plenty of others before me, including all my *Bruders*. But the difference was, they didn't know the truth.

And I did.

More than worrying about exposing the bishop, I couldn't violate *Gott's* commands.

When the sermon finally ended, Mordecai and I stepped forward to give our vows. I had been to enough weddings to know this was my last chance. After I answered the bishop's questions in front of the People about our future marriage, I could not turn back.

Before I knew it, Mordecai had finished his vows and it was my turn. I could have easily spoken the words the congregation expected to hear. But I just couldn't contribute anything else to the bishop's lie. I had to put a voice to what Mammi had kept secret for so many years.

I took a deep breath, steadied my trembling hands, and I spoke. A whisper came at first, but then I coughed and found my voice.

"I cannot marry Mordecai Zook today."

Despite clearing my throat, my voice still hadn't been loud enough, and most of the congregation looked confused. Mamm's eyes grew bigger though, and those closest to me started to fidget in their seats.

I cleared my throat and tried again, louder this time. "I can't marry Mordecai Zook."

Mamm's sigh of relief sounded even louder than my words.

Mordecai scowled.

I took a deep breath and pulled Mammi Miriam's journal out from the folds of my cape dress. Looking around, I found Judah standing in the back. He smiled and gave me a slight nod.

Taking another deep breath, I held the journal up with both hands above my head for all to see and began my story.

"Amos Zook is a—"

A quick movement from the front of the room stole my attention, and then the journal was snatched out of my hands.

I had never felt the cold blade of a knife on my throat before, but Bishop Amos, or whoever he was, seemed pretty comfortable holding it there.

"It's time we left." His breath felt hot in my ear.

I could hear Mamm scream as the bishop dragged me away from the front of the room and out the back door, the knife pressed tightly to my throat. My *Bruders*, trained pacifists and brought up under the bishop's thumb, hesitated in their response just a half-second too long.

"Wait!" Judah's voice came along with noise of scraping chairs. "Somebody stop him, he's not who you think he is!"

Before I knew what happened, I was thrown into a buggy, its owner nowhere in sight. The horse seemed just as surprised as me at the sharp crack of the whip on its back.

"You couldn't leave it alone, could you?" Bishop Amos sneered at me and then turned back to the horse.

What was he talking about?

"Don't act like you don't know. I don't know how you did it. This journal was supposed to burn in the fire. And you"—he jutted his bearded chin in my direction—"you were supposed to die."

I took a breath and prayed as the buggy swayed violently from side to side. Even when my *Bruders* secretly participated in buggy races, they had never gone this fast.

FORBIDDEN GIFT

"I don't know what you're talking about. I didn't find the journal in the fire."

Realization hit me then and memories came rushing back. The journal was supposed to burn in the fire, and I was supposed to die?

"You were in the *Dawdi Haus* when I was looking for the journal!"

Amos kept looking straight ahead and cracked the buggy whip hard again on the horse's backside.

I put my hand on my head, still sensitive around my scar.

"*You* hit me?" My panic turned to rage. "You hit me!"

His face glistened with sweat despite the swift chill air slamming into us.

"You were supposed to either die or marry my grandson and then forever shut up. And this"—he held up the journal—"was supposed to burn in my fire."

His fire? I lunged for the journal. I had worked too hard to get it and still had the dirt and blood under my fingernails to prove it.

Amos slapped me hard across the face with it, and I realized where his grandson got his manners.

The buggy made a quick lunge to the left, and I nearly flew out. I gripped the side of the buggy and did all I could to hold on.

"Where ... where are ya taking me?"

"Somewhere where you ... and this"—he gave the journal a shake—"will finally stop reminding me of my past."

"How could I ever remind you of your past?"

He hated me because of my weakness in disobeying the *Ordnung*—sometimes daily. I just couldn't stop writing. But what did that have to do with his past?

He gave me a sidelong glance. "You remind me of *her*."

Mammi.

The look in his eyes frightened me then. By taking me at knifepoint, he had gotten himself to a point of no return with the People. He had to know that. I began to wonder if his plan was for neither of us to return.

CHAPTER 32

Hilton violated all kinds of traffic laws on their way to Willow Brook, and Bertram hoped they wouldn't be stopped. After finding what they needed, they had contacted Nora. She assured them that someone from the sheriff's office would meet them out there. Despite everything, Bertram knew they were going to be late. And he hated that.

The information they now had could indict Bishop Amos for the rest of his life. That was a good thing, but a certain sadness came with knowing that Johanna would already be wed to his abusive grandson. The way things sometimes worked with the Amish, this grandson could rise to be the next bishop. So what good would our hard work do?

Nobody's rough with my patients.

Alfreda's face came to Bertram's mind, and he prayed that, by some miracle, they wouldn't be too late.

As they neared the house, an Amish buggy came racing down the lane. Hilton had his eyes on the road in front of him, but the speed of the buggy alarmed Bertram.

He took out his phone and grabbed a video of it as it passed by them. Then, watching the video as Hilton drove, Bertram took a still of the riders and zoomed in.

"Turn the car around, Hilton."

"What? Aren't we almost there?"

Bertram didn't have time to explain. "Let me drive."

"What?"

"Something's wrong. That was them."

Too shocked to argue, Hilton turned the car around, and then they made the switch. A call came in from Judah then, and Hilton answered.

Hilton put down the phone and swallowed hard. "Straight ahead."

JOHANNA

The horse wouldn't last much longer at this rate. I watched as it shook its head from side to side, foam coming off the mare's lips.

The bishop's plan didn't make any sense to me until he started slowing just enough to take shortcuts across fields. The tractor paths were now cold and hard enough to traverse. After a few turns, even I felt confused about our location.

I realized anyone pursuing us would find the task difficult.

I looked down at the dirt path flying past and wished I had the courage to jump. I almost did once or twice, but words needing to be said niggled inside of me. Yet, I didn't want to say any of them.

Everybody deserves another chance.

Mammi's words. And at a time like this.

Surely, she hadn't meant someone like Bishop Amos. He had lied about who he really was and cheated his way into his position, violating *Gott's* holy selection by lot all these years. And not only that, he had played a big part in my broken relationship with Mamm. If he hadn't convinced the community to add such strict rules against writing in the *Ordnung*, things might have been different between us while I was growing up. So many years wasted.

And on top of everything else, he'd set our house on fire and tried to kill me while I was inside. Surely Mammi Miriam wouldn't think that someone like Bishop Amos deserved another chance. She had no idea what he had done.

I caught myself on that one. Mammi did know most of what he had done—at least some of the really bad parts. I had read it with my own eyes just this morning.

Everybody deserves another chance.

I swallowed hard. Where to begin?

Begin at the beginning.

"Bishop Amos?" I didn't want to do this. Everything inside me screamed no. My head pounded from where he had hit me with the rock and I still felt his knife on my throat.

He turned to me—a little bit of white foam from the horse clung to his beard.

Oh, Gott. Help.

I started at the beginning then and everything sort of spilled out—my passion for writing and what it meant to me, what it had meant to my grandmother. I told him how his rules had caused such a great conflict in our family. How they had practically driven my relationship with my mother into the ground.

And in the end, I told him about Jesus. That part was for Mammi, if I had no honor for the bishop, I had honor for her. Using her words, I told him about *Gott*.

Many of the People believed their good works would get them into heaven—especially after so many years of the bishop's teaching. But Mammi knew different. She believed Jesus had died for her sins and that salvation came only through faith in him.

It felt a little silly speaking to someone as high up as the bishop about salvation, but after what Judah had said, I knew Amos was really not a bishop.

"That hogwash is from your grandmother," he said quietly, keeping his eyes on the road. "And talking about *Gott* that way violates the *Ordnung*."

"It's the gospel," I said the word as quietly and as respectfully as I could.

The bishop kept his eyes on the road but glanced at me from time to time. I could tell he felt surprised about my boldness. But that was okay. I was a little surprised at myself, as well.

The train took forever to pass. By the time he could ease the car across the tracks, a line of sweat had begun down Bertram's back. By his estimation, the buggy should be just ahead, but they could not see it anywhere. Bertram stopped the car and clambered up to its roof to get a better look around.

Hilton walked out to the buggy lane for a better view.

"Do you see them?"

His boss shook his head. "They should be just ahead of us."

"Well, they're not, and I don't get it." Bertram scratched his head.

"Maybe there's a turn up ahead. Keep going. We're not going to find them sitting here."

Bertram could tell by Hilton's tone that he had grown tired of the chase. He hoped he wasn't thinking of giving up. Something inside told him to hang on.

JOHANNA

"You have no idea what I've been accused of doing."

The bishop looked tired. Old even. He had finally brought the horse to a canter. It would have been easy to jump out now, and I was sure I could outrun him. But I knew I was supposed to stay put.

"*Gott* knows." How many times had Mammi told me that?

The bishop stopped the horse in a spot where a small stand of trees shielded us from the road. He stared straight ahead while he told me about his life in prison.

I tried to keep my jaw from dropping. I had no idea.

"I can't go back."

I thought of Susanna, his children, and grandchildren. I even thought about Mordecai and wondered how losing his grandfather would impact him.

"You have to. You have family."

He winced and squinted up at the sky which had turned overcast and threatened a storm. "They would be better off without me." He shook his head and turned to me. His face filled with regret. I hadn't seen this look from him before. "It's all been a lie, Johanna. Miriam, your grandmother, knew what little I told her. The truth of who I am drove her away from me. I thought that somehow telling her would draw her to me, but I was wrong. She was too honest for that."

I nodded. "I read about some of it in her journal."

He seemed surprised to see he still had it in his hand.

"I've been after this thing all my life as an Amish man." He slipped the journal onto my lap. "You have it. It doesn't matter now how many people know the truths that are in there now, I suppose." He clicked his tongue and guided the horse back onto the road.

"Bishop Amos—"

"I'm not your bishop." We came to an intersection with a blinking yellow light and he craned his neck to see if any cars were coming. "The lot fell on Gideon that day."

I nodded. "Did he know?"

"I think so, but he kept quiet. Seemed to think I needed it more than him." Amos shook his head and his voice fell to a whisper. "All these years, it should have been Gideon."

In the distance, I heard a train whistle. He brought the horse to a gallop again. The jolt surprised me, and I grabbed the side of the buggy and hung on.

"I'm done running, Johanna. You can tell my wife that too."

I was ever so glad for that, but something seemed wrong. I needed to reassure him that somehow everything would be okay, even though I had a feeling it wouldn't be.

"We can go back. It will work out ... somehow."

"*Nee*, it won't, Johanna." His knife dropped to the floor of the buggy. "Now I need you to do something for me."

I nodded.

"I need you to take the journal and start walking toward the last intersection we passed. Wait for an Amish buggy to come by and tell them the bishop told them ... er, tell them you need a ride to Mose's house."

Was he letting me go?

The horse slowed, and the buggy came to a stop on the curb.

He gave me a long look. "I'm sorry I hit you with that rock."

I nodded.

"I was so sure the fire was the answer to all the torment and fear I was having about being discovered—and about going back to jail. And when you got in the way ..."

I told him I understood and got out of the buggy. Clutching the journal, I ran down the road for a bit. If I had my directions right, after crisscrossing over all those fields, we were three or four miles away from the community. Hopefully, a buggy would be by soon. I had to make it quick if I was going to make it back before dusk. Mamm was probably crazy with worry.

The thought of Mamm being concerned about me brought some comfort. Then I thought of Judah.

The train's horn grew louder, and I saw it wind around the curve of its tracks in the distance. Focusing again on the road in front of me, I searched for a buggy that might be able to help me get back home.

The horn blew again, but this time it seemed different, more urgent. I turned my head and suddenly the scene all made sense.

"Wait. No!"

I held my hands over my ears as the train's screeching brakes pierced the air. I couldn't muffle the splintering crash that followed.

Bertram turned down yet another desolate country road. Where had that buggy gone? They'd been searching now for nearly an hour. Johanna could be dead by now.

Hilton played the video on Bertram's phone over and over again. "Where are you, Ima?"

"Hilton, you know her name is really Johanna, right?"

He cradled the phone. "She's Ima to me."

After Bertram and Hilton had been down what seemed every Amish road in the county, Hilton turned from the phone to Bertram.

"Maybe we ought to head back to Willow Brook. Start talking to some of the people there. See what really happened. I'd hate to not be there for Ima … Johanna, but maybe we can do some good after we're able to put some pieces together."

"Just one more road, Hilton. It'll be getting dark soon. There has to be somehow that we can help."

Hilton opened his mouth to speak, but his words were drowned out by the angry horn of a train and then a loud crash.

Bertram sped toward the wreckage. Up ahead he saw broken pieces of buggy fiberglass strewn all over the road.

"God, no!"

The horse lay dead on the side of the road as the engineer searched through the wreckage for Amish passengers. Bertram brought the car to a halt, and Hilton jumped out to help.

Then Bertram spotted her. Sitting on an outcrop in the edge of a field of ryegrass sat a lone Amish woman dressed in purple. The color matched Johanna's dress in the video.

Bertram let out a sigh of relief, texted Judah, and stepped into the field. He could hear the whine of a siren in the distance.

JOHANNA

Everything had happened so fast. I wondered if there was something I could have done to stop the bishop from following through with his plan.

I felt sad he had chosen death over life. We both knew things would be tough for him from here on out, but at least they would be honest and he would be alive. I thought about his family and began to weep. My hatred for the bishop had changed to compassion. Only *Gott* could have done that.

Judah's newspaper friend came up to me then and introduced himself, offering me a kind smile and his handkerchief which I gladly took.

Looking past him, I felt grateful to have his company as a policeman started picking his way across the field over to us. We both watched as the tufts of ryegrass almost tripped him up a time or two.

I started to shiver. I hadn't paid attention to the cold until now, and there had been no time to grab my shawl when the bishop took me from Mose's house.

The policeman tipped his hat at me, and I nodded.

"Do you know where Matthias Fisher is, miss?"

"Who?" His question confused me at first, and then I remembered the name from Mammi's journal. Still the question didn't make sense to me. Didn't we all know where he was? I pointed to remains of the crushed buggy. "Isn't ... isn't he somewhere over there?"

"No, miss. We can't find any evidence of a body. We've circled the area, but he's nowhere to be found. We believe he escaped from the crash."

JUDAH

Gideon and I had been searching the roads in his buggy with no luck. But then my phone beeped, and I gasped as I read Bertram's text.

Bertram didn't give us much to go on regarding their location, but it was enough. Gideon knew the area well and turned his buggy around. Letting out a soft clucking sound, he gave his horse a quick flick of the reins, and I had to hold on to my felt hat as our buggy darted forward.

When we arrived, police and EMT workers had swarmed the scene. The train had pulverized the buggy, and I squatted down to pick up a bent orange safety triangle.

I spotted Johanna and a rush of emotion ran through me. It had been a long time since I felt this way about anyone.

I felt a hand on my shoulder, and I turned around to see Bertram.

I gave him a hug. "Thanks, Bert. It means a lot to me that you were here."

He grinned. "Well, I didn't do so hot on these back roads. It took me a while to finally find her."

"The point is you found her. And that she's not hurt."

He looked down at the ground and pushed some sod with his toe. "They haven't found a body yet, Judah. They're covering the perimeter, but a train can only throw a person so far."

I let his news soak in, but couldn't get the image of Johanna being taken away at knifepoint out of my head. "If he's alive, do you think he'll come back to hurt her?"

Bertram shook his head. "Johanna said she had the opportunity to ... ah, talk with Amos about her faith. He let her go before he decided to take a pit stop on the train tracks."

"I wonder if he changed his mind about dying at the last minute."

"Either that or God took him up like Elijah."

I gave Bertram a nervous laugh. He would have been shocked to know I understood his Bible reference. But I gave him a blank look instead. I wasn't quite ready to share with him, or anybody for that matter, what was going on inside of me.

As the sheriff and EMTs walked away from Johanna, I fought the urge to rush up to her. Instead, I stood my ground and waited for her with Hilton and Gideon. After a few moments passed, she clutched the blanket one of the EMTs had given her around her shoulders and walked over to us.

I watched Hilton closely. Afraid of what he might say to her, I guess. This young Amish lady could be the one to determine whether the *Mountain Laurel Star* lived or died after all. But he kept his cool and I felt that some of his desperation was now gone. He chatted with Gideon about Matthias Fisher and what he'd been in jail for. My jaw dropped open when I heard but then turned to Johanna as she came closer.

"I just wanted to thank you ... all of you." She swept an arm out from under her blanket. "For caring. You... you really helped to saved my life."

Bertram gave her a quick side hug.

"Bishop Amos or ... Mr. Fisher was a bit ... well, confused when he took me from the wedding. But I don't believe he really meant to hurt me." She thought about that for a minute. "Well, at least not after we talked. When I heard the train crash into the buggy, I was already down to the end of the street." She looked down at her sneakers and was quiet then.

"You know they haven't found a body," I said, wondering if the sheriff had told her.

Johanna looked up at the sky and then nodded. "Judah, Gideon, would ya take me to Mose's house? I'm sure Mamm is pretty worried."

Gideon turned to untie his buggy reins from a fence post and then handed them to me with a wink.

"I'd like to finish up my conversation with Hilton, and maybe get a ride back with him. You don't mind, do ya, Judah?"

I smiled and shook my head. Hilton asked permission to visit her the next day and, after she'd nodded, I led her to the buggy.

Matthias wasn't ready to die. He knew that. He'd made some bad choices in his life, but he wasn't about to make suicide one of them. He was glad he'd had the strength to jump right before the train hit.

Matthias thought of his brother Ernst for the first time in years, unsure whether he was still alive. Being the younger brother of the mayor had had its benefits, but also its drawbacks. Prison had been one of them. He'd taken a lot of hits for his brother over the years.

Murder didn't look so good on a mayor's reputation.

As Matthias walked through the woods, he came to a fork in the path and stopped. He couldn't go any further, and he knew it. He had lived over forty years of his life trying to be someone he wasn't. And look how that turned out.

He didn't know how he would do it, but he needed to figure out what really happened the night he supposedly killed three men. And then he had to set his record straight. With Ernst—if he was still out there—and with the world. And he knew a good writer who might be willing to help.

Chapter 33

Judah

Johanna and I stayed quiet for most of the ride back to Mose's house. Somehow, the silence seemed comfortable between us.

When we arrived at Mose's house, she gave me a light kiss on the cheek.

"*Denki*, Judah, for being there for me so many times."

Gideon had filled me in on the rules against Amish dating *Englishers*. I didn't know how things would work out, but I did know that, somehow, I would be back. I squeezed her hand and boldly told her so.

Her mother, brother, and what seemed like thirty other people came out of the house then. She squeezed my hand back and turned to greet her great big family.

Going home to an empty apartment made my chest ache. Even Liza Lou probably had forgotten me by now. But then I thought of my own mother and the ounce of faith in my heart slowly began to swell.

I smiled then, watching Johanna with her mother, knowing I had some mending to do of my own.

Hilton and Bertram later came to the carpentry shop to drop off Gideon and to take me home. After saying goodbye to Gideon and promising to come back and help him on my days off, I got into the car.

We rode most of the way in silence until Hilton turned in his seat and gave me a strange look.

"I need to tell you a little something about your mother."

"My mother?" I felt a stab of fear thinking maybe something had happened while I'd been living with the Amish.

He waved his hand. "No, it's nothing like that."

Hilton proceeded to tell me about Mom's involvement with the paper, and I felt a familiar tightness in my chest thinking she was barging into my life once again. But then, I let it go. What this news really meant was Mom had saved the paper from going under. I had done nothing to deserve that kind of help.

Hilton then told me how Mom had already made steps to expand their web presence with a better design that made it easier for online readers to experience their stories. She had also been working on their social media marketing and had increased their advertising base. None of what he said surprised me.

"I guess my mother and I have a lot to talk about."

Hilton smiled.

I didn't bother going into my own apartment when Bertram and Hilton dropped me off, but went down to Consuelo's instead. With my Amish get-up, she didn't recognize me at first and almost didn't let me in until Liza Lou nearly knocked me over in greeting.

"Wait ... Judah! Is that you?"

After I'd told Consuelo the whole story and filled my stomach with more of her beef empanadas than I wanted to admit, I took Liza Lou and trudged off to my apartment. I hadn't much choice when I'd told Consuelo I planned to visit my mom next. She'd practically pulled my ear off trying to get me on my way.

I took a shower but put my broadfall trousers back on. I wasn't getting rid of those babies for a long time. Then, I grabbed a ball cap to help cover my bowl cut, and jumped into the Swagon.

From the warm glow of the streetlamp, I saw Mom's dried sunflowers still hung over the top of the white picket fence in front of her house, just like they always had in the fall. It was just like her to wait to throw them in the compost until some hungry bird ate the last seed.

I tightened my collar against the late September chill and opened my car door.

I wondered if she would recognize the sounds of the Swagon's signature creaks and open the front door like she had when I was younger.

I almost left then, not sure if I could do this.

My ear still stung a little where Consuelo had pinched it. Then I got out of my car. Come what may, I was going to do this thing. Mom deserved it. And I guess I did too.

A fluffy orange cat met me on the porch. She rubbed against my leg and actually jumped into my arms when I bent down to give her a pat.

I was still rubbing her belly when Mom opened the door.

JOHANNA

A freezing cold breeze blew out here at the riverbank, but all my *Bruders* came to watch with Mamm and me as David climbed the sturdy limbs of a black walnut just a stone's throw from the old oak.

The tree, just a sapling when the original swing was hung, offered an even better plunge into the swimming hole. David found the best branch, and Mose hoisted up a new swing Gideon had made just for the occasion.

Now, all my nieces and nephews wouldn't be disappointed come summer with nowhere to jump out into the river.

Smiling at my *Bruders*, I thanked David and told everyone Judah had agreed to let Mose teach him to swim that coming year. They all let out a hurrah and gave hugs all around.

Mamm and I lingered on the riverbank despite the cold after all the *Bruders* had left. As we looked out at the river, I told her I had taken a part-time job writing for the *Mountain Laurel Star* with Bishop Gideon's permission. I chose part-time so I could still maintain my life among the Amish.

Mamm let out a gasp and held her hand to her mouth. I felt like I was ready for anything after all I'd been through, but I'd really hoped to have her blessing on this new stage of my life. When she turned to look at me, her eyes held tears, but she smiled.

"You know how proud your Mammi would be of ya right now?"

I squeezed her hand and together we walked back to the buggy.

But not before I took out my journal and pen.

ABOUT THE AUTHOR

Debra Torres is an author of inspirational Amish fiction. She writes romantic suspense for readers who are looking for relatable characters dealing with raw and real-life issues. Forbidden Gift, a touching story of self-discovery, forgiveness, and healing set in a small Amish community in Northwestern Pennsylvania, is her debut novel.

For eleven years, Debra and her family lived in rural Northwestern Pennsylvania where she was able to observe the Amish in the grocery stores—and in the "buggy lanes." For several of these years, Debra and her family lived on a twenty-nine-acre farm sharing the land with a herd of white face beef cows, two carrot-loving horses, and a barn full of cats. Here, Debra kept a large "kitchen" garden and learned from locals how to "put up" her produce.

Debra is currently a web content specialist where she writes and strategizes compelling web content for one of the largest Christian universities in the world. Debra has been a Christian devotional blogger and a newspaper columnist as well as a freelance copywriter and web writer. She holds a BA in Communication and a MA in Journalism. While in graduate school, Debra was editor in chief of two university newspapers.

Debra and her writer husband, Michael, live in Virginia, and have five wonderfully gifted children.

And if you've enjoyed book one of Willow Brook—Secrets of the Pen, read on for chapter one of book two—*Forbidden Truth*.

BOOK TWO: FORBIDDEN TRUTH

WILLOW BROOK—SECRETS OF THE PEN

CHAPTER ONE

JOHANNA

Deleting my typing mistakes for the tenth time, I resisted the urge to throw my new laptop across the floor.

My scalp prickled with heat under my prayer *Kapp*.

The computer had been my friend when Hilton, the editor in chief of the *Mountain Laurel Star* first handed it over to me. I'd rubbed my hand across its silver smooth cover and stopped to trace the still-warm logo embedded in its center.

But my new friend quickly turned into an enemy when I'd discovered that my fingers, rough and calloused from a lifetime of work on my family's veal farm didn't fare well with its keys. Stretching out my hands in front of me, I was embarrassed to still see the oily grey film under my nails that came with handling the animals.

Ach.

I thought of Chelsea, the receptionist who sat upfront. Her cherry-red fingernails glistening under the fluorescent lighting.

Being able to work at the newspaper was a dream come true, really. And one that came under very special circumstances for my Amish district. But it brought along with it an onslaught of questions in my head I wasn't prepared for. Questions a typical Amish woman tucked in safely among the People, didn't have to deal with.

Looking around the newsroom, the scent of antiseptic wipes stung my nose. Lost in a cluster of fabric-walled cubicles, I realized I wasn't "tucked in safely" anywhere. And that feeling was boring a small hole in my already sensitive heart.

The sound of bubbling water on the other side of the cube wall broke into my thoughts, and I stood up looking in. The gurgling was coming from an electric teapot of sorts and grew louder. Its owner, a sports reporter named Trevor, was nowhere to be found. Chelsea's heels coldly clicked nearby, and I hesitated to say anything. But surely the liquid would overflow or something if I didn't get help. I had no idea how these things worked.

I took a deep breath and stood up so she could see me. Coming down my row, Chelsea jumped back a little and her heels screeched to a stop on the linoleum.

"Um, Chelsea, would you tell Trevor his tea is ready?"

She looked at me like I was a *Dummkopp*.

"His teapot or, maybe it's his Kaffi?" I pointed to Trevor's cube. "It's boiling." Only now it wasn't, I quickly realized. The sound had stopped.

Chelsea's smile was thin, and she gave short nods while she spoke. "It has an automatic shut-off."

"Oh ... I didn't know." I attempted to explain myself, but Chelsea had already moved on. Her dress clung to her curves as she made her way back to the front desk.

The snub hurt and reminded me of my latest encounter with my sister-in-law Mary over the weekend. It was a small thing – but it was still festering in me like a fence post sliver. Esther Bish had called a frolic for making and canning Yankee bean soup for the winter.

The ladies were always interested in my work with the *Star*, and I was doing my best to share without trying to sound prideful. I figured that if word got out that I was enjoying it too much, Bishop Gideon may have his hands full with requests from single women in the community to do things other than sew, teach school, or work in neighboring restaurants.

"So how does it work?" Esther asked over her shoulder as she chopped carrots while her toddler clung to her skirted leg.

We were in the *Küche*, and I was in charge of sifting through the dried beans—removing dirt clods and small rocks. I was glad to be facing the wall and focusing on my work. I had ignored her question—hoping it wasn't directed towards me. I wasn't up for a conversation about my work. These women wouldn't understand anyway, and I wasn't sure where they stood on the issue.

I was up to my elbows in beans when the room grew silent.

Pulling my arms out, I turned around to see that all eyes were on me. Several beans smattered down to the green linoleum.

I crouched to retrieve them. "What?"

"You're work at the paper—what's it like?" Esther, finished with the carrots, pulled the toddler up to her hip.

I turned back to the beans and took a slow breath. Digging through, I worked on a response. These women had known me all my life. Some had known Mammi. Most knew the struggles we'd been through as a family. Some understood while others didn't want to.

"It's fine." I'd found an especially large clod of dirt and crushed it hard between my fingers. It felt soft and silky. I would wash it out later in the sieve.

"*Nee*, that's not what she asked, Johanna." The high-pitched voice belonged to Mary.

Shutting my eyes, I took another deep breath.

Gott?

Mary's voice leveled. "She wants to know how it works when you leave the People and go work among *Englischers* doing something that was against the *Ordnung* until just a few weeks ago."

A thousand responses fired into my brain, and I bit my tongue to not say any of them. These ladies didn't need to hear an argument. Plus, my thoughts ran to what Mammi had once said about mean girls.

They bite because they hurt on the inside.

A buzz had started in the room again, the ladies filled the room with nervous talk, obviously not sure how or if I would respond to Mary.

In the end, I remained silent. There wasn't anything to say really. Mary had her way of looking at my work at the Star, and it was doubtful that anything I had to say would make a change.

Soon after, when the room was filled with laughter and easy talk again, Esther had stepped over to me. "I'm sorry," she had mouthed. I gave her a half-smile, squeezing her hand.

Although different, Chelsea's treatment towards me stung just the same as Mary's. Squinting up at the fluorescent lights, I sat back down hard into my office chair.

Trevor had returned and must have made his tea because with every sip came a loud slurp. I was surprised no one else was bothered by the noise until I remembered that most of the reporters had plastic things in their ears that canceled out sound. So, it was just up to me to deal with it.

Great.

A wisp of hair had escaped my *Kapp*, and I blew it out of my face. I tried again with the keyboard, but I was all thumbs. Learning to type on the computer for the *Mountain Laurel Star* was harder than I thought it would be.

DEBRA TORRES

The keyboarding lessons Judah set up for me were a game really, but after so many times typing letters, my fingers ached, and I longed for my pen and journal.

Composing a story on this thing just seemed wrong. How I was supposed to get something out of my heart and into this machine was beyond me. No wonder the Amish, for the most part, weren't permitted to deal with them.

Bishop Gideon and the ministers had given me the special permission I needed. But thankfully, my use of the computer was limited to the newsroom. Who would want one of these in their home, anyway? All the options that came with a computer: links, videos, and web pages were enough to give me a headache. It made me appreciate the simple life of the People.

My eyes wandered over to the small pile of newspapers that sat dog-eared on my desk. For the past few weeks, the Star's homepage had filled readers in on the latest news on my former bishop, Amos Zook. I gently ran my fingers across the newsprint and prepared for another read. Judah was out even now, working on a story that would add to the pile. Even though I already poured over each article, I wanted to read through them again. Maybe I'd missed something about the Bishop's escape.

Maybe all of us had missed something.

"Finished yet?"

My editor in chief wasn't a patient man. I learned that soon after joining his team as a staff columnist.

I know that he had gone through quite a bit of change in his personal life recently, Judah and Bertram had filled me in on that. And, he had worked hard to get me here.

But he also demanded a lot.

Hilton Hughes' salt and pepper hair poked over my cube wall, and he squinted at me, waiting for an answer.

"Umm ... not quite."

335

Hilton tapped his watch. "We go to print in two hours."

I nodded. His deadline wasn't new information to me. If he didn't stop interrupting me, I was going to have to do something desperate. And how was I supposed to write with all these thoughts about Amos Zook swirling around in my head?

"Psst."

I swung around to see Bertram peeking over the back wall of my cube.

"You've got this." He wore a contagious smile and offered a big thumbs up. I grinned back.

Focus. Focus. I massaged my temples.

My column was a difficult one to write not to mention type. After the incident with the bishop just a few weeks ago, I just couldn't seem to get my head on straight.

Feeling under my desk for my bag, I pulled out my journal and ran my thumb over its worn leather cover. It came to me then—what I was really thinking about—and I decided to put it on paper.

The story wrote itself.

It was an installment in an ongoing novel I had been submitting to the Star for over a year. My characters— some Amish, some Englisch—faced daily struggles that my readers seemed to relate to.

I finished it, pleased. Fumbling over the keys with greater determination, I typed the story out. And, using the email tool Judah had taught me, I sent it to Hilton—even though his office was just a few steps away.

I was putting on my heavy black cape when Hilton appeared again. Two pieces of paper sagged in his grip.

"I can't print this."

"What? Why?"

"You wrote this about Amos."

"Well, maybe. But ..."

"Johanna, we don't know where he is or what exactly is going on with him. Our readers will see right through this."

"Not to be disrespectful, Hilton." Bertram had popped up again, and I sat while the words flew just above my head. "But so what if they do? I mean ... everyone is thinking about it anyway. It could be just what our audience needs right now."

"Yeah, except for one thing." Hilton's tone was at a low growl.

"What's that?" Bertram had given me the courage I needed, and I stood as I spoke.

"You don't think he's guilty." Hilton jabbed a thick finger in my direction while Chelsea snickered at the front desk.

Get your free Amish/ Mennonite digital cookbook when you subscribe to my author newsletter.

Love Amish recipes almost as much as Amish stories? Get in on the heritage of the Amish and Mennonites with recipes used in their own kitchens. You'll get full-color images of Amish life along with recipes like Chicken Soup with Rivels, Friendship Bread, and, of course, Whoopie Pies!

AMISH AND MENNONITE

Plain & Simple Recipes

RECIPE COLLECTION
by Debra Torres
Photos by Jim Fisher
All recipes used with permission
©2021 Debra Torres - All Rights Reserved

Sign up here for your free cookbook: https://free-amish-cookbook.ck.page/1e28014298

CONNECT WITH ME!

Facebook:
https://www.facebook.com/DebraTorresWrites
YouTube:
https://www.youtube.com/channel/UCByOkkufDm8uHA8tzdcNQfQ
Instagram:
https://www.instagram.com/debratorreswrites/
Twitter:
https://twitter.com/DebraTorresBook
MeWe:
https://mewe.com/p/amishfictionauthordebratorres2
Website:
https://www.debratorres.com/

CPSIA information can be obtained
at www.ICGtesting.com
Printed in the USA
BVHW040056270621
610451BV00006B/1779